CCH BUSINESS OWNER'S TOOLKIT

BUSINESS PLANS THAT WORK

FOR YOUR SMALL BUSINESS

A *CCH Business Owner's Toolkit* Publication

Edited by Susan M. Jacksack, J.D.

CCH INCORPORATED
Chicago

This publication is designed to provide accurate and authoritative information in regard to the subject matter covered. It is sold with the understanding that the publisher is not engaged in rendering legal, accounting, or other professional service, and that the authors are not offering such advice in this publication. If legal advice or other expert assistance is required, the services of a competent professional should be sought.

Cover designed by Tim Kaage, Laurel Graphx, Inc.

Books may be purchased at quantity discounts for educational, business or sales promotion use. For more information please contact:

Small Office Home Office Group
CCH INCORPORATED
2700 Lake Cook Road
Riverwoods, Illinois 60015

ISBN 0-8080-240-6

Printed in the United States of America

THE CCH BUSINESS OWNER'S TOOLKIT TEAM

Susan Jacksack is frequently quoted as a small business expert in national publications including *The Wall Street Journal, The New York Times, Money,* and *Worth,* and has made several guest appearances to discuss small business issues on CNBC. She has over 10 years of experience advising and writing for small business owners and consumers on tax, personal finance and other legal topics. Susan is an attorney and a graduate of the University of Illinois, Urbana-Champaign.

Alice Magos has over 35 years of experience running the operations of numerous small businesses. She is the author of the *CCH Business Owner's Toolkit* online advice column "Ask Alice," and serves as a member of *Home Office Computing* magazine's expert team of advisors. Alice is an accountant and a Certified Financial Planner, and holds degrees from Washington University in St. Louis and Northwestern University.

Joel Handelsman has 20 years of experience writing about business, tax, and financial topics. He has experience with multiple new product and business ventures in the publishing industry, and has held a variety of management positions. Joel is an attorney and holds degrees from Northwestern University and DePaul University.

John Duoba has more than 10 years of experience in book and magazine publishing, fulfilling various roles in editorial and production management. He has been involved in the publication of scores of titles, with multiple editions and issues raising the total well into the hundreds. John is a professional journalist and holds a degree from Northwestern University's Medill School of Journalism.

Martin Bush has 15 years of experience providing legal, financial and tax advice to small and large businesses in various industries. He is a frequently quoted small business expert and has appeared on CNBC and National Public Radio. Martin is an attorney and a CPA, and holds degrees from Indiana University and DePaul University.

Steve Crow is the founder and owner of A Better Business Plan, a business planning and consulting firm in suburban Chicago. He has 20 years of experience in business planning, management, marketing, sales, and training, and has provided advice, support and direction to a broad range of businesses, from small startups to multi-million dollar expansions. Not only an author of business plans, related documents, and articles on business planning, Steve also regularly presents seminars on the importance and the process of business planning.

We would also like to acknowledge the significant efforts of others who contributed to this book: Bob Barnett, Ron Hirasawa, and Todd Matta. In addition, we would like to thank Drew Snider and LaVerne Dellinger for their contributions in the production of this book.

FOREWORD

There are dozens of articles and books being written about business plans today. Many provide very good, thorough advice about the process of writing a planning document and, incidentally, how to run your business effectively.

But very few of them are willing to show you what an actual business plan, for a real business, looks like. Most of the business plans that have been published are works of fiction, created as an illustration of an "average" small business, rather than real, working plans created by the business people who will actually have to live with those plans.

Yet knowing what a real business plan looks like is *exactly* the information that you need most, in order to write your first plan. In fact, what you really need to see are plans that have performed successfully for their business owners — plans that have helped the owner obtain needed financing, get a new business started, or embark on an expansion or change in direction.

Why are real business plans so difficult to find? One reason is that it takes a substantial amount of time and effort to create a high-quality plan. Much research and thinking goes into the process. Once the work is done, the creators are often unwilling to share the fruit of their efforts.

In view of these facts, we are grateful for the assistance of Steve Crow, a professional business consultant and planner in Mundelein, Illinois. Steve was willing to share his expertise with us in the form of five plans that he has developed for real, live businesses that are starting up or already operating. By reading through these plans, you can get a clear sense of the type of information and the level of detail that you'll need to include in your own plans.

Business Plans that Work for Your Small Business will also help you understand the elements that must be included in a planning document, and the information you need to gather to create your own plan. You'll see that creating a business plan need not be difficult, and the time you spend planning will save you many, many hours of time you'd otherwise spend dealing with major problems in the future.

Why should you turn to us? CCH INCORPORATED is a leading provider of information and software to the business and professional community. More than four generations of business advisors have trusted our products, and now you can too.

A caution and an invitation — the discussions and plans contained in this book are current as of the date of publication. But remember, things change. To keep abreast of the latest new affecting your business, visit *CCH Business Owner's Toolkit* on the Internet (www.toolkit.cch.com) or on America Online (keyword: CCH).

While you're there, take a look at the other interactive information and tools we offer to assist you in running your business. You can also ask follow-up questions of our team of small business experts. We welcome and look forward to your questions and comments.

Martin Bush

Publisher, Small Office Home Office Group

Table of Contents

Table of Contents

Part I

Creating A Business Plan That Works

Coming up with a great idea for a new business, or for a way to turn around or expand an existing business, can be a tremendous challenge in itself. While there's never a shortage of raw ideas, finding one that's solid enough to support a successful company for an extended period of time takes a great deal of investigation and research, good judgment, timing, and even luck.

But coming up with a great idea, difficult as it may be, is not enough. Countless businesses have started out well, sailed through the first few months or even years, and then foundered as soon as the first real problems cropped up.

How can you make sure this won't happen to you? You can't, of course. But you can greatly improve your chances by taking the time to thoroughly research your business idea before plunging into it. Then you can take the most important step: using what you've learned to create a detailed plan that plots out your objectives, your marketing strategy, operations procedures, and the right combination of expertise, equipment, location, and sheer capital that will be required to convert your ideas into reality.

Creating a business plan need not be difficult. However, it does require a step-by-step approach, and a willingness to persist in digging for information and thinking through all the essential factors that will contribute to your operation. You'll find that the time you spend creating your plan will be some of the most valuable hours in your entrepreneurial career. By creating a business plan, you'll know exactly what pieces must come together at the right time, place, and amount to make your project a success. What's more, you'll be able to explain your idea to others whom you must convince to write a loan, invest in your business, or join you as a partner or co-owner.

While the planning document itself can be important, particularly if you're going to use it to obtain necessary capital, the planning process is even more important. It's during the process of creating the plan that you round out your knowledge base by gathering information, consider numerous alternatives, and make dozens, if not hundreds, of decisions about how to proceed.

Where available, you can and should enlist the help of others (e.g., your accountant, lawyer, consultant, or even a professional business plan developer) to help you pull together the physical document. A review of the financial section by an accountant can be particularly helpful. But *you* must ultimately do the essential thinking and decisionmaking yourself. Your plan must reflect your own individual strengths, personality, and intentions for your business, and no one knows them as well as you.

In Part I, we'll describe the process of creating a plan, and the important elements you need to include in the formal document. We'll also describe some ways that you can use your plan in the future to manage your business more effectively.

Chapter 1: Preparing to Put Your Plan Together shows how to shape your plan to match your reason for creating it, and the audience to whom your plan is directed.

Chapter 2: Format and Introductory Elements presents an overview of your written plan, discusses format and presentation issues, and describes the executive summary, table of contents, and appendix portions of the plan.

Chapter 3: The Company Summary discusses the parts of your plan that will describe the ownership, mission, objectives, and keys to success of your company. Where appropriate, it may include descriptions of your facilities and your company history.

Chapter 4: Market Analysis explains the portions of your plan that describe your industry, your target market, and your competition. We suggest you include a Strengths, Weaknesses, Opportunities, and Threats (SWOT) Analysis and a Needs Analysis.

Chapter 5: Product or Service Description discusses the part of your plan that provides a detailed description of what your company's offerings are or will be.

Chapter 6: Marketing and Sales Plans explains how to present your marketing strategy and plans for implementing that strategy.

Chapter 7: Operations and Management Plans discusses the portions of the plan that address your management team and employees, important processes, and other operations issues that are important to your business.

Chapter 8: Financial Plans, discusses the financial statements that must be included, as well as the assumptions and projections you must make in order to complete them.

Chapter 9: Using the Completed Plan explains how a business plan can become an important tool for keeping your business on track, long after the plan is completed.

Chapter 1

Preparing To Put
Your Plan Together

Before you sit down to write your business plan, it's important to think about your reasons for doing it, and what you hope to get out of the process and the plan itself.

Remember that no two business plans will look alike. There are a number of key considerations that will play an important role in shaping the scope and contents of your particular plan. What's more, your plan should reflect your personality and your management style. You'll want the readers to feel as if they know you, and have a good handle on what your business is all about.

Work Smart

Try to avoid the cookie-cutter template effect that you can get by using some business planning software. Software can be a tremendous time-saver, certainly, but some business owners are tempted to just "fill in the blanks" without attempting to consider whether another organization or style might be more appropriate for their business. This can be a serious error if you're applying for a loan, and your banker has read dozens of plans using the same software (and boilerplate language) already. Resist the temptation — make sure that your plan expresses your creativity and individuality.

Obviously, your business's position in its life cycle will have a significant impact on the type of planning that's needed. A startup may need extensive planning of all its aspects, while an ongoing business might require a plan that relates primarily to a new market that it wants to enter, or a new product that it wants to introduce.

The most important consideration will be the uses to which you expect to put your plan, and the audience who will read it. Will people outside the business see your plan? Will you be seeking outside financing, and if so, from whom? The type of lender or investor you're pursuing will dictate the type of information and details you need to include. On the other hand, if the plan is to be used primarily as a management tool for yourself and/or other owners or key employees, you can be more flexible about the length and contents of the plan.

A PLAN FOR AN OUTSIDE AUDIENCE

Just as a person seeking a job prepares a resume that outlines qualifications, experience, and other relevant information, a business that is seeking debt financing or an infusion of capital from an outside investor will benefit from having a "resume" of its own.

You can think of your business plan as a rather lengthy resume. To the extent that it reflects the reasonable plans of a good manager, it gives your audience a positive image of what your business is and what it can be expected to do.

For Lenders and Investors

Starting a new business, or expanding an existing one, may require more money than you can get together on your own. This means turning to an outside source for financing. While you might consider taking on a partner or finding an investor, you'll most likely go to a bank for a loan.

If you're just starting out, you obviously won't have a history of profitable operations to indicate that you can function successfully enough to make all your loan payments. In the past, this lack of a history made most banks extremely hesitant to lend money to new, unproven businesses. However, there are indications that bankers are becoming somewhat more open to financing startup operations.

Nevertheless, with the majority of conventional lenders, a workable business plan is essential to getting startup financing. It is one of the first things that a potential lender will want to examine (along with a list of your *personal* assets).

If you've been in business for a while and you need financing to expand or introduce a new product or service, your lender might not require you to submit a full-fledged business plan. However, a solid plan that illustrates a successful track record can provide strong support for your loan request, and should increase your chances of getting the amount and type of loan you want.

Venture capitalists, prospective partners or shareholders, and even relatives who might loan money or invest in your business will want some assurances that they have used their money wisely. A business plan demonstrates how their money will be used and what they, and the business, can expect in return.

Finally, if you expect an ongoing need for funding, showing that the business is meeting or exceeding planned goals can help you build a history that might let you borrow under more desirable rates and conditions in the future.

For Prospective Employees

In some cases, portions of a business plan can serve to introduce prospective employees to your business. Particularly if you intend to hire long-term or high-level employees, you'll want to present a fair picture of what your business is and what types of work need to be performed. You can also establish expectations regarding income and growth opportunities based on the plan's projections.

Shaping the Plan for an External Audience

If you are writing a plan primarily to be shown to an external audience, you'll want to pay close attention to the established conventions of business plan documents. There are certain elements and types of information that your lender or potential investors will expect to see, and it doesn't pay to disappoint them. Similarly, a business plan is expected to have a "professional" appearance, which means that it must look somewhat like every other business plan.

For any outside lender or investor, the executive summary is the most important part of your plan. Venture capitalists, in particular, typically receive hundreds of plans and don't have time to read them all cover to cover. If your summary doesn't capture their attention, they won't go any farther.

A plan destined to be shown to a banker must include a financing proposal or statement that succinctly describes the type of loan(s) you are seeking, the purposes to which the funds will be put, and how you will pay the money back. In the lender's view, this is the most important part of the plan, so place it up front, in the executive summary or immediately afterward.

Any plan for an outside investor will have to emphasize the financial side of your business. The section that includes your financial statements is often the second section a banker will turn to, so make sure that it is complete, accurate, and reasonable in its assumptions.

Venture capitalists and outside investors will want all the financial information that a banker would need, plus a good deal of marketing, operational, and personnel information. These types of investors view themselves as owners, so they tend to want a lot of detail. They also need to get a strong sense of your vision, experience, and commitment to the company.

Venture capitalists tend to be short-term investors, and it's important that you include an exit plan if you are seeking VC backing. You'll need to show that you have a workable plan for cashing out the investor, generally by selling stock to the public or by selling the business to a larger company. There may be some other options, depending on the particular investor, but you should at least consider the possibility that your own involvement in the company's management will be greatly reduced within the foreseeable future.

However, with any plan for an outside audience, keep the reader's attention span in mind. If the plan is too short, it won't provide all the answers that the reader is looking for; if it is too long, the reader may give up before coming to the conclusion. Somewhere around 20 to 30 pages should be the right length for most small businesses.

For an example of a plan that was created for the purpose of getting financing, see the Plan for Jumpin' Java Cybercafe on page 237.

THE BUSINESS PLAN AS A MANAGEMENT TOOL

An extremely important, but too-often overlooked, reason for creating a business plan is to help you manage vital business activities better.

If you're just starting out in business, the time it takes to create your first plan will be more than repaid by the insight you gain. If you're in business already but have never created a business plan, you'll be in a much better position to assess opportunities and risks that accompany the various changes you may be considering.

You should consider creating a business plan if:

- You want to open a new business.

- Your business has grown significantly since you last did any significant planning.

- You want to introduce a new product.

- You want to enter a new market.

- You want to acquire a new business or a franchise.

A Business Plan for a New Business

For most entrepreneurs, it's only when you take the time to create a written document that embodies your thoughts that you realize the scope and magnitude of what's involved in running a business. In your head, you've concentrated on the idea. In your plan, you can examine the nuts and bolts of running a business to exploit your idea.

Since you're considering a wholly new business, a big part of the planning process is going to involve developing an initial set of assumptions. You'll have to make assumptions regarding costs, labor, the number of potential customers, pricing, and many other factors.

Your business plan will also identify the essential events that must occur and actions that must be taken, and set forth a clear timetable for accomplishing them. You may want to show these important activities in a chart — as an example, see the plan for African Adventure Tours on page 91.

Perhaps the most important component of the business plan is your marketing plan, which identifies your target audience and explains how you will position your product or service to reach that audience. Your specific advertising and promotional activities will be linked to sales targets. Your operational plans will explain how your business will conduct its day-to-day activities. The timing of these activities in relation to marketing plans is crucial; for example, there is little point in running ads for a product that isn't available for sale.

A good business plan also includes a substantial amount of detail regarding cash flow projections that set forth the projected timing of revenues and expenses. These projections help establish whether and how the business will meet its obligations to vendors and others who provide the business with goods or services. Most of these projections are tied directly to planned operational results. For example, the sales projected to occur in one month are supposed to generate the income necessary to pay expenses that are due the following month.

Work Smart

If you work hard to create a business plan and your plan demonstrates that you can't profitably exploit your idea without making some pretty wild assumptions, you haven't lost anything. To the contrary, you've saved yourself the time, money, and heartache you would have expended on a hopeless cause. It is far better to realistically appraise your chance for success before you commit your time and money to a new enterprise.

In a well-crafted plan, the overall rhythm of the business will be realistically reflected. If some portion of the business is cyclical, as is often the case, the cycle will be identified and accounted for. For example, many retail outlets rely on the Thanksgiving-to-Christmas period for a substantial part of their annual sales volume. This cycle is reflected in the plan by, for example, increasing inventory as November approaches, planning for the addition of temporary workers to handle the expanded sales volume, and clumping expense payments directly following the busy season when cash is most available.

For examples of business plans that were created to get a new business off the ground, see the plans for All Church Sound on page 125, African Adventure Tours on page 91, and Jumpin' Java Cybercafe on page 237.

Business Expansion

If your business experiences gradual growth, at some point that expansion alone will make it worth your while to create a plan to explore the opportunities that growth might provide. For example, a production-based business might be able to acquire additional or better production equipment because the volume of business has reached a level that justifies the expense. Or, it might be time for a retail establishment to consider the costs, benefits, and risks of opening a second business location.

Planning for growth also can reveal some of the disadvantages of getting bigger. For example, as your sales volume increases, your need for working capital may increase correspondingly. Careful planning can help you to become aware of the magnitude of your future cash needs, and make arrangements to meet them. As another example, as your business expands you may need to hire more employees, or train your existing employees for expanded duties. By thinking through your needs ahead of time, you'll be able to make better hiring decisions.

Ideally, before launching a new product, moving into a new market, or developing a new distribution channel, you would revisit your existing business plan and integrate the new product or project into the overall plan. As an alternative, you might create a plan that is limited in scope to the impact that the change will have on your existing operations.

For an example of a business plan that was created to help an existing business expand, see the plan for Computer Solutions, Inc. on page 193.

Acquisitions and Franchise Opportunities

If you're considering the purchase of an existing business, how do you know how much to pay? Will the business provide you with the income you need three years down the road? While there's no substitute for a thorough investigation, a business plan can be a useful tool to help you assess whether you should buy a business or let the opportunity go by. In fact, many sellers will create a selling memorandum, which is really a business plan in reverse, to fully acquaint prospective buyers with their business and convince them that the opportunity is a good one. You can use this as a starting point for creating your own plan for the future.

Similarly, deciding whether to purchase a franchise is a serious issue. By becoming a franchisee, you agree to conform to a wide variety of very specific requirements. A business plan provides the framework for considering whether the benefits of holding a franchise outweigh the associated costs and restrictions. The plan is the perfect tool for modeling how your business will perform as a member of the franchise. If you're already operating as an unaffiliated business, you can compare your current operations to the costs and opportunities presented by joining the franchisor.

Managing an Existing Business

Obviously, no one likes to take big risks to obtain a small return. A business plan can be used as a modeling tool to look at a variety of scenarios.

Suppose you decide to drop your prices, which generally means that you'll accept a somewhat lower gross margin in exchange for greater sales volume. How much will sales increase? Will you have enough production capacity? Will you need additional help, or storage space? Can your suppliers provide the raw materials you need? Will lower prices fit your mission and image? Answers to these questions are more readily available if your business plan is used as a baseline, so you can see what happens as you change some of the variables.

For a plan that was created to help an existing business take stock of its current situation and make some changes in direction, see the plan for Bob's Big Pencils on page 159.

Tracking Your Progress

It probably comes as no surprise to you that, until recently, even some very large companies used a "cigar box" approach to tracking business results. That is, every dollar that comes in to the business goes *into* the cigar box. All the expenses are paid *from* the cigar box. As long as the box isn't empty and there's adequate money left over for the business owner, everything is just fine.

But there are better ways to stay on top of how your business is doing.

A business plan can provide the foundation for a tracking system that lets you evaluate your business's progress. This tracking function gives you, as the business owner, real-time feedback regarding operations. Deviations between actual and planned results provide clues that you can use to tweak or fine-tune certain elements of the plan.

Shaping the Plan for an Internal Audience

If your primary reason for business planning is to use the planning process and the document itself as management tools, you can be quite flexible about the length, scope, and style of your plan.

While you'll want to include all the elements that are customarily found in a plan for an outside audience, you may choose to emphasize certain areas where you feel your business is weak. You may also decide to create a longer plan that provides more detail in terms of the specific tasks you want to undertake during the year. For example, you may want to use your cash-flow statement as the basis for a more detailed budget that you'll attempt to adhere to during the year.

You may also want to do more thinking about various contingencies that may occur during the year, and create a plan to deal with the most likely scenarios. For example, you may want to consider what you'll do if a major new competitor enters your market, if a key supplier goes out of business, or if a natural disaster forces you to close down for a while. The time to unearth all the potential pitfalls is in the planning stage, not later on when unexpected events tend to be unfavorable and costly.

There may be others within the business with whom you will share the business plan, or substantial pieces of it. Clearly, if you have partners, co-owners, or a Board of Directors, those individuals should see the plan after its completion. They may also be able to provide you with significant input into the plan as it's being developed.

If you have employees, many of the goals that you set for them will be derived from the plan. For example, your sales projections might translate directly into the level of sales your representatives must achieve. In general, your people will be able to do a better job if they see exactly where they fit in with your business objectives.

Example

Let's say that your business plan provides a detailed strategy for achieving a 50 percent increase in sales over the next 12 months. It would be a good idea to share the strategic analysis and your mission statement with your sales people. Your sales force will have a much better idea of what is expected of them, and they'll have a solid understanding of where they fit within your organization.

Obviously, there may be parts of the plan that you won't want to share with your employees. This is particularly true of portions that might reveal more than you want them to know about your personal finances. Similarly, you may not choose to share information regarding how the business finances its operations.

You'll have to use your judgment regarding the type and amount of detail that will be relevant to each of your employees. In many cases, you may want to share with them only your executive summary and the top-line goals for the year. In other cases, greater detail will be necessary and helpful in motivating key employees to "get with the plan."

HOW FAR OUT CAN YOU PLAN?

When you hear an extended weather report, you know that the predictions for today and tonight are more likely to be accurate than the five-day forecast. Similarly, many of the variables that can affect businesses in general or your business in particular aren't easily predicted. The value of the dollar compared to foreign currencies, interest rates, and many other factors that can affect a business's profitability change constantly. There are no guarantees. So how far out do you plan?

The answer is: *it depends*. For example, there were no doubt dozens of aspiring entrepreneurs in Atlanta who figured out a way to profit from the Olympic Games held there in 1996. Some of these businesses came into being and shut down in less than a year, as one-time opportunities.

On the other hand, some businesses may spend months or years in a product development stage before any sales activities begin. A software business may expend tremendous amounts of money and time developing a product, with the expectation that the product will be sold, and upgraded, for a number of years to come. Obviously, the planning horizon for the software business would be far longer than a business designed around the Olympics.

As a general rule, for an "average" business, a three-year plan is a reasonable starting point. But that doesn't mean that you need to map out, month-by-month, or week-by-week, what is going to happen over the next 36 months. The level of detail will drop as your plan covers periods further into the future. The cash flows that are tracked monthly during the first year of operation may be projected by quarter or by year for the second and third years. Just how this transition from detail to the big picture is managed will depend on your specific situation.

Example

If your goal is to obtain a five-year term loan, you may want to project your plan out for five years to better convince your banker that the loan will be paid off on time.

Predicting your sales, costs of goods, or what the prevailing wage rates will be one, two or five years down the road is no easy matter. Obviously, the assumptions relating to the very near future are more likely to be accurate than those relating to periods further out. For example, if interest rates have held reasonably steady for the past year or so, assuming that the interest rate on a variable-rate loan won't increase by more than a point in the next six months is a fairly safe bet. But you would be much less certain where the rates might be in 12 or 24 months.

PLANNING FOR YOUR TYPE OF BUSINESS

Very few businesses deal exclusively in the provision of goods *or* in the performance of services. For planning purposes, however, it is useful to consider whether your business is primarily a service provider, a seller of goods, or both. Issues that might be extremely important to a product-based business, such as inventory, can have vastly less significance for a service provider.

Service Businesses

One of the first things the owner of a service business must consider will be the question of who, exactly, who will be providing the services that your business sells? Will you be the sole provider, or will you need to recruit other employees or independent contractors to serve your customers?

If someone other than yourself will be providing the services, you'll need to build in some procedures to ensure that the quality is up to your standards. This may involve screening prospective employees very carefully, providing special training to workers, and following up to check on their work.

Many personal service businesses require the owner to spend substantial time doing presentations, preparing bids or estimates, or doing other sales-related activities to acquire future business. To the extent that your time must be spent on sales activities, you can't devote time to actually providing the services. If performing services is what you do best (or even, what you *like* to do best), you may need to plan to hire a manager, or at least an administrative assistant, at some point down the road.

Another issue service providers face relates to billing and collections policies. When goods are sold, there is a clear event that triggers the need for payment. For some service providers, the event that should trigger payment might not be so clear. For example, a contractor may feel that payment should be made when he or she informs the homeowner that the job is complete. The homeowner, however, may feel that he or she has a right to have the work inspected before tendering payment.

One way to reduce the possibility of this type of problem is to include clauses in all your contracts for larger jobs stating that customers must make progress payments of a specific percentage of the total price as a job proceeds. Another is to establish credit terms and consider offering a discount to customers who pay earlier than required. Ultimately, you must plan your cash flow requirements realistically, allowing for the possibility that a certain portion of what you are owed might not be immediately forthcoming. For examples of business plans for service businesses see the plans for All Church Sound on page 125, and African Adventure Tours on page 91.

Product-Based Businesses

Retailers, wholesalers, and manufacturers can all be considered product-based businesses. In each case, the business plan will have to include some type of inventory planning. Even if you intend to carry little inventory but order it from suppliers as you make a sale, you'll need to state that fact in your business plan. In some cases, you'll have a lot of money tied up in inventory, and your financing needs may be more extensive.

Your needs for employees may also be an important issue that needs to be addressed in your business plan. Will you use part-timers or full-timers? How will you recruit and retain these workers? What pay and benefits will you need to offer, and what raises should you budget within the time frame that your plan will cover?

Businesses engaged in manufacturing typically need a good deal of equipment in order to operate. Leasing or buying, maintaining, repairing, and insuring your equipment must all be part of your plan. You'll also need to plan for the eventual replacement of obsolete equipment. Similarly, retailers and, to a lesser extent wholesalers, must plan for the shelving, counters, lighting, and other fixtures and decorating their particular business will need.

Since a retailer's business can sink or swim based on its location, a business plan for a retailer must place some importance on this issue. Your plan should explain what a "good" location means in your industry, and how the location you've chosen fits the bill.

For an example of a business plan for a small manufacturer, see the plan for Bob's Big Pencils on page 159. For an example of a retailer's plan, see the plan for Computer Solutions, Inc. on page 193.

Mixed Goods and Services

A business that provides its customers with both goods and services will probably have a somewhat more complicated business plan than a business that primarily provides either goods or services. There are many logistical considerations relating to managing the interaction between the delivery of goods and the performance of services.

Example

Take the case of a restaurant, where customers expect to receive good food and to be served by an attentive wait staff. Everything has to come together for *each* customer in order to meet his or her expectations. This is no mean feat for the business owner. Probably everyone has experienced an "almost good" meal, where one small aspect of the meal didn't go quite right. Perhaps the food was excellent but too long in coming, or maybe you had to ask for the check three times before you finally got it. Whatever the reason, it is clear that people expect both the product and the service to meet their standards. If either fails, customer satisfaction will suffer.

The financial aspects of a mixed goods and services business require careful scrutiny. The relative mix between goods and services must be managed to maintain a reasonable return on the entire enterprise. Pricing is more of an issue because you are trying to cover the wide variety of components that make up the entire package. The business planning process affords you with an opportunity to examine this and other relationships that can impact on the profitability of your business. For an example of a plan for a mixed goods-and-services business, see the plan for Jumpin' Java Cybercafe on page 237.

Chapter 2

Format And Introductory Elements

After you've considered the purpose of your plan and done some background preparation, it's time to consider the actual elements that you'll include in the written document, and the format your plan will take.

A business plan customarily has a number of major elements or sections. Each of these elements serves a particular purpose in the overall presentation of your plan. The following list identifies and briefly describes each of the documents or document categories that will make up your plan.

Components of a Written Business Plan

Cover page: this page identifies you and your business, and dates the plan.

Table of contents: this element makes it easy for readers to find and examine particular documents.

Executive summary: this is arguably the most important single part of your document. It provides a high-level overview of the entire plan that emphasizes the factors that you believe will lead to success.

Company summary: this section provides company-specific information, describing the business organization, ownership, mission, objectives, and history. If location is important in your business, you can include a description of your business facilities here.

Market analysis: this section or sections presents an analysis of the industry, target market, and competition that the business faces.

Product or service description: this section describes exactly what your company will offer its customers.

Marketing and sales plans: these sections set forth the marketing strategy that the business will follow, and provide details of your marketing activities to support sales.

Operations and management plans: depending on your type of business, your operations and management plans may include production and inventory plans, customer service and order fulfillment plans, facilities and equipment plans, management and personnel plans, expansion plans, and any other pertinent issues.

Financial plans: this section includes your projections (and historical financial information, if you have it) that demonstrate how the business can be expected to do financially if the business plan's assumptions are sound.

Appendix: this is the place to present supporting documents, statistical analysis, product marketing materials, resumes of key employees, etc.

These items are presented in the order in which they *usually* appear in the plan. But don't feel constrained to follow this exact format if another way makes more sense because of the nature of your business.

Work Smart

Remember that there is no requirement that these items be *created* in the order shown. In fact, conventional wisdom has it that the executive summary, which is preceded only by the cover sheet and table of contents, should be prepared after the rest of the plan is complete.

The relative mix of product and services to be offered will affect the content of a plan. For example, a business that relies on the services of many professional employees would provide substantial details about acquiring and retaining these vital workers. Issues relating to suppliers, production, inventory, etc., become more significant as the product/service mix moves toward a purely product-based business.

In any event, it pays to at least mention all the major issues discussed here, even the ones that are relatively less significant to your particular business. This is particularly true if you're developing a plan with the object of obtaining financing. Someone who's reading your plan will be more confident about your assessment of the situation if you identify such issues and resolve them, however quickly.

Example

If you plan to work alone and perform all services personally, you might note that you don't anticipate a need to hire employees or engage independent contractors if the business succeeds at the levels projected in the plan. You don't want to raise any questions in the mind of your audience that aren't resolved somewhere within the plan document.

FORMAT AND PRESENTATION ISSUES

First of all, remember that the business plan is a clearly recognizable type of document, and your audience will have some expectations with respect to style and contents. Just as your teachers in school expected you to conform to certain standards, the people who will look at your business plan will have certain expectations.

You want your plan to look professional and be a useful tool. There are a number of things you can do to ensure that is the case:

- Print the plan on a high-quality white or cream colored paper. Print on one side of the paper only.

- Incorporate a cover page that includes your logo, company motto, or other identifying information or graphic. Be sure to include an address and phone number for the business and to name the person who should be contacted about the plan.

- Use a typeface that is easy to read, and a font size that is large enough to prevent eyestrain. This may require financial projections to be spread over several pages in order to maintain readability.

- Maintain reasonable borders for your pages. Allowing one inch of white space all around is a good rule of thumb.

- If those in your business use specialized language or acronyms, use them sparingly and be sure to define any terms that someone outside your area of expertise wouldn't readily know.

- Number the pages, and be sure that the page numbers are accurately reflected in the table of contents.

- Keep the plan short and concise: 20 to 30 pages should be sufficient for most small businesses. You can always provide additional details in an appendix, if required.

- Be certain to carefully edit the document. Spelling and grammatical errors do not make a good impression.

- Don't go overboard on expensive binders, paper, printing, etc. Elevating the form of the plan over its substance can raise doubts among those reading the plan. If the plan is for an outside audience, a simple plastic spiral binding will allow your plan to lie flat while opened, without adding too much to the weight and bulk of the plan. If the plan is for internal use, you may want to use a three-ring binder so that you can insert additional materials as needed.

THE COVER PAGE

If you have spent any time and effort at all on a company logo, slogan, or other identifying graphic or text, the cover page is the place to highlight it.

If you haven't considered these basic marketing tools, we strongly suggest that you do so. Building an identity is vital if you want people to recognize and remember your business.

In addition, the cover sheet contains all the usual and appropriate identification information about the business. This includes business address, telephone numbers, facsimile numbers, etc.

The cover sheet should state the date that the plan was prepared. It should identify the person to contact regarding any questions about the plan (generally, you). If you have prepared multiple copies of your business plan, you might also put a copy number on the cover page to help you ensure that none go astray.

THE TABLE OF CONTENTS

The table of contents should clearly and simply lead a reader to each of the documents in the plan. Be sure that page numbers are accurately reflected. If the plan is long, consider dividing it up into subsections, if that will make it easier for readers to find specific documents. For shorter plans, just numbering the pages in sequence is fine.

If your table of contents is more than two pages long, reconsider the length of the section headings, the length of your plan, and the number of documents you've included.

THE EXECUTIVE SUMMARY

The executive summary is the most important section of the business plan. Its purpose is to summarize the highlights of the plan and to provide a brief snapshot of the business. It must be concise, specific, and well-written.

The summary emphasizes those factors that will make the business a success. It must give the reader a fix on the size and type of company for which the plan is written, its management, and the types of products or services it offers. It should briefly present some basic information about the industry, the size of the target market, and company financial goals in terms of revenue and profits, and indicate any funding required.

For new businesses or businesses seeking funding, credibility and excitement are key elements of the executive summary. Venture capitalists receive hundreds of plans each month, and just a few are actually read from cover to cover. A quick 20-second scan of the executive summary is often the basis for determining whether the plan will be read and whether your company may be considered for investment. When the plan is the vehicle used to attract financing or investment, the executive summary should make it clear to the reader who is a potential source of funds why the company is a sound investment.

If your business plan is designed to help you get a loan, the executive summary must include some information on the amount and purpose of the funds you are seeking, and indicate how you intend to pay the money back. The more specific you can be about the type(s) of loan you are seeking (e.g., a term loan, a working capital line of credit, a mortgage on real estate), the more you will favorably impress the lender. Some business owners choose to highlight this information by placing it in a separate subsection, entitled "Financing Proposal" or something similar.

THE APPENDIX

The appendix is the repository for those items that aren't part of the plan itself but that are helpful or persuasive to someone reading the plan. While it will appear at the very end of your plan, we mention it here to remind you that you can add to it as you develop each section of your plan.

Your plan document is intended to present a concise summary of your business; in the process of creating it, you'll uncover a lot of interesting information that won't actually be included in the plan itself. If you think it is likely that a reader will seek further information regarding some portion of your plan, you can include the appropriate supporting material in the appendix.

The appendix may also house sample marketing materials such as brochures, ads, sales scripts, letters of reference from customers, and good product reviews. If you are just starting out, consider including resumes of key employees if you are relying on their skill and experience. Consider material for inclusion only if you believe that it adds to or clarifies the rest of the plan.

Chapter 3

The Company Summary

The company summary section of your business plan generally consists of four to six subsections that, when considered together, present information that gives a general overview of the nature, structure, and goals of your business.

For many businesses, the information that needs to be presented is your company's ownership and organization structure, a mission statement, and a list of your business objectives. Depending on your business, you may need to include a description of your location and facilities, your company's history, and/or startup information. For all businesses, we recommend that you include a listing of what you perceive to be the keys to your business's success. This will help you to prioritize your goals and your activities throughout the year.

Note that startup businesses face a special challenge when drafting the company summary. In the absence of an existing operation, the background will be couched in terms of what the business *will do*, not what it has done. This makes it even more important to have a clear picture in mind as to how your business will look and operate once it's up and running. When you have a track record, it's easy to point at the results you've achieved as an indication of your potential for success. Without any history, you'll have to work a little harder to make sure that you've developed, and presented, a realistic idea of what it will take to make your business work.

COMPANY OWNERSHIP

The company ownership portion of the plan provides information that describes the form of organization of your business — that is, whether it is a sole proprietorship, partnership, corporation, or limited liability company.

For a sole proprietorship, a simple one-line statement to that effect may be all you need. If the business has more than one owner, this subsection should list the owners and the percentage or number of shares that they own. If the owners are active in the business, you may want to briefly describe their role, although you should also include a lengthier description of each principal's responsibilities in the "management and employees" section of the plan (see page 59).

If the structure of your business has changed over the years, you may want to include that information and a brief statement as to why you decided to make the change. For example, you might say that "in 1992 the business was incorporated to facilitate succession planning for the owner."

THE MISSION STATEMENT

A company mission statement can be a powerful force to clearly define your company's purpose for existence, and to determine the direction that all future activity should take.

Your mission statement will not necessarily describe what your business provides to customers, right now, but rather expresses your vision for the company. It should focus on the future and present an expansive view of what your company is all about.

The most successful company missions are measurable, definable, and actionable project statements, with emotional appeal, that everyone involved with the company knows and can act upon. For an example from corporate America, a mission to "be the best health-care provider in the world" for a multi-national HMO organization sounds good. But a simple mission statement from Honda — "beat GM!" — is better because it's a project statement that can be measured every day by every employee.

Case Study — Creating a Company Mission Statement

As an example of how a company mission statement can serve as a focus for improvement in your business's performance, consider the case of Fred's Grocery, a small one-store business, which suffered sales declines when a large chain supermarket opened in the neighborhood.

Fred initially considered lowering prices and adding many new items to compete, at great expense and lower margins. However, a family discussion about the "mission" of Fred's Grocery caused Fred to respond in a less direct, less costly, and less risky manner.

Fred and his family realized that their *mission was to serve the convenience needs of local, upscale neighborhood shoppers for specialty items and "fill-in" grocery items that they needed.*

The majority of Fred's shoppers spent an average of only $12 ($5-$25 per visit), considerably less than at the larger chain store. Fred and his family decided they would offer more services and specialty items than the larger chain store. Their array of specialty goods, prices, and services also separated them from convenience store chains like Seven-Eleven.

Fred's carried all groceries to the shoppers' cars and apartments and delivered gift baskets/flowers, at no extra charge within a five-block radius of the store. They also added specialty items to their store, putting in an espresso coffee bar, wine kiosk, and food/flower gift assortments. They upgraded and limited the amount of fruits and fresh vegetable selections and added fresh, warm breads and cookies.

After one year, Fred's Grocery realized its best year ever and increased both shopper traffic and average sale by 100 percent to an average of over $25 per shopper. Fred felt the new chain store was the best thing that ever happened to his business, thanks to the time he took to discuss and refine his mission statement!

YOUR COMPANY OBJECTIVES

The statement of objectives in your business plan is basically your short list of goals for the year, or for the time period covered by the plan.

Most business owners find it helpful to set a number of annual financial goals. For example, you may set goals of hitting a certain volume of sales in dollars or units, maintaining a certain percentage of gross margin, achieving a certain inventory turnover rate, or increasing your market share to a certain percentage. For a startup business, one of your goals may simply be to become profitable within a certain number of months (or years) after you open for business.

You may also have some non-financial goals, such as opening a new location, establishing a training program for employees, reducing customer complaints to a certain number per month, introducing a certain number of new products, or modifying your customer base (for example, transforming a 50/50 split between retail and wholesale, to a 35/65 split in favor of wholesale).

It's important to keep your goals realistic and limited in number. If outsiders are reading your plan, they will generally expect to see at least three financial goals, and they will expect you to set goals that are reasonably achievable.

But even if you are writing a plan that no one but yourself will see, your goals should be set high enough to motivate you into action, but not so high that you'll give up in disgust after three or four months.

Work Smart

One of the most difficult parts of running a small business can be prioritizing your time. Particularly if you're just starting out, it can be tempting to get caught up in the thousands of details that go into the business's operation, and to feel overwhelmed by all the decisions you need to make. It can be extremely helpful to keep your goals in sight at all time, to remind yourself of what's really important, and to stay focused on relentlessly pursuing those tasks that will help you reach your goals.

KEYS TO SUCCESS

While not absolutely essential to every plan, we believe that an effective business plan should list, early on, the most important of the actions that you must take to reach your goals.

Identifying these key activities can itself be an art, not a science, and the keys to success portion of your plan will illustrate your style as a manager as much as it will tell the reader about your business. You may find it useful to hold off on writing the keys to success until you have completed the rest of your plan. When you know how all the pieces of the plan fit together, you can identify those tasks that are most crucial.

One important point: your keys to success should be things that you can control.

Example

As a very simple example, a snow removal company may know that it will have more work if there is a heavier than normal amount of snowfall this year, but there's obviously nothing the business owner can do to control the weather! There's little point in listing, as a key to success, "snow on at least 40 days this winter."

In this instance, the key to success might be to increase the percentage of sales made to customers who are willing to pay a monthly charge for snow removal, regardless of the number of times that the plowing must actually be done. That way, the uncontrollable but important factor can be effectively neutralized.

COMPANY LOCATION AND FACILITIES

The company summary section of your business plan may include information about your business's location and facilities (e.g., your retail store, manufacturing plant, etc.), although you may need to devote a separate section to this subject if your facilities are very important to your business (see page 57).

At a minimum, the facilities description should list the type, address, and size of each business location you own or rent. It should also briefly describe the surrounding area (i.e., is your store located in a commercial strip mall with off-street parking, or are you located on the second floor of an indoor shopping galleria). Is the area zoned residential, commercial, or light industrial? Is it convenient to major transportation routes? Is there adequate parking? What are your hours of operation?

You may want to describe your most immediate neighbors, if relevant. For example, if you have a small retail store, the presence of a major department or food store in the vicinity may be an important source of walk-in business, and a major advantage to your company.

COMPANY BACKGROUND AND CURRENT STATUS

For a business that has been in operation for a while, you need to set the stage for the business plan with a narrative that explains how your company came into being and what were the major milestones you've passed along the way.

This will give the reader a sense of why you chose the business you're in, where you currently stand in the business lifecycle, and a general overview of your major strengths and weaknesses.

This section of the business plan need not be lengthy and filled with facts and figures — those will have their place later on, in the marketing, operations, and financial sections. The emphasis here should be on conveying the broad outlines, in a way that presents a very positive image of your company. It's a good opportunity for you to express your personal style.

For examples of different ways to handle the company background section of the business plan, see the plans for Bob's Big Pencils on page 159 and Computer Solutions, Inc. on page 193.

STARTUP SUMMARY

If your business is in the startup phase, you should include a section that provides detailed information about the costs you expect to incur in starting your business. The chart that follows can be used as a starting point to determine your business startup costs.

Initial Cash Requirements for the New Business		
One-Time Startup Expenses		
Startup Expenses	*Amount*	*Description*
Advertising		Promotion for opening the business.
Building/Remodeling		The amount per contractor bid, materials, etc.
Decorating		Estimate based on bid if appropriate.
Deposits		Check with the utility companies.
Equipment Lease Payments		The amount to be paid before opening.
Insurance		Bid from insurance agent.
Licenses and Permits		Check with city or state offices.
Miscellaneous		All other.
Professional Fees		Include CPA, attorney, engineer, etc.
Rent		The amount to be paid before opening.
Services		Cleaning, accounting, etc.
Signs		Use contractor bids.
Supplies		Office, cleaning, etc. supplies.
Unanticipated Expenses		Include an amount for the unexpected.
Total Startup Expenses		Total amount of expenses before opening.
Cash		Requirements for the first 90 days.
Beginning Inventory		The amount of inventory needed to open.
Other Short-Term Assets		
Total Short-Term Assets		
Building		Use the actual price of the property you want.
Fixtures and Equipment		Use actual bids.
Installation of Fixtures and Equipment		Use actual bids.
Other Long-Term Assets		
Total Long-Term Assets		
Total Startup Expenses		Total expenses and assets before opening.
Left to Finance		Amount of financing still needed.

You'll also need to explain how you expect to finance these costs. If you are seeking a short-term line of credit, equipment financing, a mortgage, or other type of loan, this should be explained in your startup summary. If the initial costs will be borne by yourself and any other owners, be sure to state that fact.

The amount that you've invested in the business will be a point of interest to any prospective lenders, since owners with significant personal investment are considered to be much stronger credit risks. This information may also be presented in the form of a "sources and uses of funds" statement that you include in the financial statement section of the plan.

Funding Source	Amount	Description
Funding Plan for the New Business		
One-Time Startup Expenses		
Investment		
Investment from Owner A	_____	Investment by individual owner, if appropriate.
Investment from Owner B	_____	Use if necessary.
Investment from Owner C	_____	Use if necessary.
Total Investment	_____	Total investment by business owners.
Short-Term Borrowing		
Unsecured Short-Term Loans	_____	Often, credit cards are used for fill-in cash.
Line of credit	_____	
Other Short-Term Loans	_____	
Total Short-Term Borrowing	_____	
Long-Term Borrowing		
Mortgage	_____	On business property or on your home.
Equipment Loans	_____	
Other Long-Term Loans	_____	
Total Long-Term Loans	_____	
Total Borrowing		Total amount of short and long-term loans.
Loss at Startup	( )	Total amount of startup expenses (not assets)
Total Equity		Total investment
Total Debt and Equity		Add your total investment to total borrowing.

Chapter 4

Market Analysis

A business plan is the blueprint for taking an idea for a product or service and turning it into a commercially viable reality. The Market Analysis section provides the evidence that there is a niche in the market that your company can exploit. It consists of:

- an industry analysis, which assesses the general industry environment in which you compete

- a target market analysis, which identifies and quantifies the customers that you will be targeting for sales

- a competitive analysis, which identifies your competitors and analyzes their strengths and weaknesses

- a SWOT and/or needs analysis may be included to further describe the Strengths and Weaknesses of your business and the market Opportunities and Threats you face (SWOT), or the met and unmet needs that you perceive in the marketplace

The precise way in which you choose to organize this information is up to you. As long as you include all the basic facts, there are a number of outline forms that can work well. Just keep the purpose of your plan in mind, and highlight or expand the sections that have the greatest application to what you're trying to accomplish.

It's also important to realize that as you go about planning a business startup or expansion, you should be doing a lot of research and learning an enormous amount about its marketing environment. Your business plan is not intended to include everything you've learned. It will just summarize the highlights, in a way that shows the reader that you understand your industry, market, and individual business.

THE INDUSTRY

The industry analysis is the section of your business plan in which you demonstrate your knowledge about the general characteristics of the type of business you're in. You should be able to present some statistics about the size of the industry (e.g., total U.S. sales in the last year) and its growth rate over the last few years. Is the industry expanding, contracting, or holding steady? Why?

Who are the major industry participants? While you might not compete directly against these companies (they are likely to be large national or international corporations), it's important that you can identify them, and have a good understanding of their market share and why they are or aren't successful.

You should also be able to discuss the important trends that may affect your industry. For example, significant changes in the target market, in technology, or in other related industries may affect the market's perception of your product or your profitability.

This kind of information is often available for free from the following sources:

- trade association data

- industry publications and databases

- government databases (e.g., Census Bureau, state trade measurements)

- data and analysts' opinions about the largest players in the industry (e.g., Standard & Poor's reports, quotes from reputable news sources)

The *Directory of On-Line Resources* and the *Data Base Catalog* are popular services listing many resources available over your computer modem. Or, if your prefer to do research the old-fashioned (print-based) way, consult a book called *Knowing Where to Look: The Ultimate Guide to Research* by Louis Horowitz, published by the Writer's Digest. The American Marketing Association (the "other" AMA) may be able to help you as well. You can reach it by phone at 1-800-AMA-1150, or on the Internet at http://www.ama.org.

THE TARGET MARKET

How do you determine if there are enough people in your market who are willing to purchase what you have to offer, at the price you need to charge to make a profit? The best way is to conduct a methodical analysis of the market you plan to reach.

You need to know precisely who your customers are, or will be. If you've been in business for a while, you may know many of them by name, but do you really know what type of people or businesses they are?

For example, if you sell to consumers, do you have demographic information (e.g., what are their average income ranges, education, typical occupations, geographic location, family makeup, etc.) that identifies your target buyers? What about lifestyle information (e.g., hobbies, interests, recreational/entertainment activities, political beliefs, cultural practices, etc.) on your target buyers?

You may very well sell to several types of customers — for example, you may sell at both retail and wholesale, and you may have some government or nonprofit customers as well. If so, you'll want to describe the most important characteristics of each group separately.

Directly surveying your current customers can be expensive. For planning purposes, it's acceptable to substitute published industry-wide information; for example, "the average U.S. household computer owner is between the ages of 31 and 42, has graduated from college, and earns $40,000 to $60,000 per year."

Once obtained, this type of information can help you in two very important ways. It can help you develop or make changes to your product or service itself, to better match what your customers are likely to want. It can also tell you how to reach your customers through advertising, promotions, etc.

Example

A company that sells athletic shoes may know that its typical customer is also a sports fan. Thus, if it can build shoes good enough to be worn by professional athletes, it will have a convincing story about quality to tell. It can also benefit by using well-known athletes as spokespersons in its advertising, and by placing advertisements in sports magazines where its customers are likely to see them.

It is also important to be able to estimate the size of your target market, particularly if you're thinking about a new venture, so that you can tell if the customer base is large enough to support your business or new product idea. Remember that it's not enough that people like your business concept. There must be enough target buyers on a frequent enough basis to sustain your company revenues and profits from year to year. Small businesses have a strong advantage here, in that they can often be profitable while serving a relatively small niche — one that a Fortune 500 company would consider too small to pursue.

Niche Marketing

Most marketers know that "20 percent of buyers consume 80 percent of product volume." If you could identify that key 20 percent and find others like them, you could sell much more product with much less effort.

The heaviest users of your product or service can be thought of as a market "niche" that you should attempt to dominate. The driving force behind niche marketing is the need to satisfy and retain those consumers who really love your products or services. It is much more efficient to continue selling to the same customers, than it is to continually go out and find new ones.

Therefore, in your target market analysis, you'll want to identify your ideal customer niche as narrowly as possible, keeping in mind that your niche must be large enough to profitably support your company.

Influences on Consumer Behavior

If your customers are primarily the ultimate consumers or end users of your product or service, identification of your target market is generally done in terms of demographic and lifestyle factors.

Demographics are tangible, measurable facts that distinguish one group of people from another, whereas lifestyle analysis is more concerned with the intangibles.

Demographic Factors

- ethnic background
- age
- income
- education
- sex

- location
- occupation
- number of people in family
- children's ages

Lifestyle Factors

- cultural background
- religious beliefs
- political beliefs

- music preferences
- literature preferences
- food or menu preferences

- value systems
- recreation and hobbies
- social interaction patterns
- entertainment preferences
- travel preferences
- media habits

For example, heavy coffee, liquor, and tobacco users are not easily identified with demographic information. They may be found in any age group or socio-economic category. However, lifestyle analysis shows high correlation with certain characteristics, including media habits, recreational pursuits, social interaction patterns, music, and other attributes.

Influences on Channel Buyers

If you sell to other businesses that turn around and resell your products and services, your buyers are predominantly channel buyers. Examples of channel buyers from the grocery and drug industry are:

- national master distributors

- local/regional distributors

- chain store wholesaler buyers

- individual retail store buyers

Influences on channel buyers may include things that have little to do with what you consider the key benefits of your products.

Influences on Channel Buyer Decisions

- **Profitability of the item** — the higher the margin and dollar profit per item as compared to competitive category products, the more likely the trade will accept it, regardless of product quality.

- **Availability of discount deals** — they can increase margin, volume, and velocity of the item. For example, 10 percent to 25 percent off invoice for all purchases during a quarter is a typical discount range for grocery and drug retailers.

- **Advertising and promotion support programs** — multi-media TV, radio, print, and PR support, plus heavy consumer couponing, sweepstakes, or contests are typical consumer packaged goods programs that may be run one to four times per year.

- **Other cash deals** — for example, new item "slotting fees" are the subject of controversy and frustration for many manufacturers supplying grocery, drug, and mass merchandiser retailers. Slotting fees are cash payments and/or free goods that are not refundable, even if the products are dropped after six months by the retailer. Slotting fees range from a few hundred dollars to over $25,000 per item in some chains.

- **Availability of free goods** — for example, one free case per store is common for new grocery item distribution.

- **Personal buyer/seller relationships** — there will always be personal relationships influencing buying decisions as long as there are people selling to people. That's why you hire good salespeople!

- **Sales incentive programs** — these programs may spur salespeople on to greater productivity and sales of a particular item or offering.

THE COMPETITION

Once you've identified what's unique about your business and who your target buyers are, you need to take a good, long look at your competition.

In the industry overview section of your business plan, you may have identified the largest players in your industry. Not all of these businesses will be directly competing with you, however. Some may be located in geographically distant locations, and others may have pricing or distribution systems that are very different from those of a small business.

Therefore, in your competition analysis, you'll focus on those businesses that directly compete with you for sales.

Levels of Competition

It may help to think of your competitors as a series of levels, ranging from your most direct competitors to those who are more remote.

- **First level** — the specific companies or brands that are direct competitors to your product or service, in your geographic locality. In many cases, these competitors offer a product or service that is interchangeable with yours in the eyes of the consumer (although, of course, you hope you hold the advantage with better quality, more convenient distribution, and other special features). For example, if you operate a local garden center, you may compete against the other garden centers within a 10-mile radius.

- **Second level** — competitors who offer similar products in a different business category or who are more geographically remote. Using the example of the garden center, a discount chain that sells garden supplies and plants in season is also your competitor, as is a landscaping contractor who will provide and install the plants, and a mail-order house who sells garden tools and plants in seed or bulb form. None of these competitors provides exactly the same mix of products and services as you, but they may be picking off the most lucrative parts of your business.

- **Third level** — competitors who compete for the "same-occasion" dollars. Inasmuch as gardening is a hobby, third-level competitors might be companies that provide other types of entertainment or hobby equipment; inasmuch as gardening is a type of home-improvement, competitors might be providers of other home-improvement supplies and services.

The point of this analysis is to consider carefully, from the buyer's point of view, all the alternatives that there are to purchasing from you. Knowing that, you can attempt to make sure that your business provides advantages over your competitors, beginning with those who are the most directly similar to you. In fact, you can even borrow ideas from second- or third-level competitors in order to compete more effectively against your first-tier competitors.

Competitors' Strengths and Weaknesses

It's to your advantage to know as much as you reasonably can about the identity of your competitors, and the details of your competitors' businesses. Study their ads, brochures, and promotional materials. Drive past their location (and if it's a retail business, make some purchases there, incognito if necessary). Talk to their customers and examine their pricing. What are they doing well that you can copy, and what are they doing poorly that you can capitalize on?

Secondary data, as well as information from your sales force or other contacts among your suppliers and customers, can provide rich information about competitors' strengths and weaknesses. Basic information every company should know about their competitors includes:

- each competitor's size and market share, as compared to your own

- how target buyers perceive or judge your competitors' products and services

- your competitors' financial strength, which affects their ability to spend money on advertising and promotions, among other things

- each competitor's ability and speed of innovation for new products and services

There may be a wealth of other facts that you need to know, depending on the type of business you have. For example, if you're in catalog sales, you'll want to know how fast your competitors can fulfill a typical customer's order, what they charge for shipping and handling, etc.

Even for new businesses, company data from competitors may be available by interviewing competitor company executives, attending industry trade shows, and asking the right questions from industry "experts." They may be unaffordable as consultants but willing to direct you to free databases that you would not ordinarily know of or have access to. And don't overlook your competitor's suppliers. They can be excellent sources of information to aid your research.

Future Competition

Along with your current competitors, your business plan should give some consideration to the possibility that other competition will arise in the near future.

So, you should discuss the barriers to entry for a new business in your industry and market. Is it relatively easy, or relatively difficult, to join the fray in terms of capital, staffing, inventory, distribution control, workforce, relationships with suppliers, etc.?

If your business is new, you'll have to show how you can overcome these hurdles yourself.

What other types of businesses (or other entities) are most likely to be able to overcome these hurdles? What is the likelihood of new entrants to the market in the next few years? Remember that, with the increasing influence of the Internet and catalog merchants, companies that are geographically remote from you may already be selling directly to your customers.

(SWOT) ANALYSIS

One useful way to organize information about your company and its marketing environment is to do a Strengths, Weaknesses, Opportunities, and Threats (SWOT) analysis. While this section is not mandatory for all business plans, it can help you to think more creatively about the factors that will affect your business.

Strength and weakness analysis is an internal company exercise to gauge your ability to compete effectively. Opportunity and threat analysis is an external exercise centered on competitors and the external environment that affect your company's ability to compete. Almost every business can come up with a list of at least five or six items, for each of these four categories. Some key questions are:

Strengths and weaknesses:

- What are your company's greatest strengths in terms of product or service, name recognition and reputation, production processes, workforce, location, distribution channels, favorable supplier relationships, management knowledge and experience, and creativity?

- What are your greatest weaknesses in these areas?

- Are some or all of the items you sell subject to varying product life cycles? How do your products compare to competitors' product life cycles?

Opportunities and threats:

- How does the overall economic outlook, and the economic outlook in your geographical area, affect you? Is the local population growing? Is the job market growing? Are income levels increasing?

- How big are your competitors, and what are their financial resources? Is your competition actively seeking to grow through new product or service introductions, new outlets, new distribution channels, or acquisitions?

- Are competitors' market shares growing, or are they loosing their grip on your target buyers? What types of competitive spending, promotions, advertising, and field sales response will your business encounter?

You may need to network with potential customers, industry associations, suppliers, and competitors to answer these questions.

In the case of weaknesses and threats, you should give a considerable amount of thought to how you'll go about compensating for (or better yet, eliminating) the problem, and discuss that in your plan. In the case of positive factors, you may want to give some thought to how you'll preserve your edge.

For an example of how SWOT analysis might be conducted for a small service company, consider the following case study.

Case Study — Life Designs Architecture

An independent architect who specializes in designing residential homes, Life Designs, has a strengths, weaknesses, opportunities, and threats (SWOT) list that includes:

Strengths:

- ability to respond quickly to customer demands and changes
- ability to make acceptable margins on small jobs, with low overhead
- high quality of work and experience
- reputation for being affable, honest, and easy to work with
- reputation for good value of services and prices
- appeal to customers of working directly with the architect/principal

Weaknesses

- very limited financial, personnel, and time resources
- a limit of three to four projects at any given time
- inability to sell and work on a project at the same time
- not having a personal relationship with influential local business leaders
- being known for a limited number of architectural design "styles"

Opportunities

- a growing market for new homes and more upscale homeowners moving to the area, fostered by a growing local economy
- a chance to contract with a local developer for an exclusive agreement
- a chance to work with the university architectural design department as a visiting lecturer
- a chance to relocate his office from his home to a co-op business office center, with shared secretaries, receptionist, conference rooms, and computers
- the availability of hiring independent sales reps to work with residential owners, real estate firms, and contractors

Threats

- a growing amount of advertising and business inroads by outside regional and national firms in the local area

- new local zoning codes and state/federal legislation increasing the cost of new home and remodeling/addition work

- increasing costs of building materials

- a possible shortage of skilled building trade people in the area

- a new competitor in the area specializing in residential home design, especially in his known "style" of design

NEEDS ANALYSIS

While not absolutely essential for all business plans, a needs analysis can help you to further refine your expectations for the success of your business.

Particularly for new business owners, it's important to remember that, while you may be drawn to a particular type of business because of your knowledge of its operations or your affinity with the type of product or service you're planning to offer, ultimately your success will depend on how well you satisfy your customers' needs.

Example

A small business that operates an auto repair shop must remember that customers patronize the shop because they need reliable transportation. Everything that the shop does must come together to serve that need. By focusing on the customer's need, the shop owner can devise ways to improve service *in the eyes of the customer,* such as by offering loaner cars, providing free rides to the customer's workplace, or guaranteeing the service performed for a specified period. The typical auto shop customer is less likely to be concerned about the decor of the shop or about bargain-basement prices, since those don't immediately impact on the need for transportation.

Once you've come up with what you believe to be the customer's most important needs in relation to your products or service, and to your category of business in general, you can divide your list into two parts: needs that are already being successfully met in the marketplace, and needs that remain unfilled. You can then describe how your business will fill these gaps in the marketplace.

You need to be aware of the needs that are already being filled, so that you can avoid being simply a "me-too" business with little chance of breaking down your customers' already established loyalty to another provider. Particularly if the competition is well-established with a substantial market share, it will be difficult to break in unless you do a noticeably better job of meeting more of your customers' needs.

On the other hand, there are few customer needs that go unnoticed and unserved for long. If you believe that you've discovered a huge, gaping hole in the marketplace, chances are that either (a) the need isn't as large as it appears, (b) the need can't be profitably satisfied, or (c) your competitors are already making plans to move into the market.

Although there are a few exceptions, particularly where new technology is being employed, most small businesses can thrive by becoming more closely attuned to their customers' needs, and offering a product or service combination that meets those needs in a significantly superior way.

Warning

You may discover that virtually all of the customer's needs are already being filled. If so, you'll have to reexamine the situation a bit. Either you must dig deeper to uncover more unmet needs, or rethink your business plan more dramatically. Perhaps going into a slightly different type of business would allow you to function in a marketplace that's not quite as saturated.

Chapter 5

Product Or
Service Description

If you've reached the point where you are trying to write a description of what it is that your business actually does or sells, you've probably been thinking about your product or service for quite some time. Now is the time to take a step back and reflect.

What's the view from 40,000 feet? What's the big picture overview of your product lines or the services you offer? How would you categorize them and describe them for a reader who's unfamiliar with the terrain?

Remember that the product or service idea you have hasn't been kicking around for months in the heads of the people who might read your plan. You may have to set the stage a little bit to make sure that a reader understands exactly what your product or service is. On the other hand, don't go overboard with detail. For example, you won't need to list every single product that will be carried in a retail store, or every item that will be on the menu for a restaurant.

The starting point is a clear statement of what the product is or what service your business will provide. Focus on those factors that make your offering unique and desirable to customers. Explain what it does, how it works, how long it lasts, what options are available, etc. Especially if your plan is being written for an external audience, be sure that you explain any special terms with which people outside your industry might be unfamiliar.

If you're a service provider, what categories of services do you offer, and approximately how long does it take to provide each unit of service? Are packages available?

Explain whether you are selling a standalone product (e.g., lunch) or a product that must be used with other products (e.g., computer software or peripheral devices). Be sure to describe the requirements for any associated products (especially vital for software). And, if there are special requirements for successful sales, say so.

Another issue to consider is whether you hope to sell items on a one-time or infrequent basis, or whether repeat sales are the goal. If you're opening a bakery or restaurant, you're going to count on the same customers returning on a regular basis. But a heating contractor installing a new furnace or a consultant helping to implement a new order processing system probably isn't going to do that again for the same client any time soon (we hope!).

If there are certain products or services that your competitors carry but you don't, take some time to explain why so that the reader isn't left to question your judgment.

If you will be operating a retail environment, you'll want to describe the store or restaurant, as well as the items you'll offer there. You might consider adding a picture or a diagram of the layout in your appendix, as well, unless you'll be discussing these things in detail in a separate "Business Facilities" section of your plan (see page 57).

COMPETITIVE COMPARISONS

Your product or service description should give the reader a complete picture by comparing your offering to similar services or products offered by others. This is especially important for a new business seeking financing. The potential lender or investor will want to mentally position you among the other companies in your category, with which he or she is more familiar.

In the competitive comparison section, it's natural to focus on how your products are bigger, better, longer lasting, better tasting, or generally more exciting that those of your competitors. There's nothing wrong with being very positive about your business's offerings. However, if your competitor's products are clearly superior in some respects, you should mention that as well. Your business plan is a planning document, not a sales brochure, and readers will not be favorably impressed by unrealistic hyperbole.

As a general rule, your plan should always address potential problems, including the strengths of your competition, rather than avoiding all mention of them. The fact that you can recognize where legitimate problems might exist reflects well on your management abilities. Most lenders and outside investors will be more impressed by the fact that you can identify problems and deal with them, than they would be if no problems existed in the planning document.

SOURCING

To some extent, all businesses are dependent on their relationships with suppliers. Even if you make nearly all the products you sell, you'll need to get your raw materials from somewhere. Service providers must locate sources of supplies used in rendering those services. And if you resell products, the source of those products can be extremely important.

Your business plan should address the type of vendors you will use, and if possible, identify them by name. You'll want to show that the issues of price, quality, and availability have been covered. Knowing which vendors you want to use, what products or services they can provide, and what business terms they require is an important part of getting your business on its feet.

In some cases, the readers of your plan will be more familiar with the vendors you use than they are with you, and you have the opportunity to gain favorably by association. You might include copies of important contracts in the appendix of your business plan, to reinforce this favorable impression.

FUTURE PRODUCTS AND SERVICES

Successful small businesses generally find that other businesses will eventually discover their formula and attempt to imitate them. Particularly if you've done a good job of identifying an important unmet need of your target market, you'll find that copycats seem to spring out of the woodwork all too quickly, and some of them may even threaten your hard-won market share.

So, small business owners need to embrace and seek out change, rather than avoid it or wait until change is forced upon them by competitors. One way to do this is to constantly be on the lookout for ways to expand your business by offering new products or services to your customers, or by combining products or services in new ways.

Your business plan should address the future in some fashion, by outlining the opportunities you see for growth beyond your current capabilities. To some extent, you've done that by creating an expansive mission statement (see page 24). But you should also include at least a few paragraphs, in the product or service section of the plan, that describe your expectations for the next round of new products or services, or an update/upgrade of your current ones.

Work Smart

Timing is also an issue to address. Be realistic about the time it will take to develop the new product or service. It's generally better to set a far-off deadline and come in early, than to continually have to revise and extend your introduction date (witness the credibility gap that some giant software companies have experienced when promised software takes months or years longer than expected to materialize).

Chapter 6

Marketing And Sales Plans

Your marketing and sales plans explain how you plan to reach your targeted customers and how you will effectively market your product or service to those customers. In essence, the marketing plan provides an answer to the market analysis that you've done. It sets forth the specific steps you will take to promote and sell your product or service and provides a timetable for those actions to occur.

Traditionally, the marketing plan portion of the business plan addresses four main topics: product, price, place, and promotion.

PRODUCT

What are the goods or services that your business will offer? How are your offerings better than those against which they will compete? Why will people buy from you? These questions will be answered in the "product" section of your marketing and sales plan.

First, you'll want to provide a very brief overview of your products or services, primarily to set the stage for readers who may not yet have read the detailed product or service description that you've provided in a separate section of the business plan (see Chapter 5).

Then, highlight the aspects of your offerings that will surpass those of your competitors. For example, if you offer a superior warranty or a broader range of services, this is the place to say that.

PRICE

How much will you charge? How will you strike a balance between sales volume and price to maximize net income? Will you be testing a variety of price points? Will you offer discounts and, if so, under what circumstances? This section of your business plan will discuss your pricing policy in some detail.

All pricing strategies depend on balancing three influences:

- Cost — to produce the item and to cover your overhead

- Competition — what other businesses are charging for comparable offerings

- Demand — what customers are willing to pay, and how many of them are willing to pay it

The basic concern for almost all small businesses is to price products at a level that will cover all expenses and that customers will accept, which generally means pricing that's fairly close to that of your competitors.

Analyzing Market Size and Composition

In setting prices for your product or service, one of the first calculations you must do is to estimate approximately how large your potential sales volume could be, based on a reasonable assessment of your potential market share in the product category, at different price levels. Knowing the size of the existing market is critical to determining if there are enough customers to establish and grow a business.

In an established market, in order to sell your product you must cut into your competitors' market shares. Who will you compete against? What are their strengths and weaknesses? Are any direct competitors vulnerable to your products? Are any competitive products priced too high or not providing product "value" for the price? The competitive analysis, described on page 36, should help you to answer these questions.

Researching Product Price Elasticity

If demand for your product or service changes significantly with slight changes in price, the product category is considered to be *elastic* with respect to price.

If no significant volume changes occur, even with significant price changes, the category is *inelastic.*

Example

Grocery store items are often very price sensitive, with a 10 percent price increase or decrease resulting in significant share and volume changes per brand. Consumers are less price-conscious when shopping for gourmet foods, and a price increase or decrease of 50 percent may be required to create any perceptible changes in consumers' behavior.

The greater the price elasticity for a product you offer, the closer you should price your products to similar competitive products and vice versa. While your product may be unique, consumers will not pay much of a premium for it if there are similar competitive choices at lower prices.

To find out more about price elasticity, you might study secondary data sources for your industry or talk to trade association experts.

Evaluating Your Product's Uniqueness

The closer your product resembles competitive products, the smaller the price differences that buyers will tolerate. And the closer the product differences between brands, the greater the likelihood that brand-switching will occur when products go on sale.

Product uniqueness does not guarantee a significant price premium over a competitive product, if the product differences aren't recognizable and meaningful to consumers. And depending on the category of product or service, even recognizable and meaningful product differences may not be enough to get buyers to switch to the new product at equivalent pricing, let alone at a premium price over the competition.

Field testing on a small market basis is highly recommended for testing new product differences or unique new products.

Analyzing Your Costs and Overhead

The most common errors in pricing are:

- pricing products or services based only on the cost to produce them

- pricing products based only on competitors' prices

Instead, you need to take both of these strategies into account and find the proper balance between them. At the very least, your pricing policy must allow you to meet your breakeven point. For more on how to calculate breakeven, see page 66.

Wholesaling and Retailing Markups

Retailers and wholesalers need to consider the issue of markups in their pricing structure, and manufacturers or other product producers need to be aware of the average markup in their industry.

A Few Definitions

"Markup" is the percentage of the selling price (or sometimes the cost) of a product which is added to the cost in order to arrive at a selling price.

"Markdown" is a percentage reduction from the selling price.

Be aware that there are two different ways to calculate markup — on cost or on selling price. So when someone asks you about your markup on an item, you must specify whether it is "20 percent of *cost*" or "20 percent of *selling price*." In retailing, the industry standard is to compute markup as a percentage of selling price.

Example

Joel received a shipment of clocks that he will sell in his gift store. He paid $12.00 for each clock and plans to make $4.00 on each one. The selling price is then $16.00.

The markup percentage on cost is the dollar markup (4.00) divided by cost (12.00) = **33%.**

However, the markup percentage on selling price is the dollar markup (4.00) divided by selling price (16.00) = **25%.**

As a product wends its way through a distribution channel, each step along the journey adds a "markup" before selling the product to the next step. Here's an example of how markups work based on selling price:

Level	Category	$	%
Producer	Cost	20.00	80.0
	Markup	5.00	20.0
	Selling Price	25.00	100.0

Level	Category	$	%
Wholesale Outlet	Cost	25.00	71.5
	Markup	10.00	28.5
	Selling Price	35.00	100.0
Retailer	Cost	35.00	70.0
	Markup	15.00	30.0
	Selling Price	50.00	100.0

Markups vary widely among industries. For example, average retail markups (on selling price) are 14 percent on tobacco products, 50 percent on greeting cards, 8 percent on baby food, and often more than 50 percent on high-end meats.

Considering Other Pricing Strategies

In addition to the primary goal of making money, a company can have many different pricing objectives and strategies. Larger companies may utilize product pricing in a predatory or defensive fashion, to attack or defend against a competitor.

Example

Maxwell House Coffee introduced a second, low-priced brand into their own dominant eastern United States markets during the 1970s to slow and confuse the introduction of Folger's Coffee into their markets. This new product was packaged and designed to resemble Folger's familiar red can, with pricing set below Folger's Coffee. The new temporary product clogged grocer shelves and made it more difficult and expensive for Folger's to introduce their coffee into new eastern markets.

If you have a premium quality product, with premium packaging, graphics, and unique features and benefits, perhaps a premium price is necessary to reinforce the premium brand image. Higher margins than normal may be one benefit. High prices confirm perceptions of high value in consumer minds.

A good pricing strategy will also indicate guidelines for action in the case of price increases or decreases. For example, "We will price at or near the share leader's pricing on a per unit basis. We will increase prices to follow a share leader price increase, but only if we can preserve margin objectives."

Work Smart

Be sure to consider variations that may come up to affect your pricing. You may wish to use discounting for prompt cash payment or for quantity purchases. Seasonal items may warrant special pricing from time to time. How about senior citizen and student discounts? And promotional incentives may motivate your dealers. These are but a few of many variables you'll want to consider when you formulate your pricing strategy.

The pricing levels you finally select for your products should have flexibility for both increases and discounts to customers. Price increases may be inevitable because of component, ingredient, and processing cost increases. The market may or may not absorb price increases without decreasing volume effects.

Work Smart

If in doubt, price on the high side, where possible. It is always easier to discount prices than to raise them.

PLACE

Which sales channels will you use? Will you sell by telephone or will your product be carried in retail outlets? Which channel will let you economically reach your target audience? The "place" discussion in your marketing plan should explain the distribution choices you've made, and how you will go about implementing those choices.

Small businesses may have products that would appeal to many different markets, or channels of distribution in a single market. However, when you have limited resources, it's often best to select a single distribution channel or a limited number of distribution channels that offer:

- greatest ease of entry against the competition

- least financial risk and long-term commitment

- sufficient volume potential to reach short-term company goals

- pricing levels to provide acceptable profit margins

PROMOTION

Whatever you're selling, you'll need to communicate about it with your target buyers. Most businesses find that they need all three components of marketing communications (promotion, advertising, public relations), in some combination. But how do you narrow down the available choices and build a communications program that makes sense? Here's how:

1. **Know who the target buyer is.** Identify the target buyer in demographic, lifestyle, and other descriptive terms.

2. **Determine what is meaningfully unique about your product.** "Meaningful" differences are those business or brand attributes *that buyers or end users consider in making purchase decisions* among different available choices.

3. **Construct a business positioning strategy statement.** It is important to be consistent in all promotion, advertising, and PR programs, particularly with the scarce resources of most small businesses. A good business positioning strategy statement will address who the target buyer or end user is, what the competitive environment is, and what the meaningful differences in the products or services are when compared to the competition. The statement might also communicate some idea of a business "personality" that will be created and fostered in all marketing programs.

4. **Determine the best message to communicate your product positioning to target buyers.** Use your positioning statement to construct a memorable "slogan" or ad message that correlates with the needs and wants of your target buyer.

5. **Determine promotion options and costs in terms of available budget.** There is never enough money to do everything desirable to build the business. Often a promotional budget reality check means a choice between a little promotion, advertising, or PR, but not all three at the same time. Here are some options to consider.

    *   Advertising — consider print, radio, cable television, billboard, and Internet ads; packaging; display and point-of-purchase signs; direct mail; catalogs; brochures and flyers; doorhangers; posters; and the yellow pages and other directories.

- Sales promotions — consider grand openings, games and contests, premiums and gifts, coupons, rebates or "frequent buyer" programs, product demonstrations, low-interest financing, and trade shows.

- Publicity and public relations — consider press releases and press kits; public service activities; and speeches or seminars. These types of activities are often "free" except for the time you'll spend on them.

The marketing and sales plan usually includes a calendar that ties marketing and sales activities to specific operational events. For example, an advertising campaign may begin some months before a new product is ready to be sold. As the date of the new product introduction approaches, the ad campaign would be stepped up. Once the new product hits the market, additional advertising is used to support specific sales objectives.

If your target market is divided among several different types of customers (for instance, you sell both wholesale and retail), you may find it necessary to address promotions for each group separately.

YOUR SALES PLANS

Your sales plans may be included in the "promotions" part of your marketing plans; however, if personal selling is a large part of your strategy and especially if your business will have a sales force, you may wish to devote a separate section to your sales plans.

One challenge that you face in developing your business plan is selecting the sales channel that is most effective. For instance, if you're in a business where you provide services personally, your participation in the sales process can be extensive. In contrast, if your business deals in the sale and production of large quantities of product with little associated service, then you face a different challenge. Customers may not know or care who you are.

Planning for selling is, therefore, based on the particular mix of goods and services that you plan to offer and on the way you intend to reach potential customers. Some tools to consider are sales presentations, product samples and giveaways, and incentive programs for sales reps.

If you are going to have a sales force of some kind, be sure you know what you will expect them to do. When making hiring decisions, do your best to find people who can do what you want. If *you* will be the entire sales force, at least initially, try to quantify the activities and time involved.

Chapter 7

Operations And Management Plans

The operations and management portions of your business plan will explain how you will actually produce the goods and services your business will deliver to its customers. These sections also address the back office or "overhead" activities that all businesses must undertake.

Operations and management include activities such as:

- hiring and managing employees or contract workers

- choosing and maintaining your business facility

- supervising and improving your production processes

- filling orders

- collecting money from customers

- providing customer service and support after the sale

- dealing with unexpected occurrences or changing conditions

These types of issues can be grouped into two major categories for purposes of dealing with them in your plan. The categories are: the operations plan, and the management and human resources plan.

PLANNING YOUR OPERATIONS

Creating the operations plan forces you to think through each step that must be completed before your customers receive whatever it is that they purchase from you, and also how you will interface with customers after the sale. For the reader of your business plan, the operations planning section should provide a good overview of the types of activities your business must routinely perform in its core business activities.

The types of operational issues that you'll face will vary tremendously based on the type of business you own. For example, a consultant who deals primarily in assisting customers with network communications isn't going to have an extensive manufacturing or inventory control plan.

For some service businesses, the operations issues may be adequately addressed in the section of your business plan in which you describe your services. It may be most efficient to describe how you're planning to provide services in the same place where you describe exactly what they are. In that case, the services description section (see page 43), in combination with the human resources section (see page 59), may avert the need for a separate operations section.

Production Plans

A fast food vendor, in contrast, will have to carefully plan for purchasing the food and related supplies, inventory storage and turnover, the cooking process, employee sanitation, disposal, etc. Similarly, a manufacturer will generally have to plan for facilities, equipment, and inventories of raw materials and finished goods, not to mention the production processes themselves. Owners of these types of businesses should include a fairly detailed operations section in their business plan. They may even want to divide the operations section into several subsections, such as production, facilities, inventory control, and customer service/order fulfillment.

In writing the production section of the business plan, you may find it useful to look at your business as if it were a linear process that starts with raw materials and ends with a delivery to a satisfied customer. You'll probably be surprised at how many steps there are and how critical the timing and duration of each step is.

While it is easy to relate to production issues in a manufacturing process where goods are fabricated, the concept may also be applicable to other types of businesses.

Example

As a consultant you are engaged to help a company convert from a paper-based billing system to a computer-based system. The end "product" that you will deliver is assistance in selecting the appropriate software and hardware, training on that new equipment, and supervision of the process by which the data is converted to electronic format.

You can do a great job without "producing" anything tangible beyond, perhaps, documentation of the process. This doesn't mean that you can ignore "production." Consider all the work that you would have to do. First, a working knowledge of the client's existing system has to be acquired. Then, software and hardware combinations are evaluated in light of the client's needs and budget. A conversion process has to be developed so that those portions of the existing data that carry over to the new system are available in the new format. Documentation must be prepared to train the client's employees in using the new system. Whether you thought of them that way or not, each of these activities would be part of your production process.

Business Facility Assessment

There are a number of issues you should address in your business plan regarding the choice of a facility.

The first question to address is why you need a business facility, and what kind. At one extreme, a consultant may perform most services in space provided by clients. That consultant may not need a facility at all and may maintain a small home office to store reference materials and business records. At the other extreme, a manufacturing business may require access to rail transport, room for manufacturing operations and storage, parking facilities for a lot of employees, etc.

The success of a retail outlet or a restaurant may depend to a large extent on its location. Is it situated in the right part of town, on a street with sufficient foot traffic, parking, or public transportation? Are the neighbors conducive to drawing customers who might also patronize your business? Don't give these issues short shrift, either in actually choosing your location, or in explaining your choice in your business plan.

Your business plan should also describe the basic aspects of your facility (age, square footage, location on first or second floor, etc.), as well as the important aspects of any equipment, furniture, or fixtures that you may need for operation. You may want to augment your explanations with maps, site plans, floor plans, or even architectural drawings.

If you've already obtained a lease, you may want to attach a copy to the plan in an appendix. If you're seeking financing in order to purchase a facility, you'll want to include a lot of detail about the property you're considering and how it suits your needs.

Inventory Control

Businesses that are required to carry an inventory often find that a significant amount of their working capital is tied up in inventory. This applies to those engaged in retailing, wholesaling, and manufacturing, but may also apply to some service businesses. For example, restaurants must maintain inventory of the food they will be serving and perhaps also supplies such as napkins, straws, sugar packets, etc.

If your business maintains an inventory, we suggest that your business plan should discuss how you plan to manage it. For example, how many weeks' or months' worth of raw materials will you attempt to keep on hand? How many months' supply of finished or retail products? Who will be in charge of keeping track? Will you have a computerized system? Will your suppliers help you to stay on top of your inventory?

Being able to answer these questions in your plan will show that you've considered the implications of maintaining adequate stock, without tying up too much money in inventory that may become obsolete or unsalable. If you're just starting out, your suppliers should be able to give you ballpark estimates of what you'll need; trade associations may also provide some helpful information.

Order Fulfillment and Customer Service

Providing superlative customer service is often the most important way in which small businesses can distinguish themselves from the competition. If you've established a customer service policy, be sure to include it in your plan. Your policy may be as simple as saying that "all customers will be treated in a friendly, professional manner" — and if you have employees, you may need to reinforce it often.

If your business is one in which customers place advance orders and then receive their products later, consider including a section in your business plan that discusses your procedures for taking and fulfilling orders. What shipping methods will you use? Will you charge a flat rate for shipping, or will you base your shipping charges on what the carrier charges, plus (or minus) a fixed percentage?

Will you set a target fulfillment period within which the customer should receive the order? Will you set a time limit on returns, or will you state that only exchanges are available (i.e., no cash returns)?

MANAGEMENT AND HUMAN RESOURCE PLANS

A business plan should help you to organize the roles and responsibilities of all the people involved in your business. Therefore, virtually every plan will have a section describing its management. Some businesses will also need a description of their other staffing or the independent contractors they plan to use.

Management Plans

Whether your business has one owner/employee — you — or dozens, you'll need to describe the management strengths and expertise of your business in your business plan.

If your plan is designed to be shown to an outside investor or lender, the quality of management can be a deciding factor in whether you get the desired capital or not. Generally "quality" is interpreted as meaning "experience," so be sure to explain any previous related job experience, any pertinent experience working for community or other voluntary organizations, and even your family background if that will indicate that you know what you are doing in running the business. Also highlight any special skills or education you have. You may wish to include a formal resume in your appendix.

If your business has more than one owner or manager, you should explain how the important roles and duties will be divided between you. For example, will one of you focus on sales, while the other takes care of the production plant? Or will each of you be in charge of a separate business facility, such as a store or restaurant?

It's generally better to establish business roles with some definition, rather than just assuming that "everyone will pitch in with whatever needs doing." Although in fact you may all need to cover each other's roles from time to time, most owners find that the business runs more smoothly if everyone knows what their primary responsibilities are.

Also consider the "key person" concept. Is there anyone whose presence in the business is vital? For instance, yourself? If so, it makes sense to consider what your business would do in the event that a key player is lost. This may be especially important to lenders who would be concerned if the business's revenue stream were interrupted.

Management Gaps

For some businesses, particularly those just starting out, there may be important positions in the business that remain to be filled, or there may be some gaps in the owner's experience or skills that need to be addressed.

If that's true in your case, your plan should explain the situation. If, for example, you're launching a new magazine but are still searching for the right managing editor, you should explain the importance of the position and the fact that finding the right person is crucial to your success. You may want to outline the qualities and experience you're looking for. Be sure to list a ballpark salary that you expect to pay — you'll need it to complete your financial projections.

If you recognize gaps in your own experience, you should explain what they are and how you expect to compensate. In many cases, you can hire a business or an individual to take care of the tasks that are not your strengths. For instance, you can hire an accountant if you don't know much about recordkeeping, and you can hire a salesperson if personal selling is not your strong suit. The fact that you admit your potential weaknesses will generally not diminish your business's potential in the eyes of an outside reader, as long as you have a realistic plan to fill the gaps.

Staffing Plans

It can be difficult to predict how many people your business is going to need, particularly if you're in a new business. You should find that the process of creating a business plan will be very helpful in this respect. As you consider each of the key areas, you'll develop a picture of all the activities that go into running your business. Then you can estimate how many and what kind of employees you'll need, how much you'll need to pay them, and what your total payroll and contractor costs will be.

At one extreme, your business plan can make it clear that you won't ever have any employees. What little you can't do, you'll contract out. Many businesses built around performing services tend to be near this end of the spectrum. At the other extreme, your plan may reveal a need for an exponentially expanding sales force until you have reps in every major city in the United States.

Even if it's just for your own benefit, a description or even a checklist of all the different tasks performed by individuals (or classes of individuals, if you have many employees) may be useful. You may want to include an organization chart to show who reports to whom, if that is a part of your business's structure.

Chapter 8

Financial Plans

Unless you are thinking of starting a religious or charitable organization, the main reason you're starting a business is because you think you can make money at it. The drive to be your own boss might have caused you to quit being an employee and *start* your business, but the quest for income is what keeps it going. When you develop a business plan, financial projections and cash flow analysis are among the most critical elements.

You have a close personal interest in the financial performance of your business. So does everyone else who might be looking at your business plan. Not surprisingly, the portions of your plan dealing with expected financial performance will usually come under the closest scrutiny. A potential lender will want to know what you'll be doing with the money it lends you and how you plan to generate the necessary income to pay the money back.

Fortunately, or perhaps unfortunately, the financial projections are the most formalistic and stylized documents that you will have to prepare. There are certain accounting conventions that you are expected to follow. Simple accounting or business planning software can be extremely helpful in formatting the statements and doing the math. For example, the plans in this book were originally formatted using Business Plan Pro™ from Palo Alto Software. You can generally purchase such software for under $100, and it's well worth the price.

In some cases, you may need to prepare the financial portions of your plan in conformance with "generally accepted accounting principles" (GAAP). This usually occurs when the business owner is creating a plan in an effort to obtain a loan or line of credit, and the bank or potential investor requests that you follow these formally established accounting rules. It also means that you'll need to get an accountant involved in preparing that portion of the plan. If the financial material was created in conformance with GAAP, that should be noted within the plan. The same is true if the financial statements have been audited.

Important Financial Information to Include

- **important assumptions** — statements that must be assumed to be true as the premise for all your projections

- **breakeven analysis** – a description of the sales volume needed to cover all your costs (may be omitted for businesses that have been operating for some time)

- **projected sales volume** – your assessment of how much you can realistically sell at your chosen price points, in a given period of time

- **projected profit and loss** – the statement that details your income, your expenses, and the difference between the two which equals your profit or loss

- **projected cash flow budget** – the statement that shows the timing of cash inflows and outflows for your business

- **projected balance sheet** – the statement that shows your business's projected net worth after operating for a specified period of time

---

The type of financial information that you're going to need to prepare your analysis will depend on whether your business is an established enterprise or is just starting out.

As a general rule, however, you should plan to include three years of projected financial statements, unless your lender requests five years. The first year's statements should be broken down by month; later years' information can be presented on a quarterly or annual basis.

STARTUP BUSINESS FINANCIAL INFORMATION

If you're just starting out, you face a special challenge because there is no history of operations, profitable or otherwise. You're going to have to rely almost entirely on financial projections; that is, *prospective* ("pro-forma") statements based on assumptions that you've made as to how your business will perform in the future.

You'll also have to rely heavily on your ability to sell yourself as a potentially successful business owner. In large part, your ability to capture the readers' imagination and get them excited about the possibilities is a substitute for the historical information that doesn't exist.

Startup businesses, or business expansions, frequently involve a startup budget that is different in character from the operating budget of an ongoing business. These startup costs will be detailed separately, in the startup summary of the company summary section of your plan (see page 23).

The startup funding plan will show how your personal investment will be used to fund the business (see page 27). If you plan to contribute any personal assets to the business, such as a car, truck, office machines or computers, etc., you should provide specific details on that as well. Other documents that may be required, particularly if you're trying to obtain outside financing, are a personal financial statement and your income tax returns for the last few years.

As with an established business, you're also going to need to provide a statement of important assumptions, a breakeven analysis, and projected sales forecasts, profit and loss statements, cash flow budget worksheets, and balance sheets. These documents quantify the results you expect to achieve through your operations.

HISTORICAL FINANCIAL INFORMATION

An existing business can bolster the credibility of its business plan by documenting the results of its ongoing operations. A proven track record is very persuasive evidence of your chances for continued success.

Hopefully, you've been creating and maintaining financial records since the inception of your business. If so, most of your work is done. You'll already have balance sheets, income statements, and cash flow budgets for the last three to five years (or since inception if your business is less than three years old). As always, the relative importance of each type of document will vary with the characteristics of your particular business.

These financial statements are the most objective pieces of evidence that lenders will look at to either support or contradict your forecasts for future performance. Generally speaking, the reader of your plan will expect that "history will repeat itself" and that your business's future will be an extension of the trends that are shown in your historical statements. Therefore, if you expect that the picture will improve dramatically, be sure your plan provides solid evidence as to why that will happen.

Our sample business plans (beginning on page 89) have left out the historical financial statements, in the interest of saving space. But be sure to include them in your own finished plan.

ESTABLISHING REASONABLE ASSUMPTIONS

When you draft a business plan, you need to make many different types of assumptions. Some of these are so basic that they remain, appropriately, unstated. For example, although the U.S. economy might cease to function predictably if the country were invaded by Canadian armed forces, it's safe to assume that no such invasion will occur.

Beyond that, there are several broad types of assumptions that you're going to have to make. These assumptions are what support and quantify the financial projections that you'll make in the plan.

Assumptions About the Business Environment

As you draft your business plan, you may feel somewhat overwhelmed by the sheer number of external factors that can dramatically impact your business. Most of these factors are simply beyond your control. For example, if you're planning to take out a variable-rate loan, you'll have to make an assumption about the interest rate during the planning period, which may be dependent upon the general state of the economy.

Work Smart

If you feel very uncomfortable predicting an average interest rate, you may want to draw up several sets of financial projections using best-case, worst-case, and most-likely-case interest rate assumptions. However, this is rather time-consuming and most business owners will simply choose the most-likely-case scenario, for initial planning purposes.

As another example, while Census data may tell you how many people are physically located in your geographic market, the percentage of people who will actually buy your product or service isn't so easy to nail down. But such assumptions are an absolute requirement when it comes time to project sales.

Besides the assumptions about interest rates and about market demand for your product, your business plan should list any other assumptions on which the financial statements depend. For the reader, and for yourself as well, the list serves as a warning that if an assumption later turns out to be false, your business may not perform as expected.

Examples

Here are some examples of the wide variety of types of statements you may want to include in your assumptions:

- We assume continued stable government and political structure in the African countries we will tour.

- There will be no major competitive threat from a currently unknown source.

- No sales will be made on credit.

- Fifty percent of sales in our retail gift shop will occur during the last three months of the year.

- Personnel burden (the extra costs of payroll taxes and benefits for employees) will be 15% of total payroll.

Despite the difficulty in ensuring that your assumptions are reasonable, there is a lot of help available. For example, a bank can provide you with historical information regarding rate changes, and possibly even a prediction about future rates. Vendors can tell you about product availability issues. Get as much information as you need to feel comfortable with your ability to make reasonable assumptions. Remember, however, that no one is likely to be right all the time. If the assumptions on which you base your planning are generally "in the ballpark," you have done a good job.

Assumptions About Your Business

As you work your way through the planning process, you will be called on to take your best guess regarding the key operational issues facing any business. You'll have to make estimates regarding productivity, capacity, cash flow, costs, and a hundred other interrelated factors. For example, if you are considering a manufacturing business, how many units of product can you expect a particular piece of equipment to produce? What assumptions can you make about the equipment's reliability and potential down-time?

From a practical standpoint, there are two potential sources for the information you need to make reasonable assumptions. If you have an existing business, you have your personal experience on which to rely. You know how much to expect from an employee or how reliable your production equipment is. Even if you're taking on a new product or trying to enter a new market, your experience in the industry in general will serve you well.

But what about the business owner who has relatively little experience in a particular field? The best bet is to tap into existing sources of information. One excellent source is industry groups or associations. These organizations exist to further the aims of business owners within a specific industry or field of endeavor. They can provide information regarding a wide variety of topics. Local chambers of commerce and other civic organizations can often provide valuable demographic information regarding the specific geographic market in which you will compete.

Potential vendors and suppliers can also be consulted to get information regarding costs, product availability, timing requirements, etc.

While there is no substitute for personal experience, you can learn a lot by drawing on the experience of those around you. Unless you're starting a wholly new type of business, there will be someone around with experience at what you're planning to do. You'd be surprised how willing even potential competitors are to share information, if asked in the right way. This is particularly true if your business will serve a limited geographic market and won't directly compete with a similar business located some distance away.

BREAKEVEN ANALYSIS

The "breakeven point" for your business is the sales volume you need to achieve in order to cover all the costs of your business. It's extremely important for you to know what your breakeven point is, and to have confidence that you can achieve that volume of sales within a reasonable period of time — otherwise, you need to do more work on the marketing portion of the plan, or to rethink your business idea altogether!

Also, it's a good idea to recalculate your breakeven point periodically, because it will change whenever your costs or your pricing structure changes. Knowing your breakeven point is a good way to keep a handle on all your costs over time.

Fixed and Variable Costs

So, how do you calculate breakeven? Start by determining all the costs of doing business. You may want to use your income statement form as an aid (see page 72).

Virtually all of your business's costs will fall, more or less neatly, into one of two categories:

- "Variable costs" increase directly in proportion to the level of sales in dollars or units sold. Depending on your type of business, some examples of variable costs would be the price you paid for the items you sold (cost of goods sold), sales commissions, shipping charges, delivery charges, costs of direct materials or supplies, wages of part-time or temporary employees, and sales or production bonuses.

- "Fixed costs" remain the same, at least in the short term, regardless of your level of sales. Depending on your type of business, some typical examples would be rent, interest on debt, insurance, plant and equipment expenses, business licenses, and salary of permanent full-time workers.

Your accountant can help you determine which of your costs are fixed and which are variable, but here the key word is "help." In order to be accurate, the ultimate classification has to be done by someone who's intimately familiar with your business operations—which probably means you.

Combination Costs

Some costs are a combination of fixed and variable: a certain minimum level will be incurred regardless of your sales levels, but the costs rise as your volume increases. As an analogy, think about your phone bill: you probably pay an access or line charge that is the same each month, and you probably also pay a charge based on the volume of calls you make. Strictly speaking, these costs should be separated into their fixed and variable components, but that may be more trouble than it's worth for a small business.

Save Time

To simplify things, just decide which type of cost (fixed or variable) is the most important for the particular item, and then classify the whole item according to the more important characteristic. For example, in a telemarketing business, if your phone call volume charges are normally greater than your line access charges, you'd classify the entire bill as variable.

Variable Costs Per Unit

If you add up all your variable costs for the accounting period, and divide by the number of units sold, you will arrive at the cost per unit. This cost should remain constant, regardless of how few or how many units you sell. If yours is a service business, you may be able to divide your variable costs by the number of jobs performed (if the jobs are essentially similar) or by the hours spent on all jobs (if the jobs vary greatly in size).

Calculating the Breakeven Point

Once you know what your variable costs are, as well as your overall fixed costs for the business, you can determine your breakeven point: the volume of sales needed to at least cover all your costs. You can also compute the new breakeven point that you'd need to meet if your cost structure changed (for example, if you undertook a major expansion project or bought some new office equipment, thus increasing your fixed costs). The computation is best explained through an example.

Example

Assume that the financial statements for Lillian's Bakery reveal that the bakery's total fixed monthly costs are $4,900, and its variable costs per unit of production (loaf of raisin coffee cake) are $.30.

Further assume that each loaf sells for $1.00. Therefore, after the $.30 per loaf variable costs are covered, each loaf sold can contribute $.70 toward covering fixed costs.

Dividing fixed costs by the contribution to those costs per unit of sales tells Lillian's Bakery at what level of sales it will break even. In this case: $4,900/$.70 = 7,000 loaves.

As sales exceed 7,000 loaves per month, Lillian's Bakery earns a profit. Sales of less than 7,000 loaves produce a loss.

Lillian's Bakery can see that a 1,000-loaf increase in sales over the break-even point to 8,000 loaves will produce a $700 profit, and a 3,000-loaf increase to 10,000 will produce a $2,100 profit. On the other hand, a decline in sales of 1,000 loaves from break-even to 6,000 loaves will produce a loss of $700, and a 3,000 decrease from the 7,000 break-even point produces a $2,100 loss.

Presenting this information in your business plan is generally done in the form of a graph, with sales units (or dollars) forming one axis of the graph and profits (and losses) forming the other axis. (For an example, see page 115). The reader can immediately see the effect that various sales levels will have on your bottom line.

PROJECTED SALES FORECAST

Every financial plan must include a forecast of sales for the business. Any forecast will include some uncertainty. Your sales forecast probably won't match your actual sales because of the many variables that ultimately affect the final amount. The economy, inflation, competitive influences, and a whole range of other variables will affect your actual sales. No matter how much uncertainty you associate with these variables, you must come up with an estimate of future sales.

Projecting Sales for an Existing Business

If your business has been operating for a number of years, your sales reports for the last few years are the best starting point for estimating sales for the coming year. Simply adjust last year's sales figures as necessary to reflect the conditions you expect next year.

If you anticipate making changes that will affect your sales volume in the future, the sales forecast section of the plan should explain those changes, and why they will have the effect you state. Similarly, if you expect that external changes will have an effect on your sales volume, such as a new highway, a plant closing, changing demographics in your area, or new competition entering the market, this is the place to say so.

You might also want to explain your strategy for meeting the challenges you foresee — for instance, will you hire an additional salesperson if you expect sales would otherwise drop, or will you need more production capacity if you expect sales revenue to increase dramatically?

Case Study

John Divot owns a golf supply retail store. John will use last year's sales figures to prepare his sales forecast for the next six months. Here is the sales information from the first six months of last year:

January	$18,000
February	$18,500
March	$20,500
April	$28,900
May	$32,300
June	$36,600

John expects sales for this year to be 1 percent higher in the off season and 1.5 percent higher during the golf season, which begins in April. John forecasts his sales for the first six months of this year to be as follows:

January	$18,180
February	$18,685
March	$20,705
April	$29,333
May	$32,785
June	$37,150

Projecting Sales for a New Business

Before we take a look at some ways to estimate revenues for a startup business, a word of caution. Estimating your sales will be an inexact science. Don't count too heavily on your projections and, if you're going to err, err on the conservative side in predicting how much business you'll do in your first year.

Product vendors may be an excellent source of sales data. If your new business is one that will have high inventory levels, suppliers or warehouse facilities may be a potential source of sales data.

For example, assume you plan to open a grocery store. You would purchase the majority of your product from a primary grocery distributor. Usually a distributor of any significant size will have access to other grocery stores' sales in your trade area. This could be your starting point for your sales potential. You will have to make adjustments to the sales figure based, for example, on site selection, competition, and marketing.

Warning

Be careful when dealing with product vendors to determine sales potential. Some may just tell you what you want to hear in order to get your business. Back up their forecasts with other sources.

Most libraries have a wide range of information available for specific types of enterprises. The trade publications and trade associations are good sources of overall sales information for your specific industry. These publications will generally break out sales by geographic region and by business type.

The Bureau of the Census publications, available in larger libraries, can provide you with a lot of information on sales volume for various business types by geographic location. This information is usually a few years out of date, so if your new business is one that will be greatly affected by the time lag, you'll want to make adjustments for it. Remember that your sales figure will still be just an educated guess. Along with the sales figure, Census publications will provide other financial details, such as average cost of goods sold and payroll.

Example

Let's say you want to estimate sales for a fictitious submarine sandwich shop in Cedar Rapids, Iowa.

The Census of Retail Trade, a Census Bureau publication, showed that there were 284 eating and drinking establishments in Cedar Rapids. The average sales volume per eating establishment was $548,866. Based on other research, it was determined that this in itself was not a realistic number for the planned sub shop, and adjustments need to be made for other known facts.

Assume that the average customer will spend $4.50 per meal. Also assume that the restaurant will have between 150 to 200 customers on an average day. Multiplying the $4.50 times 175 customers (average of 150 and 200) times 365 days, the sales will compute to $287,438 per year.

PROJECTED PROFIT AND LOSS STATEMENT

Also called an income statement, a profit and loss statement lists your income, expenses, and the difference between the two, which is your net income (or loss). Your business's tax return will use a variation of the profit and loss statement to determine your potentially taxable income.

The profit and loss statement shows you a summary of the flow of transactions your business has over the entire accounting period. In other words, the statement shows you what happens during the period between balance sheets.

Three years' worth of projected income-statement data is normally presented, so that you can make comparisons and identify trends.

For a sample form that you can use to construct your own statement, see the next page. The categories provided are the ones that are most common for the average small business — be sure to add or subtract categories as appropriate to your particular company.

	JAN	FEB	MAR	APR	MAY	JUN
Your Company						
Projected Profit and Loss Statement - Annual by Month						
Revenue:						
Gross Sales						
Less: Sales Returns						
Net Sales						
Cost of Goods Sold:						
Materials						
Labor						
Other Direct Expenses						
Indirect Expenses						
Total Cost of Goods Sold						
Gross Profit (Loss)						
Expenses:						
Advertising						
Bad Debts						
Bank Charges						
Credit Card Fees						
Delivery Expenses						
Depreciation						
Dues and Subscriptions						
Equipment Rental						
Insurance						
Interest						
Maintenance						
Miscellaneous						
Office Expenses						
Operating Supplies						
Payroll Taxes						
Permits and Licenses						
Postage						
Rent						
Telephone						
Travel						
Utilities						
Wages and Benefits						
Total Expenses						
Net Operating Income						
Other Income:						
Gain (Loss) on Asset Sales						
Interest Income						
Total Other Income						
Net Income Before Tax						
Net Income After Tax						

Your Company						
Projected Profit and Loss Statement - Annual by Month						
JUL	**AUG**	**SEP**	**OCT**	**NOV**	**DEC**	**TOTAL**

The data on your projected profit and loss consist of the following:

- sales revenue

- sales returns and allowances

- cost of goods sold

- selling, general, and administrative expenses

- depreciation and amortization expenses

- interest expense

A detailed, month-by-month P & L should be provided for the first year. For later years, you may want to break down the information by quarter, or you may decide to provide an annual summary.

Depending on whether you are preparing a projected profit and loss statement for an existing business or a startup enterprise, you may have some difficulty coming up with reliable estimates for some of these figures. Dun & Bradstreet and other financial information purveyors may be able to provide information regarding industry average expenditures for cost of goods sold, general and administrative expenses, and other major categories as a percentage of sales. As you talk to suppliers and receive bids from them, sign leases for equipment or facilities, find out the going rate for employees in the jobs you'll be hiring for, etc., you should be able to fill in the blanks.

PROJECTED CASH FLOW BUDGETS

In its simplest form, cash flow is the movement of money in and out of your business. It could be described as the process in which your business uses cash to generate goods or services for the sale to your customers, collects the cash from the sales, and then completes this cycle all over again.

"Inflows" are the movement of money into your business, and are most likely from the sale of your goods or services to your customers. If you extend credit to your customers and allow them to charge the sale of the goods or services to their account, then an inflow occurs as you collect on the customers' accounts. The proceeds from a bank loan are also a cash inflow.

"Outflows" are the movement of money out of your business, and are generally the result of paying expenses. If your business involves reselling goods, your largest outflow is most likely to be for the purchase of retail inventory.

A manufacturing business's largest outflows will most likely be for payroll and for the purchases of raw materials and other components needed for the manufacturing of the final product. Purchasing fixed assets, paying back loans, and paying accounts payable are also cash outflows.

A good way to learn respect for the concept of cash flow is to compare it to the idea of profit. If a retail business is able to buy a retail item for $1,000 and sell it for $2,000, then it has made a $1,000 gross profit. But what if the buyer of the retail item is slow to pay his or her bill, and six months pass before the bill is paid? Using accrual accounting, the retail business still shows a profit, but what about the bills it has to pay during the six months that pass? It will not have the cash to pay them, despite the profit earned on the sale.

As you can see, profit and cash flow are two entirely different concepts, each with entirely different results. The concept of profit is somewhat narrow, and only looks at income and expenses over an entire accounting period. Cash flow, on the other hand, is more dynamic. It is concerned with the movement of money in and out of a business. More importantly, it is concerned with the time at which the movement of the money takes place. You might even say the concept of cash flow is more in line with reality!

Therefore, your cash flow projections will be the most important financial statements in your business plan. You need to include a month-by-month cash flow projection for at least the first year. For a sample form on which you can compute your own cash flow, see page 76. In using the form, note that the cash that remains at the end of the first month will become the beginning cash balance for the second month, and so on through all the months of the year.

For later years, you can project annually by quarter, or even annually by year, as you'll see in our sample business plans (for example, see page 117).

If you are preparing a cash flow budget worksheet for an existing business, you can base your estimates of cash inflows and outflows on historical information. On the other hand, if you're a startup business, you should base your estimates of cash sources and uses on the revenues and expenses listed in the projected profit and loss statements. Accordingly, we recommend that you complete a projected profit and loss statement before completing the cash flow budget worksheet.

If you are seeking a loan, an important feature of your cash flow statement is that it will show the lender exactly how you're going to afford the loan payments.

		JAN	FEB	MAR	APR	MAY	JUN
Your Company							
Cash Flow Budget Worksheet - Annual by Month							
Beginning Cash Balance							
Cash Inflows (Income):							
Accounts Receivable Collections							
Loan Proceeds							
Sales & Receipts							
Other							
Total Cash Inflows							
Available Cash Balance							
Cash Outflows (Expenses):							
Advertising							
Bank Service Charges							
Credit Card Fees							
Delivery							
Health Insurance							
Insurance							
Interest							
Inventory Purchases							
Miscellaneous							
Office							
Payroll							
Payroll Taxes							
Professional Fees							
Rent or Lease							
Subscriptions & Dues							
Supplies							
Taxes & Licenses							
Utilities & Telephone							
Other							
Travel							
Maintenance							
Subtotal							
Other Cash Outflows:							
Capital Purchases							
Loan Principal							
Owner's Draw							
Other:							
Subtotal							
Total Cash Outflows							
Ending Cash Balance							

		Your Company				
		Cash Flow Budget Worksheet - Annual by Month				
JUL	**AUG**	**SEP**	**OCT**	**NOV**	**DEC**	**TOTAL**

Planning Your Cash Flow

If you were able to do business in a perfect world, you'd probably like to have a cash inflow (a cash sale) occur every time you experience a cash outflow (pay an expense). But you know all too well that business takes place in the real world, and things just don't happen like that.

Instead, cash outflows and inflows rarely occur together. More often than not, it seems, cash inflows lag behind your cash outflows, leaving your business short of money. Think of this money shortage as your cash flow gap.

When creating your business plan, you have the time and opportunity to adjust your projected cash flow statements. If you notice a gap, and especially if the gap is large, try to change your operating plans until the gap disappears. For instance, if you expect a gap in October as you load up on inventory for the December selling season, consider reducing or postponing some of the expenses you'd normally pay that month. You might be able to reduce your travel expenses that month, or avoid purchasing office supplies, or change your insurance payment due dates so that none fall in October.

The point is not only to make your business plan look good (although that's important, obviously) but also to do as much as you can ahead of time to avoid any cash flow gaps and the havoc they can wreak upon your business.

PROJECTED BALANCE SHEETS

The balance sheet is a statement of your company's relative wealth or financial position *at a given point in time*. It's often referred to as a "snapshot," because it gives you a fairly clear picture of the business at that moment, but does not in itself reveal how the business arrived there or where it's going next. That's one reason why the balance sheet is not the whole story — you must also look at the information from each of the other financial statements (and at historical information as well) to get the most benefit from the data.

In your business plan, you'll want to provide at least three years of projected balance sheet information. You may want to provide detailed, month-by-month information for the first year, as our sample business plans have done.

The balance sheet consists of three categories of items: assets, liabilities, and stockholders' or owners' equity.

Assets. Assets are generally divided into two groups: current assets and noncurrent (long-term) assets. They are usually presented in order of liquidity, with current assets (cash and those that will be converted to cash within one year) appearing first. Current assets include cash, accounts and notes receivable, inventories, prepaid expenses, and any other short-term investments. Long-term assets include land, buildings, machinery and equipment, and capitalized leases, less any accumulated depreciation and amortization.

Liabilities. Liabilities are normally presented in order of their claim on the company's assets (i.e., liabilities due within one year are presented before liabilities due several years from now). Liabilities include accounts payable, notes payable, income taxes payable, the current portion of any long-term debt, and any other liabilities due within the accounting period. Long-term liabilities include a mortgage or any other debt that will become due after the relevant accounting period, deferred income taxes, or other deferred debts.

Equity. For sole proprietorships, equity is usually a one-line entry that represents the difference between the business's assets and its liabilities.

For co-owned businesses such as partnerships or limited liability companies, the statement should show the division of equity between or among the co-owners.

For corporations, stockholders' equity is presented properly when each class of stock is presented with all its relevant information (for example, number of shares authorized, shares issued, shares outstanding, and par value). If retained earnings are restricted or appropriated, this also should be shown.

See page 80 for a sample balance sheet form that you can adapt for your company. We've filled in the blanks for a fictitious company, to show you how the numbers should add up. You can also use other formats, as illustrated in the sample business plans (see page 119).

Sources and Uses of Funds Statement

If your business is seeking a loan or investment by an outsider, it's important to show prospective financiers exactly how much money you need and how you expect to spend it. The sources and uses of funds statement is the best way to highlight this information. It will also indicate the extent to which you're investing your own funds in the business — something that is highly important to an investor. With your own assets on the line, you'll certainly be more motivated to make sure the business succeeds.

Joel's Chocolate Company, Inc.
Projected Balance Sheet - December 31, ____

Assets				Liabilities and Capital		
Current Assets:				**Current Liabilities:**		
Cash		$815,840		Accounts Payable	$7,500	
Accounts Receivable	$22,000			Sales Taxes Payable	800	
Less: Reserve for Bad Debts 1,980		20,020		Payroll Taxes Payable	17,500	
Merchandise Inventory		15,000		Accrued Wages Payable	60,000	
Prepaid Expenses		5,200		Unearned Revenues	78,000	
Notes Receivable		0		Short-Term Notes Payable	0	
Total Current Assets			$856,060	Short-Term Bank Loans Payable	0	
				Total Current Liabilities		$163,800
Fixed Assets:						
Vehicles	0			**Long-Term Liabilities:**		
Less: Accumulated Dep.	0	0		Long-Term Notes Payable	50,000	
Furniture and Fixtures	25,000			Mortgages Payable	0	
Less: Accumulated Dep.	9,000	16,000		**Total Long-Term Liabilities**		50,000
Equipment	160,000					
Less: Accumulated Dep.	60,000	100,000		**Total Liabilities**		213,800
Buildings	0					
Less: Accumulated Dep.	0	0		**Capital:**		
Land	0			Paid-in Capital	758,260	
Total Fixed Assets			116,000	Additional Capital	0	
Other Assets:				**Total Capital**		758,260
Goodwill		0				
Total Other Assets			0			
Total Assets			$972,060	**Total Liabilities and Capital**		$972,060

The sources and uses of funds document should start by stating the total amount of capital you need to start operations, to finance your expansion project, or to do whatever else it is that you want to accomplish with your plan.

It should detail how you expect to spend the money, in categories such as: working capital, facilities, equipment, marketing expenses, staff hiring, initial inventory, etc.

Then, it should detail how you expect to obtain the money: investment by you, sale of stock in the company, a short-term line of credit, long-term debt, a mortgage, etc. The total funds needed should equal the total funds to be sourced, of course! For an example of what the completed document might look like, see page 281.

Chapter 9

Using The Completed Plan

Your completed business plan is a document that you can use as a blueprint as you begin or continue to operate the company. It's also a document that you can use to communicate with both internal and external audiences.

But creating a business plan should yield many benefits over and above the actual document. Most importantly, you will have established a planning process that you can use over and over again, improving it each time by incorporating the experience you have gained. The existence of both the *document* and the *process* enable you to derive the maximum benefit from the work you put into creating the plan.

The plan can also become a tracking and evaluation tool. Because your plan will set forth a number of marketing, operational, and financial milestones, you can meaningfully interpret your actual operating results against the baseline established by the plan.

Let's take a look at how you can effectively use your business plan to run your company.

MONITORING YOUR PROGRESS

A well-written business plan defines the goals and objectives that you wish to achieve over the next few years in specific, quantifiable terms. It may project a certain level of sales by a given date, the acquisition of a certain number of clients, or any of a number of other objective measures of success. Whatever the conditions that spell success, you'll want to watch your progress toward those goals over time. If you're on track, great!

If not, you're in a position to take steps to get back on track before it's too late.

The process of monitoring your business's performance can be relatively painless. The following pages discuss the issues to consider.

How Frequently Should You Look?

As a practical matter, you'll probably have a feel for how you're doing because of your involvement with the day-to-day activities of your business. If you make the bank deposits each night, if you pay the bills each month, if you balance the books at the end of the month, then you already know a lot about how your business is doing. But it's worthwhile to supplement this familiarity with some hard and fast milestones.

Using milestones is simply a decision to take a look at a specific performance measure at a particular point in time. You should select your milestones to accommodate two competing considerations. On the one hand, milestones should be infrequent enough so that there is a meaningful amount of information available to analyze. On the other hand, milestones must occur frequently enough so that you can take appropriate action if you see that interim goals aren't being reached. With luck, you'll be able to schedule these periodic business check-ups to coincide with activities you would do anyway, such as balancing your checking account.

Many larger businesses take a look, each month, at certain performance measures that they deem especially important. We suggest that your business do the same, so that you can make any necessary corrections quickly and avoid major problems. Waiting until the end of the year, or even the calendar quarter, to check your progress may be too late.

Selecting Performance Measures

Almost every aspect of your business can probably be measured against some objective yardstick of success. The ability of a salesperson can be measured by the number of sales per month or by the cumulative amount of sales, year-to-date. If your business gets most of its profit from the more expensive products or services you provide, sales revenue (or dollar amount per sale) will be of far more interest than the raw number of sales.

If possible, try to integrate all of your performance measures into the routine of your operations. For example, if a lender requires monthly statements of income and expense, use them to monitor performance. You may want to track information the lender doesn't want, but you can piggyback that data-gathering onto your required reports.

Assessing Your Performance

Once you begin operations according to your business plan, there are two possible outcomes. One is that your projections and assumptions prove to be relatively accurate. In that case, it's likely that your business will be performing as you had hoped. More likely, however, things aren't going exactly as projected. These departures from your plan may be small and not a source of concern, or they may be substantial and require immediate action on your part.

When Things Go According to the Plan

Let's consider the first outcome: you did a good job of planning and, basically, your business is operating the way you'd like to see it. Your performance measurement system is generating data showing that the goals and objectives set forth in your business plan are being met. Congratulations! As many race car drivers say, "I'd rather be lucky than good any day." If you've written a plan and your business developed just as you projected, you're definitely one or the other. So, what do you do about it?

First, make an effort to extend your planning horizon further out in time. Begin to "firm up" the numbers for periods beyond the initial planning window. Fine-tune the plan to get an even better picture of where you're heading. For you, keeping the plan current is easy.

Second, and more importantly, begin looking for ways to improve on what you've done so far. You've begun to build a track record of success and you want to keep on building. Your basic business idea was, most likely, sound (never completely discount the luck factor), and you now have an opportunity to expand, refine, and innovate. If you haven't considered the long-term future of your business, start thinking. If you've set aggressive goals (and most business owners do), consider what you'll have if your business stays on track for three years, or five.

When Things Go Wrong

Despite your best efforts, sometimes a business just doesn't take off the way you expected. The unfortunate fact is that a large percentage of new small businesses fail. But then, most small business owners don't bother to create a written business plan unless they are absolutely required to (as is usually the case if you need outside investors or bank financing). Without a written plan, it's just that much harder to cope when your business isn't meeting your goals.

You, however, will have a written plan, so let's see how it can help you out when things go wrong.

Deviation Analysis

We've included a chart, below, that you can use to compare your expected results against your actual results for any given month, and for the year to date. The difference between the actual and expected results is the deviation – and it can be positive (in your favor) or negative. In the columns labeled "Budget," you can insert the data from the pro-forma income statements in your business plan. Comparing the "actual" data with the "budget" will tell you the deviation, either positive or negative. Once you know the extent of your deviation from what you had hoped to achieve, you can decide what to do about it.

Financial Results	This Month	This Month	This Month	Year to Date	Year to Date	Year to Date	Prior Year to Date
(In 1000's)	Actual	Budget	Deviation	Actual	Budget	Deviation	Actual
Sales Revenue							
Direct Costs							
Marketing Costs							
Marketing Contribution							
New Units Sold: Line A							
New Units Sold: Line B							

When things don't go well for a business, it isn't always easy to figure out why. It could be that your business plan contains some faulty assumptions or conclusions. Or it could be that your business is having operational difficulties of some sort. In either event, you have to isolate the cause of the problem before you can correct it.

Some problems will be internal to your business, while others will result from external factors beyond your direct control.

External factors can be very widespread, such as a downturn in the entire local economy, or they can be specific to your business, such as a vendor's failure to deliver on time. Internal factors relate to the specific processes and activities that you use in running your business. An employee may not be performing as you'd like, or operating cost estimates contained in the business plan might have been too low.

In all probability, there won't be just a single root cause for your business's problems. As you look for the source of your problems, don't be surprised if you have to address several issues. The key concern is to identify all of the reasons why your business isn't going the way you'd like. Then you can consider what to do about them.

Keeping Your Plan Current

You should treat your business plan as a dynamic document that should be kept current as your business evolves. You've invested a good deal of your time and effort to create the plan in the first place. If you don't keep the plan current, you can look forward to a similar effort the next time you need a written plan. Remember, it's almost always easier to edit an existing document than to create a new one from scratch.

Planning Interval

Many people think of "planning" as an annual process. Thousands of companies publish an annual plan each year, outlining their expectations about operating results for the coming 12 months.

Realistically, though, you're probably planning all the time. Most business owners are always thinking about ways to make their business better. In discussing a "planning interval," what we're really suggesting is periodically setting aside a certain amount of time to create or update your written business plan.

So how do you select a reasonable planning interval? Start with the assumption that you'd like to have at least one planning period each year. Many factors that affect your business will be tied to some annual cycle. For example, income taxes are due yearly, and federal safety rules require posting annual summaries of information. Also, many employees will expect annual raises or bonuses. This and other factors make annual planning after tax time a reasonable starting point, though your circumstances may require a different planning interval.

Example

Consider a business located on a small chain of lakes. It operates a marina and boat repair facility from spring to fall. As the boating season ends, the business switches to servicing snowmobiles and supporting ice fishers. Even though the results of marina operations are available as of the end of the season, that information is of limited value in planning for the coming winter. The information that *is* meaningful to the business owner trying to plan for winter relates to the prior winter's operations. Planning for summer operations and for winter operations wouldn't have to occur at the same time, and there would likely be benefits from scheduling two planning sessions.

Five Sample Business Plans

Now that you have a good understanding of the elements that a good business plan should include and the purposes that each section serves, it's time to take a look at some real, live business plans that have been created by and for entrepreneurs like yourself.

In Part II, we provide you with five sample business plans written for different types of businesses, in various stages of the business lifecycle. We include a plan for a small one-person service business, a small manufacturer, a three-store retail operation, and a specialty restaurant. Three of the plans are for startups, and two are for businesses that are already operating but want to expand their scope (and profitability) in some fashion. While all of the plans have served their owners well as management tools, one was created specifically in order to help the owners obtain financing, which has been successfully obtained.

African Adventure Tours. The plan for African Adventure Tours is a good example of a small home-based service business. Otieno, the business owner, is from Kenya, and he learned the African tourism business before moving to the U.S., so this is a very logical business for him to start. This plan represents the strategic use of specialized knowledge, experience, and contacts to launch a substantial business with very little capital. At press time, Otieno is in the final stages of completing his Master's degree at Columbia University, has developed a number of important relationships with group travel coordinators, and has already conducted several small group tours to Kenya.

All-Church Sound. All-Church Sound is also starting our as a one-person service business, but in contrast to African Adventure Tours, ACS has a relatively small, very clearly defined target market. Blake built his knowledge of the church sound business with hands-on experience over a number of years, and is ready to build that experience into a profitable enterprise.

After several months of operation, Blake has had sales success in each of his service categories, but he has been especially pleased and surprised by how many new system installations he has done. He expected that not many churches would be willing to let a new business with a young owner take on major projects right away. That's why he planned that the service areas of maintenance and training would represent the bulk of his business system at first. What he's found is that the majority of his revenue is coming from total system replacements and partial system replacements at established churches. His bimonthly newsletter, *Sound Advice,* has become his most important marketing tool.

Bob's Big Pencils. Bob's Big Pencils is a very interesting company, and you will note that Bob's plan is written in "first person" — an unusual but effective technique for this "down home" business. Perhaps this style would be appropriate for your business as well. As presented in the plan, Bob has moved away from selling directly to teachers at conventions, and has focused on other markets. The last we heard, Bob and his crew were working overtime to build a thousand (maybe more) 22" giant pencils to help launch the movie *Godzilla.* Go Bob!

Computer Solutions, Inc. Computer Solutions is a 10-year-old company that competes in an extremely crowded marketplace: computer retailing. This plan lays the groundwork for continued growth in sales and profit for this multi-store operation.

In the development of their "Keys to Success," the owners of Computer Solutions make it clear that their success will be in large part determined by how effective they are in hiring and training new management and sales staff. Unfortunately, Linda and Mark were not immediately successful in these areas, and a severe cash strain forced them to close two of the three stores, focusing all of their cash and assets into the one remaining location. The single location is doing well, and the owners are working hard and smart to prevent a repeat of past mistakes.

Jumpin' Java Cybercafe. The plan for Jumpin' Java Cybercafe is a startup plan designed to guide the development and financing for a new and exciting retail enterprise. Jumpin' Java requires a substantial cash investment, and that is the key goal of the plan. Gaining the needed backing wasn't easy, primarily because of previous business debts still carried by one of the owners. Nevertheless, after diligent work and lots of contacts, complete financing was arranged, and Jumpin' Java was off and running. At last report, the business is open, the computers are in, and sales are growing. In fact, Ethan has already been approached by several different individuals and groups interested in partnerships for expansion, including nationwide franchising!

Clearly, all of these companies have benefited greatly from the business planning process. We'd like to note that the names and addresses of African Adventure Tours, Computer Solutions, and Jumpin' Java Cybercafe and their owners have been changed, to protect their privacy.

The Plan For
African
Adventure Tours

Otieno Murundi

1712 S. Dearborn

Chicago, Illinois 60605

(312) 253-8352

Copy Number _____ of Five.

THE PLAN FOR AFRICAN ADVENTURE TOURS

EXECUTIVE SUMMARY

The company. African Adventure Tours is a U.S.-based company which provides customized African safari programs to American travelers. The company is wholly-owned by its founder, Otieno Murundi, and is based on the principles of integrity, honesty, fairness, hard work, love, and respect for people and nature.

The company's services. The function of African Adventure Tours is to contract with first-quality Africa-based providers of tour services, and to make those services available to our U.S. clients, beginning in the Chicago metro area. The message of African Adventure Tours to our clients is "See the Africa of your dreams." These services will be offered predominantly as customized tours designed for individuals and groups, as "packaged tours" offered directly to customers, and as packaged tours offered through retail travel agencies.

The industry and market. The travel and tourism industry is the largest employer in the U.S., accounting for more than 6.3 million jobs and $416 billion in annual receipts. This market is served by a broad and diffuse group of providers, with many tour operators based in the U.S. and many based in Africa.

The specific market in which we will compete is best identified as "U.S. Overseas Tourism," defined as U.S. residents traveling to foreign countries not including Mexico and Canada. This market was estimated at 17,000,000 departures per year in 1993, with annual growth of 5-7%. European countries represent the largest share. African destinations account for 2% of the total, or roughly 340,000 travelers per year, spending an estimated $1.26 billion. Geographically, the Chicago metro area represents about 4% of the nationwide total, or roughly 13,600 travelers per year.

The marketing strategy. We will differentiate African Adventure Tours in the marketplace in four specific ways:

- AFRICA IS OUR ONLY DESTINATION. Our desks, minds and hearts are not cluttered with thoughts of Europe, Disney World, or Six Flags/Great America.

- WE KNOW AFRICA. Because our founder (Otieno Murundi) is Kenyan, we have a lifetime knowledge base of Africa and Africans through which all decisions pass.

- WE ARE SMALL. As a small privately-held company, we provide our clients with a level of personal service and commitment that "MegaTours, Incorporated" simply cannot provide. With African Adventure Tours, you're always dealing with the owner.

-4-

- WE ARE LARGE. We select only substantial, full-service tour operators to provide service to our clients. In fact, each potential contract service provider must pass our exclusive 10-point "African Adventure Tours Service Excellence Standards" checklist before being considered for active status.

Marketing tools will include printed promotional materials, advertising, aggressive promotional events, direct mail, trade shows, and personal selling.

Sales strategy. Our sales strategy is three-tiered:

1. We plan to achieve breakeven sales (five clients per month) in the individual/family market subset.

2. We plan to achieve "accepted vendor" status in at least 25 retail travel agencies during fiscal 1998, and add five new agencies per month in 1999 and beyond. As soon as we have demonstrated superior performance, we will begin achieving "preferred status" and then "exclusive status." This will begin to create a growing stream of clients.

3. We will attack the "group tour" subset aggressively and plan to generate two group successes of 20+ travelers each in 1998, three in 1999, and four in 2000 and subsequent years.

The sales and profit projections. As demonstrated in the chart that follows, we intend to be profitable within the first year of operation, and to grow our business as opportunities and desire permit.

Business Plan Highlights

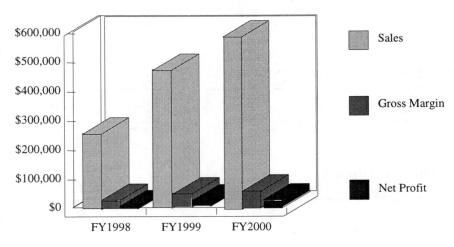

Objectives

1. To establish African Adventure Tours as a viable business, becoming profitable within the first 12 months of operation.

2. To establish a market presence in the Chicago metropolitan area that will provide a solid base of sales and profit within one year.

3. To exceed $250,000 sales during our first year of operation (FY '98), and to approach $500,000 sales in fiscal year 1999.

4. To maintain a 10% gross margin on sales.

Mission

To provide a "once in a lifetime" African touring experience to every client, on every trip. To always exceed our client's expectations, hopes, and dreams.

Keys to Success

1. The tour operators with which we contract must provide outstanding service to our clients. If we fail in this area, our business will ultimately fail.

2. We must quickly become expert at identifying potential clients and client groups.

3. We must execute a powerful marketing plan brilliantly, in order to convert potential clients into paying clients.

4. We must control costs determinedly, spending only where it will help us serve our clients better or to manage our business more effectively.

COMPANY SUMMARY

African Adventure Tours was founded on July 1, 1997 in Chicago, Illinois. It is a sole-proprietorship owned by its founder, Otieno Murundi.

Startup Summary

The initial start-up expenses total $2,200, which is mostly brochures, insurance and legal costs, and buying a copier. Also, we will open operations with $2,800 cash. The start-up costs are to be financed by direct owner investment.

-6-

Table 1: Startup Costs	
Startup Expenses	*Amount*
One-Time Startup Expenses	
Brochures	$ 500
Consultants	$ 200
Expensed Equipment, Copier	$ 450
Insurance	$ 500
Legal	$ 300
Rent	$ 0
Stationery, etc.	$ 200
Voicemail System	$ 50
Other	$ 0
Total One-Time Startup Expenses	$2,200
Short-Term Assets	
Cash	$2,800
Beginning Inventory	$ 0
Other Short-Term Assets	$ 0
Total Short-Term Assets	$2,800
Total Long-Term Assets	$ 0
Total Startup Costs	$5,000

Table 2: Startup Funding Plan	
Funding Source	*Amount*
Investment	
Otieno Murundi	$5,000
Other	$ 0
Total Investment	$5,000
Short-Term Borrowing	
Unpaid Expenses	$ 0
Short-Term Loans	$ 0
Interest-Free Short-Term Loans	$ 0
Total Short-Term Borrowing	$ 0
Long-Term Borrowing	
Long-Term Loans	$ 0
Total Borrowing	$ 0
Loss at Startup	($2,200)
Total Equity	$2,800
Total Debt and Equity	$2,800

Client Support Services

African Adventure Tours provides the following support services for its clients:

- Maintain continuous knowledge of continental Africa, its political climate, tourism status, and any developments that would be of interest to our clients.

- Identify and contract with first-quality tour operators providing services our clients desire.

- Partner with contracted providers to develop tour packages for scheduled departures that meet the needs of our scheduled departure clients.

- Be the facilitator of three-way negotiations (client, tour operator, and African Adventure) to develop customized touring packages for corporate incentive, educational, and affinity groups.

-8-

- Represent our clients in making all air and land arrangements for their tour.

- Provide extensive communication to all clients regarding the status of their upcoming tour.

- Make ourselves available (home phone included) to answer client questions.

Company Locations and Facilities

Company headquarters are located at 1712 S. Dearborn, Chicago, Illinois 60605, the residence of Otieno Murundi. As our business grows, we may find it necessary to move to larger accommodations.

MARKET ANALYSIS SUMMARY

The market in which we will compete is best identified as "U.S. Overseas Tourism," defined as U.S. residents traveling to foreign countries not including Mexico and Canada. This market was estimated at 17,000,000 departures per year in 1993, with annual growth of 5-7%. European countries represent the largest share. African destinations account for 2% of the total, or roughly 340,000 travelers per year.

U.S. residents traveling to Africa represent a unique and interesting group. One of our challenges is to accurately identify our most likely client based on a number of characteristics. This analysis appears in the following sections. We believe that there is room in this market for a new entrant, and that our marketing and sales strategies will enable African Adventure Tours to profitably niche itself in this arena.

Market Segmentation

We begin the Market Segmentation section with a basic review of the characteristics of the U.S. overseas traveler. Characteristics highly correlated to overseas travel include:

- $70,000+ annual household income.

- Two-parent household.

- Urban or suburban residence.

- High level of education.

- Under 70 years of age.

- Three or more weeks of paid vacation per year.

What we see emerging is the classic upscale professional family, with adults aged 40-60. Curiously, this demographic "client" just happens to coincide with the greatest consumer phenomenon in U.S. history, the Baby-Boom Generation. As the "Boomers" come of age (the first turned 50 in 1996), they will swell our client base to unprecedented levels. The potential for growth in international travel is clear and undeniable.

Beyond demographics, we must also examine the psychographic profile of the American overseas traveler. This person would be classified as an innovator or early adopter. They are self-confident frequent travelers who prefer to fly. They prefer destinations that are uncrowded and where they can seek out experiences that are novel. They are very interested in meeting people and exploring new cultures.

If these qualities are found in overseas travelers in general, they are found to an accelerated degree in travelers to Africa. Clearly, a safari to Africa is a more adventurous and innovative journey than a trip to see Big Ben in London.

In his book *The New World of Travel, 5th Ed.*, Arthur Frommer provides his insight into the psychographics of this group by introducing an emerging travel phenomenon he calls the "new world" of travel: "The key objective is to experience events, lifestyles, attitudes, cultures, political outlooks, and theological views utterly different from what you ordinarily encounter at home... Unless vacation travel is a learning experience, unless it leaves you a bit different from what you were when you began, it is, in my view, a pointless physical exercise."

Frommer continues, "How many people crave to enjoy this 'New World' of vacation experience? Far more than the commercial travel industry realizes. With due apologies to American Express and British Airways, to Russia's Intourist and the Caribbean Travel Association, to Carnival Cruises and all the other travel behemoths, let me suggest that they are overlooking the fastest-growing segment in travel today — one that could account for as many as 40% of all the people who travel. That figure is suggested not only by the success of the first four editions of *The New World of Travel*, but by an important statistical survey conducted by the well-respected Lou Harris organization. In a little noticed report on vacation motivations, recently issued on behalf of *Travel & Leisure* magazine, Harris concluded from hundreds of interviews that routine travel activities — sunbathing, swimming, visiting relatives — still account for the majority of all vacations. But, to his astonishment, he also discovered that a large minority — fully two-fifths of his respondents — cited personal growth as their chief vacation aim: the desire to encounter new ideas, expand horizons, meet new people. Indeed, among all the several categories of vacation desires, 'life enhancement' (with its 40% of the vote) was the single largest."

So, we now have a clear picture of the demographic and psychographic profile of our client. We must also now add the geographical profile to the mix. At startup, we will focus our marketing efforts in the greater Chicago metropolitan area. This focus will enable us to concentrate our time and money, and to minimize travel expense.

There will be instances where outside travel will be necessary, e.g., to participate in trade shows and exhibits, or to call on large-potential group accounts.

Industry Analysis

The "travel and tourism industry" is the largest employer in the U.S., accounting for more than 6.3 million jobs and $416 billion in annual receipts.

Our market, "American residents traveling to Africa," is a small fraction of this total, approximately $1.26 billion per year. This market is served by a broad and diffuse group of providers, with many tour operators based in the U.S. and many based in Africa. The following four sections will provide an in-depth analysis of the industry.

Industry Participants

There are a number of critical players involved in the process of planning and completing an African safari.

1. Accommodation sector: hotels, guest houses, lodges, tented camps, permanent camps, etc.

2. Attractions sector: National parks, wildlife parks, heritage sites, archeological sites, etc.

3. Transport sector: Airlines, bus/coach operators, local air, four-wheel drive, etc.

4. Destination organization sector: National tourist offices, local tourist offices, tourist associations.

5. Travel organizers sector: tour operators, tour wholesalers/brokers, retail travel agents, conference organizers, incentive travel organizers.

Our contracted tour operators will have primary responsibility for dealing with sectors 1, 2, 3 and 4 (except for roundtrip intercontinental air passage). African Adventure Tours will be responsible for sector 5.

Distribution Patterns

For our purposes, we will examine the distribution patterns in two distinct subsets:

1. Customized tours for corporate incentive, educational group, and affinity group travel. Negotiation and purchasing for these groups is much more centralized than subset #2 below. In this arena, we will depend much more on our marketing and sales ability to sell individual clients, which represent a large group of travelers.

-11-

2. Individual/family standardized tours. These tours, usually client-initiated, are statistically quite dependent on retail travel agents. Travel agents are cited as "information sources" by 57% of travelers (#1 response), travel agents book air travel on 68% of tours (#1 response), and travel agents book lodging for 50% of tours (the #1 response). Aside from the occasional random individual/family booking, if we intend to actively attack the "individual/family standardized tour" market segment, we will need to work with retail travel agencies.

There is a travel agent's trade organization based in suburban Chicago (Hinsdale) which may impact our ability to penetrate the travel agency market. MAST, Midwest Agents Selling Travel, represents a consortium of roughly 350 north-central states travel agencies. One function of MAST is to screen and "recommend" qualified tour operators to its membership. According to a local travel agent, the tour operators that offer the largest agency commission on sales are often those which become "recommended". Since there are more than 2500 retail travel agencies in Illinois alone, the importance of MAST remains to be seen. Since all tours booked by retail travel agents will require a commission paid to the booking agent, our gross margins on agent-generated tours will be somewhat strained.

Competition and Buying Patterns

The process that a client goes through in the selection of a tour operator is an important and complex one. Data is scarce regarding priorities of individuals, but good information is available with regard to travel agent priorities (supposedly on behalf of their clients).

Travel agents were asked to rate each of the following attributes as to their importance when choosing a tour operator, on a scale of 1 to 10:

Attribute	Rank
Reputation of the operator	9.5
Previous client satisfaction	9.4
Package quality and diversity	9.1
Price	8.7
Commission incentives	8.3
Cancellation policies	8.0
Override or compensation plan	7.9
Payment policies	7.1
Deposit policies	6.7

Clearly, the most important attributes all concern QUALITY OF PRODUCT. Each of the top three reflect directly on the tour operator's quality of work. Of secondary concern are issues of pricing, commission, and other "hygiene" factors. Our tour operators must be of top quality, and we must be able to demonstrate that quality to potential clients.

Main Competitors

All together, there are certainly more than 100 providers of tours to Africa, and perhaps several hundred, none of which has a dominant market position. A few well-known tour operators include:

- Abercrombie & Kent, Oakbrook, IL

- Brendan Tours, CA

- Carlson Travel Network, MN

- Collette Travel Service, Urbana, IL

- Safaris International, TX

- Sea Safaris Travel, CA

- SITA World Travel, CA

- Travcoa, CA

- United Touring International, PA

- Wilderness Travel, CA

These will be competitors on a national and local scale.

In addition, the following tour operators provide service to Africa, and are based in the Chicago area. They should be viewed as competitors as well:

- Caravan Tours, Chicago

- Classic Tours International, Chicago

- Design Travel & Tours, Elmhurst

- Geeta Tours & Travels, Chicago

- Great Adventure Travel Co., Chicago

- Mill Run Tours, Chicago

- Travel Plans International, Oakbrook

-13-

SERVICES

African Adventure Tours provides customized African safari programs to American travelers. Our function is to contract with first-quality Africa-based providers of tour services, and to make those services available to our clients.

Service Description

At launch, we will offer three basic types of service to our clients:

1. Standardized, off-the-rack tour packages will be offered directly to individuals and family travelers. This is intended to be a minor part of our business.

2. These same standardized packages will also be sold through travel agencies. This should produce more revenue than the first group.

3. Our largest revenue generator will be customized touring. This will involve three primary groups:

   — Corporate incentive travel — this is travel sponsored and paid for by companies for travel by employees, agents, distributors, dealers, customers, etc.

   — Educational group travel — this is travel sponsored by colleges, zoos, museums, etc.

   — Affinity group travel — affinity groups are groups from 2 to 2000 that share a special interest which dictates or influences their travel needs or desires. Examples include: travel clubs, ski clubs, golf clubs, church/ mission groups, archeology clubs, bird clubs, ethnic organizations, etc.

Competitive Comparison

African Adventure Tours will be differentiated from our competitors in several ways:

- AFRICA IS OUR ONLY DESTINATION. Our desks, minds, and hearts are not cluttered with thoughts of Europe, Disney World, or Six Flags/Great America.

- WE KNOW AFRICA. Because our founder (Otieno Murundi) is Kenyan, we have a lifetime knowledge base of Africa and Africans through which all decisions pass.

-14-

- WE ARE SMALL. As a small privately-held company, we provide our clients with a level of personal service and commitment that "MegaTours, Inc." simply cannot provide. With African Adventure Tours, you're always dealing with the owner.

- WE ARE LARGE. We select only substantial, full-service tour operators to provide service to our clients. In fact, each potential contract service provider must pass our exclusive 10-point "African Adventure Tours Service Excellence Standards" checklist before being considered for active status.

Sales Literature

African Adventure Tours has yet to design and print its sales material. A catalog from Karibe Tours and Travel, Nairobi is attached *(editor's note: catalog has not been reproduced)*. Karibe is expected to be our first contracted service provider.

Sourcing

African Adventure Tours has developed and implemented an exclusive rating system to enable us to objectively evaluate all potential contract tour operators. This system, the African Adventure Tours Service Excellence Standards, is a comprehensive tool that allows us to rank any tour operator on each of ten measurable criteria. Each operator must score positive on all ten items in order to be included on our "Active Status" tour operators roster. The Standards appear on the following page.

We are currently in negotiations with Karibe Tours and Travel, Nairobi, Kenya. Karibe Tours/Nairobi meets the African Adventure Tours Service Excellence Standards, and should become our first contracted tour operator. We expect to enjoy an exclusive arrangement with Karibe Tours, and we anticipate that they will be our sole supplier in the markets they serve (primarily Kenya, Tanzania, and Uganda).

Karibe Tours was founded and is managed by Wanyande Murundi, brother of Otieno Murundi. This close relationship, along with Otieno's knowledge of Karibe Tours, gives us an immediate and necessary foothold in the process of contracting with Africa-based tour operators.

AFRICAN ADVENTURE TOURS
SERVICE EXCELLENCE STANDARDS

Contract tour operators must:

1. Be 100% African owned and operated.

2. Have no less than 5 years of continuous service experience.

3. Maintain at least 10 full-time employees.

4. Maintain and operate its own fleet of vehicles (vans, buses, jeeps, etc).

5. Provide documentation of solid financial standing.

6. Be a member in good standing of the African Travel Association, and their own national travel association.

7. Above all else, focus on Excellent Customer Service.

8. Offer a full range of developed tours within their geographic area of service.

9. Demonstrate the ability and desire to develop customized tours to fit the needs of African Adventure clients.

10. Endeavor to promote and maintain Africa's culture, wildlife, and ecology; and to honor the traditional values of Africa's fore-generations.

Technology

African Adventure Tours' services are not protected by patents or trademarks. Our business depends on providing customization and specialization for our clients, and the processes involved are not dependent on process technology or patentable inventions.

Future Services

We will be testing client demand for tours to West African countries such as Senegal and Ivory Coast. Since much of the African-American population of the United States descended from West African slaves, there may be significant interest on the part of African-Americans (and a substantial number of white Americans, as well) to visit West African slave-trading countries.

STRATEGY AND IMPLEMENTATION SUMMARY

Our strategy is to quickly and efficiently identify potential clients in each of our market subsets (corporate incentive, educational groups, etc.), using appropriate marketing tools for each group. Once potential clients are identified, we will work diligently to convert them into paying travelers.

Marketing Strategy

We will need to focus on each of our subset markets in order to succeed during the initial two years of operation. The breakeven analysis in the Financial Plan demonstrates that we need only five clients per month in order to break even. First, individual/family travelers should generate at least that number, if not more. Second, travel agents should generate a second source of clients, although these will take longer to realize (and have lower gross margins). Finally, group travel, including corporate incentive, educational, and affinity groups, will require the longest lead time but represent the best potential for "the big kill."

Target Markets and Market Segments

Our market is U.S. residents traveling to Africa.

Of the 340,000 Americans who travel to Africa yearly, 4% (13,600) are from Illinois. We initially will limit our efforts geographically to the metropolitan Chicago area, which includes an estimated 80-90% of these 13,600 travelers. Our market is segmented as follows:

1. Individual/family travelers booking directly with African Adventure Tours. These clients must either be 1) found, in cases where they already want to go to Africa, but don't know how, or 2) created, in cases where the "right" person demographically and psychographically must be sold on the concept of an African trip.

2. Travel agent-generated clients. This market will be penetrated by convincing retail travel agents to represent and sell African Adventure Tours products. This is simple in concept, but difficult to achieve.

3. Group travel (corporate incentive, educational, and affinity groups). Again, the concept here is simple; identify the groups, contact them, and sell them on our services. And again, it is easier said than done.

The chart that follows indicates our estimate of the relative potential for each segment of the market.

Potential Market

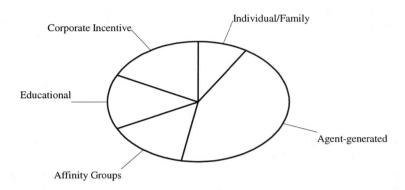

Pricing Strategy

Because we are in a market which is selling a service which will be provided in a foreign country halfway around the world, it is difficult to find established pricing "benchmarks." Kenyan safari trips of 12-14 days range in cost from $2,700 to $6,000, depending on the operator and amenities. We will generate baseline prices based on a cost-plus approach, with the goal of maintaining a 10% gross margin. This will put our retail price for the basic Kenyan trip through Karibe Tours and Travel/Nairobi at roughly $3,500 during high season, certainly within a reasonable range. We do not intend to be the low cost leader in the marketplace, nor do we intend to be the high cost leader. Our strategy for travel booked through travel agents will be to add part or all of the agency's typical 10% fee into the final selling price, yielding a final client price of $3,750-$3,850. Indications are that this price is still within viable limits.

Promotion Strategy

Our strategy is to use every effective and efficient tool available to present our company and service to our target market. These tools will include:

1.   General-use promotional materials.

2.   Advertising.

3.   Publicity.

4.   Direct mail.

5.   Trade shows and exhibits.

These programs are outlined in more detail in the next section.

Marketing Programs

General-use promotional materials:

- Basic brochure identifying African Adventure Tours, our mission, personnel, services, commitment to quality, etc.

- Quality business cards for Otieno.

- Quality letterhead for all company correspondence.

- Parchment-type certificate listing the African Adventure Tours Service Excellence Standards.

- Appropriate resume for Otieno.

- Background brochure for each contract tour operator, documenting adherence to Service Excellence Standards.

- Each contract tour operator will provide their own quality catalog/brochure to us.   The enclosed tour catalog from Karibe Tours and Travel, Nairobi, is an excellent example of the high-quality promotional material we will have available.

- Current price list for all tours offered.

- African Adventure Tours logo give-aways such as: carry-on travel bag for each client, sunscreen, sunglasses, maps, travel log/diary, wildlife identification guide, travel binoculars, shirts, etc.

- Quality video for use with potential clients.

- Quality slide presentation.

Advertising:

- Limited print advertising will be investigated in order to begin to gain name recognition with the general public.   This may include small display ads or classified ads in local newspapers.

- We will make a firm commitment to Yellow Pages advertising, since this is often a "first stop" in a potential client's search for an African adventure.

-19-

- We will identify and place ads in local travel industry publications and/or local editions of national publications.

- We will investigate placing ads in all print media targeted to the incentive travel industry and appropriate education-oriented publications.

Publicity:

- We will purposefully create events which will generate opportunities for press releases. New trip announcements, public exhibits of African art and culture, African speakers, etc., will generate public exposure.

- We will join with educational institutions such as Field Museum, Brookfield Zoo, Chicago Art Institute, etc., to create team events in which both parties benefit.

- We will provide free presentations on "The African Experience" to affinity clubs throughout the Chicago area. There are hundreds of these clubs, and most of them are looking for quality speakers.

- We will generate a portfolio of recommendation letters from satisfied clients.

Direct mail:

- Mailing lists will be obtained for appropriate potential individual/family clients, based on the demographic profile of our market, and mailings will be designed and executed specifically at this group.

- Specific mailings will be designed and executed for corporate incentive travel providers nationwide.

- Specific mailings will be designed and executed for the retail travel industry in our geographic market.

- Specific mailings will be designed and executed for affinity groups and educational institutions in our market.

Trade shows and exhibits:

- We will attend appropriate exhibitions to introduce African Adventure Tours to each subset of our market. A number of shows have already been identified as target events.

Sales Strategy

Our sales strategy is three-tiered:

1. We plan to achieve breakeven sales (five clients per month) in the individual/family market subset.

2. We plan to achieve "accepted vendor" status in at least 25 retail travel agencies during 1997, and add five new agencies per month in 1998 and beyond. As soon as we have demonstrated superior performance, we will begin achieving "preferred status" and then "exclusive status." This will begin to create a growing stream of clients.

3. We will attack the "group tour" subset aggressively and plan to generate two group successes of 20+ travelers each in 1998, three in 1999, and four in 2000 and subsequent years.

Sales Programs

1. Otieno will be fully engaged in selling tours to potential clients. He has the experience and communication skills required to be successful in this area. Selling activities will touch all targeted markets, and will include the following:

   — Phone selling work such as lead follow-up, cold-calling for appointments, etc.

   — Selling to individual/family clients.

   — Calls on travel agents.

   — Calls on significant affinity groups.

2. Marshall Field. A joint tour program is already under development between African Adventure Tours and Marshall Field Travel Service at their downtown Chicago flagship store. This tour package to Kenya is limited to 20 travellers, and should begin booking by mid-September, 1997.

Sales Forecast

Revenue should begin in October 1997, with growth as shown in the accompanying table and graph.

Table 3: Sales Forecast			
	FY1998	**FY1999**	**FY2000**
Sales	$259,000	$472,500	$590,625
Direct cost of sales	$233,100	$425,250	$531,563

-21-

Total Sales by Month in Year 1

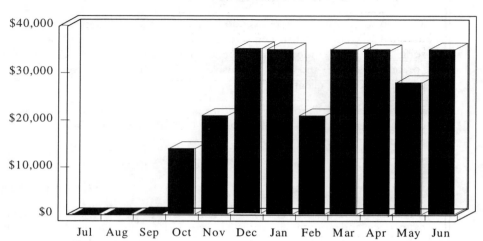

Strategic Alliances

As noted in earlier sections, we will need to develop alliances with as many retail travel agencies as possible in order to penetrate that segment of the market. This will take time and effort, but will generate significant sales over time.

Also noted earlier, we will build mutually beneficial relationships with a number of educational/cultural institutions in our geographic market. This will provide good public relations exposure for us, and will generate sales as well.

Milestones

The following table lists important program milestones, with due-dates and budgets for each. The milestone schedule indicates our emphasis on planning for implementation.

Table 4: Milestones		
Milestone	**Date**	**Budget**
Complete and confirm plan	7/1/97	$ 200
Contract w/ Karibe, Nairobi	7/15/97	$ 300
Logo/letterhead	7/15/97	$ 200
Voicemail system in	7/15/97	$ 50
Service excellence standards	7/15/97	$ 0
Introductory brochure	7/15/97	$ 500
Develop Marshall Field tour	7/15/97	$ 0
Begin market identification	7/15/97	$ 0
Begin customer calls	8/1/97	$ 0
Get copier	8/1/97	$ 450
Buy equip insurance	8/1/97	$ 500
Totals		**$2,200**

MANAGEMENT SUMMARY

African Adventure Tours is fully owned and operated by its founder, Otieno Murundi.

A native Kenyan, Otieno graduated from Utalii College, Kenya's premier tourism college, and spent two years in Kenyan tour operation. He most recently graduated from Columbia College in Chicago, Illinois with a B.S. in Business/Marketing, and is pursuing his Master's degree in Global Tourism.

At the outset, we believe that Otieno can manage the company singly, with temporary assistance during certain peak demand occasions such as the acquisition of a major group contract. As the business grows, more staff, part-time or full-time, will be required.

Personnel Plan

No additional personnel are required in the near term. The salary plan for the founder is shown in the accompanying table. Details are found in Appendix 1.

Table 5: Personnel Plan			
Job Title	**FY1998**	**FY1999**	**FY2000**
Otieno Murundi	$9,000	$18,000	$24,000
Other	$ 0	$ 0	$ 0
Total	$9,000	$18,000	$24,000

FINANCIAL PLAN

As a service business, our fixed costs are quite low. Therefore, we will finance growth through cash flow.

- The most important aspect to our success is generating sales.

- The second most important aspect is maintaining a 10% gross margin.

- The third most important aspect is controlling costs.

Important Assumptions

The financial plan depends on several important assumptions:

- We assume continued economic growth and vitality in the U.S. This will create the spending power necessary to generate adequate demand for our service.

- We assume continued stable government and political structure in the countries we will tour. While we realize that unrest will occur, we assume stable conditions will exist in at least half of our destination countries at any given time.

- We assume continued stable availability and pricing of international airfare.

- We assume reasonably stable foreign currency rates.

- We assume that we can penetrate the market as represented in the Sales Forecast.

Key Financial Indicators

- The most important indicator with regard to our business success is sales growth. In order to succeed, we must achieve early sales success and build on that success to generate sales growth. A dominant share of our launch effort will be to generate these early sales.

- Secondly, we must maintain a gross margin of at least 10%. This margin is crucial if we are to be able to afford adequate marketing and other fixed costs.

- Finally, we must control costs. Since pricing and variable costs are very difficult to control, we must operate in a consciously cost-controlling manner.

Breakeven Analysis

The breakeven analysis shows that assuming $600/month fixed business expenses and $1,120/month salaries, our breakeven point is five units (a unit equals one paid travelling client) per month.

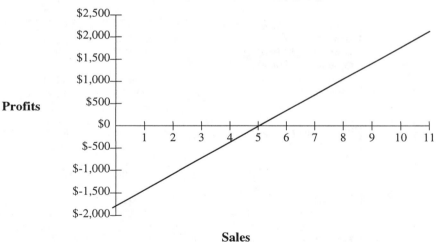

Breakeven Analysis

Table 6: Breakeven Analysis	
Monthly Units Breakeven	5
Monthly Sales Breakeven	$16,200
Assumptions	
Average Unit Sale	$3,500
Average Per-Unit Cost	$3,150
Fixed Cost	$1,720

Projected Profit and Loss

We expect to achieve or exceed sales projections. As seen in the table and chart, by maintaining a 10% gross margin and controlling marketing costs, we will achieve profitability during the first year of operation.

Table 7: Pro-forma Income Statement			
	FY1998	**FY1999**	**FY2000**
Sales	$259,000	$472,500	$590,625
Direct Cost of Sales	$233,100	$425,250	$531,563
Other	$0	$0	$0
Total Cost of Sales	$233,100	$425,250	$531,563
Gross Margin	$25,900	$47,250	$59,062
Gross Margin Percent	10.00%	10.00%	10.00%
Operating Expenses:			
Advertising/Promotion	$4,800	$4,800	$4,800
Travel	$1,200	$1,200	$1,200
Miscellaneous	$0	$0	$0
Other	$0	$0	$0
Payroll Expense	$9,000	$18,000	$24,000
Leased Equipment	$0	$0	$0
Utilities	$0	$0	$0
Insurance	$1,200	$1,200	$1,200
Rent	$0	$0	$0
Depreciation	$0	$0	$0
Payroll Burden	$1,080	$2,160	$2,880
Other	$0	$0	$0
Total Operating Expenses	$17,280	$27,360	$34,080
Profit Before Interest and Taxes	$8,620	$19,890	$24,982
Interest Expense ST	$0	$0	$0
Interest Expense LT	$0	$0	$0
Taxes Incurred	$0	$0	$0
Net Profit	$8,620	$19,890	$24,982
Net Profit/Sales	3.33%	4.21%	4.23%

Business Plan Highlights

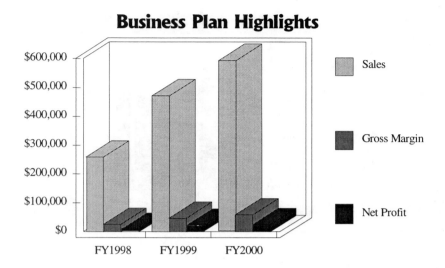

Projected Cash Flow

By running a tight operation, we plan to manage cash flow marginally for the first four months and then enjoy a growing cash position.

Table 8: Projected Cash Flow			
	FY1998	**FY1999**	**FY2000**
Net Profit	$8,620	$19,890	$24,982
Plus:			
Depreciation	$0	$0	$0
Change in Accounts Payable	$0	$0	$0
Current Borrowing (Repayment)	$0	$0	$0
Increase (Decrease) Other Liabilities	$0	$0	$0
Long-Term Borrowing (Repayment)	$0	$0	$0
Capital Input	$0	$0	$0
Subtotal	$8,620	$19,890	$24,982
Less:			
Change in Accounts Receivable	$0	$0	$0
Change in Inventory	$0	$0	$0
Change in Other ST Assets	$0	$0	$0
Capital Expenditure	$0	$0	$0
Subtotal	$0	$0	$0
Net Cash Flow	$8,620	$19,890	$24,982
Cash Balance	$11,420	$31,310	$56,292

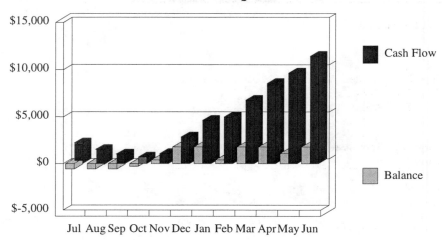

Cash Analysis

Jul Aug Sep Oct Nov Dec Jan Feb Mar Apr May Jun

Projected Balance Sheet

As shown in the balance sheet table that follows, we will begin to see our net worth grow beginning in December of 1997, exceeding $11,000 by the end of the first 12 months of operation.

-28-

Table 9: Projected Balance Sheet			
	FY1998	**FY1999**	**FY2000**
Short-Term Assets			
Cash	$11,420	$31,310	$56,292
Accounts Receivable	$0	$0	$0
Inventory	$0	$0	$0
Other Short-Term Assets	$0	$0	$0
Total Short-Term Assets	$11,420	$31,310	$56,292
Long-Term Assets			
Capital Assets	$0	$0	$0
Accumulated Depreciation	$0	$0	$0
Total Long-Term Assets	$0	$0	$0
Total Assets	$11,420	$31,310	$56,292
Liabilities and Net Worth			
Accounts Payable	$0	$0	$0
Short-Term Notes	$0	$0	$0
Other Short-Term Liabilities	$0	$0	$0
Subtotal Short-Term Liabilities	$0	$0	$0
Long-Term Liabilities	$0	$0	$0
Total Liabilities	$0	$0	$0
Paid-in Capital	$5,000	$5,000	$5,000
Retained Earnings	($2,200)	$6,420	$26,310
Earnings	$8,620	$19,890	$24,982
Total Equity	$11,420	$31,310	$56,292
Total Debt and Equity	$11,420	$31,310	$56,292
Net Worth	$11,420	$31,310	$56,292

Appendix 1: Sales Forecast and Personnel Plan

Sales Forecast

	Jul 97	Aug 97	Sep 97	Oct 97	Nov 97	Dec 97	Jan 98	Feb 98	Mar 98	Apr 98	May 98	Jun 98	FY1998	FY1999	FY2000
Sales	$0	$0	$0	$14,000	$21,000	$35,000	$35,000	$21,000	$35,000	$35,000	$28,000	$35,000	$259,000	$472,500	$590,625
Direct Cost of Sales	$0	$0	$0	$12,600	$18,900	$31,500	$31,500	$18,900	$31,500	$31,500	$25,200	$31,500	$233,100	$425,250	$531,563

Personnel Plan

Name	Jul 97	Aug 97	Sep 97	Oct 97	Nov 97	Dec 97	Jan 98	Feb 98	Mar 98	Apr 98	May 98	Jun 98	FY1998	FY1999	FY2000
Otieno Murundi	$0	$0	$0	$1,000	$1,000	$1,000	$1,000	$1,000	$1,000	$1,000	$1,000	$1,000	$9,000	$18,000	$24,000
Other	$0	$0	$0	$0	$0	$0	$0	$0	$0	$0	$0	$0	$0	$0	$0
Total	$0	$0	$0	$1,000	$1,000	$1,000	$1,000	$1,000	$1,000	$1,000	$1,000	$1,000	$9,000	$18,000	$24,000

Appendix 2: Projected Profit and Loss Statement

Pro-forma Income Statement

	Jul 97	Aug 97	Sep 97	Oct 97	Nov 97	Dec 97	Jan 98	Feb 98	Mar 98	Apr 98	May 98	Jun 98	FY1998	FY1999	FY2000
Sales	$0	$0	$0	$14,000	$21,000	$35,000	$35,000	$21,000	$35,000	$35,000	$28,000	$35,000	$259,000	$472,500	$590,625
Direct Cost of Sales	$0	$0	$0	$12,600	$18,900	$31,500	$31,500	$18,900	$31,500	$31,500	$25,200	$31,500	$233,100	$425,250	$531,563
Other	$0	$0	$0	$0	$0	$0	$0	$0	$0	$0	$0	$0	$0	$0	$0
Total Cost of Sales	$0	$0	$0	$12,600	$18,900	$31,500	$31,500	$18,900	$31,500	$31,500	$25,200	$31,500	$233,100	$425,250	$531,563
Gross Margin	$0	$0	$0	$1,400	$2,100	$3,500	$3,500	$2,100	$3,500	$3,500	$2,800	$3,500	$25,900	$47,250	$59,062
Gross Margin Percent	0.00%	0.00%	0.00%	10.00%	10.00%	10.00%	10.00%	10.00%	10.00%	10.00%	10.00%	10.00%	10.00%	10.00%	10.00%
Operating Expenses:															
Advertising/Promotion	$400	$400	$400	$400	$400	$400	$400	$400	$400	$400	$400	$400	$4,800	$4,800	$4,800
Travel	$100	$100	$100	$100	$100	$100	$100	$100	$100	$100	$100	$100	$1,200	$1,200	$1,200
Miscellaneous	$0	$0	$0	$0	$0	$0	$0	$0	$0	$0	$0	$0	$0	$0	$0
Payroll Expense	$0	$0	$0	$1,000	$1,000	$1,000	$1,000	$1,000	$1,000	$1,000	$1,000	$1,000	$9,000	$18,000	$24,000
Leased Equipment	$0	$0	$0	$0	$0	$0	$0	$0	$0	$0	$0	$0	$0	$0	$0
Utilities	$0	$0	$0	$0	$0	$0	$0	$0	$0	$0	$0	$0	$0	$0	$0
Insurance	$100	$100	$100	$100	$100	$100	$100	$100	$100	$100	$100	$100	$1,200	$1,200	$1,200
Rent	$0	$0	$0	$0	$0	$0	$0	$0	$0	$0	$0	$0	$0	$0	$0
Depreciation	$0	$0	$0	$0	$0	$0	$0	$0	$0	$0	$0	$0	$0	$0	$0
Payroll Burden	$0	$0	$0	$120	$120	$120	$120	$120	$120	$120	$120	$120	$1,080	$2,160	$2,880
Contract/Consultants	$0	$0	$0	$0	$0	$0	$0	$0	$0	$0	$0	$0	$0	$0	$0
Other	$0	$0	$0	$0	$0	$0	$0	$0	$0	$0	$0	$0	$0	$0	$0
Total Operating Expenses	$600	$600	$600	$1,720	$1,720	$1,720	$1,720	$1,720	$1,720	$1,720	$1,720	$1,720	$17,280	$27,360	$34,080
Profit Before Interest and Taxes	($600)	($600)	($600)	($320)	$380	$1,780	$1,780	$380	$1,780	$1,780	$1,080	$1,780	$8,620	$19,890	$24,982
Interest Expense ST	$0	$0	$0	$0	$0	$0	$0	$0	$0	$0	$0	$0	$0	$0	$0
Interest Expense LT	$0	$0	$0	$0	$0	$0	$0	$0	$0	$0	$0	$0	$0	$0	$0
Taxes Incurred	$0	$0	$0	$0	$0	$0	$0	$0	$0	$0	$0	$0	$0	$0	$0
Net Profit	($600)	($600)	($600)	($320)	$380	$1,780	$1,780	$380	$1,780	$1,780	$1,080	$1,780	$8,620	$19,890	$24,982
Net Profit/Sales	0.00%	0.00%	0.00%	-2.29%	1.81%	5.09%	5.09%	1.81%	5.09%	5.09%	3.86%	5.09%	3.33%	4.21%	4.23%

Appendix 3: Projected Cash Flow

Pro-Forma Cash Flow

	Jul 97	Aug 97	Sep 97	Oct 97	Nov 97	Dec 97	Jan-98	Feb-98	Mar 98	Apr 98	May 98	Jun 98	FY1998	FY1999	FY2000
Net Profit:	($600)	($600)	($600)	($320)	$380	$1,780	$1,780	$380	$1,780	$1,780	$1,080	$1,780	$8,620	$19,890	$24,982
Plus:															
Depreciation	$0	$0	$0	$0	$0	$0	$0	$0	$0	$0	$0	$0	$0	$0	$0
Change in Accounts Payable	$0	$0	$0	$0	$0	$0	$0	$0	$0	$0	$0	$0	$0	$0	$0
Current Borrowing (Repayment)	$0	$0	$0	$0	$0	$0	$0	$0	$0	$0	$0	$0	$0	$0	$0
Increase (Decrease) Other Liabilities	$0	$0	$0	$0	$0	$0	$0	$0	$0	$0	$0	$0	$0	$0	$0
Long-Term Borrowing (Repayment)	$0	$0	$0	$0	$0	$0	$0	$0	$0	$0	$0	$0	$0	$0	$0
Capital Input	$0	$0	$0	$0	$0	$0	$0	$0	$0	$0	$0	$0	$0	$0	$0
Subtotal	($600)	($600)	($600)	($320)	$380	$1,780	$1,780	$380	$1,780	$1,780	$1,080	$1,780	$8,620	$19,890	$24,982
Less:															
Change in Accounts Receivable	$0	$0	$0	$0	$0	$0	$0	$0	$0	$0	$0	$0	$0	$0	$0
Change in Inventory	$0	$0	$0	$0	$0	$0	$0	$0	$0	$0	$0	$0	$0	$0	$0
Change in Other ST Assets	$0	$0	$0	$0	$0	$0	$0	$0	$0	$0	$0	$0	$0	$0	$0
Capital Expenditure	$0	$0	$0	$0	$0	$0	$0	$0	$0	$0	$0	$0	$0	$0	$0
Subtotal	$0	$0	$0	$0	$0	$0	$0	$0	$0	$0	$0	$0	$0	$0	$0
Net Cash Flow	($600)	($600)	($600)	($320)	$380	$1,780	$1,780	$380	$1,780	$1,780	$1,080	$1,780	$8,620	$19,890	$24,982
Cash Balance	$2,200	$1,600	$1,000	$680	$1,060	$2,840	$4,620	$5,000	$6,780	$8,560	$9,640	$11,420	$11,420	$31,310	$56,292

Appendix 4: Projected Balance Sheet

Pro-forma Balance Sheet

	Jul 97	Aug 97	Sep 97	Oct 97	Nov 97	Dec 97	Jan 98	Feb 98	Mar 98	Apr 98	May 98	Jun 98	FY1998	FY1999	FY2000
Short-Term Assets															
Cash	$2,200	$1,600	$1,000	$680	$1,060	$2,840	$4,620	$5,000	$6,780	$8,560	$9,640	$11,420	$11,420	$31,310	$56,292
Accounts Receivable	$0	$0	$0	$0	$0	$0	$0	$0	$0	$0	$0	$0	$0	$0	$0
Inventory	$0	$0	$0	$0	$0	$0	$0	$0	$0	$0	$0	$0	$0	$0	$0
Other Short-Term Assets	$0	$0	$0	$0	$0	$0	$0	$0	$0	$0	$0	$0	$0	$0	$0
Total Short-Term Assets	$2,200	$1,600	$1,000	$680	$1,060	$2,840	$4,620	$5,000	$6,780	$8,560	$9,640	$11,420	$11,420	$31,310	$56,292
Long-Term Assets															
Capital Assets	$0	$0	$0	$0	$0	$0	$0	$0	$0	$0	$0	$0	$0	$0	$0
Accumulated Depreciation	$0	$0	$0	$0	$0	$0	$0	$0	$0	$0	$0	$0	$0	$0	$0
Total Long-Term Assets	$0	$0	$0	$0	$0	$0	$0	$0	$0	$0	$0	$0	$0	$0	$0
Total Assets	$2,200	$1,600	$1,000	$680	$1,060	$2,840	$4,620	$5,000	$6,780	$8,560	$9,640	$11,420	$11,420	$31,310	$56,292
Debt and Equity															
Short-Term Liabilities															
Accounts Payable	$0	$0	$0	$0	$0	$0	$0	$0	$0	$0	$0	$0	$0	$0	$0
Short-Term Notes	$0	$0	$0	$0	$0	$0	$0	$0	$0	$0	$0	$0	$0	$0	$0
Other ST Liabilities	$0	$0	$0	$0	$0	$0	$0	$0	$0	$0	$0	$0	$0	$0	$0
Subtotal ST Liabilities	$0	$0	$0	$0	$0	$0	$0	$0	$0	$0	$0	$0	$0	$0	$0
Long-Term Liabilities	$0	$0	$0	$0	$0	$0	$0	$0	$0	$0	$0	$0	$0	$0	$0
Total Liabilities	$0	$0	$0	$0	$0	$0	$0	$0	$0	$0	$0	$0	$0	$0	$0
Paid-in Capital	$5,000	$5,000	$5,000	$5,000	$5,000	$5,000	$5,000	$5,000	$5,000	$5,000	$5,000	$5,000	$5,000	$5,000	$5,000
Retained Earnings	($2,200)	($2,200)	($2,200)	($2,200)	($2,200)	($2,200)	($2,200)	($2,200)	($2,200)	($2,200)	($2,200)	($2,200)	($2,200)	$6,420	$26,310
Earnings	($600)	($1,200)	($1800)	($2,120)	($1,740)	$40	$1,820	$2,200	$3,980	$5,760	$6,840	$8,620	$8,620	$19,890	$24,982
Total Equity	$2,200	$1,600	$1,000	$680	$1,060	$2,840	$4,620	$5,000	$6,780	$8,560	$9,640	$11,420	$11,420	$31,310	$56,292
Total Debt and Equity	$2,200	$1,600	$1,000	$680	$1,060	$2,840	$4,620	$5,000	$6,780	$8,560	$9,640	$11,420	$11,420	$31,310	$56,292
Net Worth	$2,200	$1,600	$1,000	$680	$1,060	$2,840	$4,620	$5,000	$6,780	$8,560	$9,640	$11,420	$11,420	$31,310	$56,292

The Plan For
All Church Sound

BLAKE ENGEL

18841 W. Marian Dr.

Lake Villa, IL 60046

(847) 543-8840

Copy Number ____ of Ten.

-2-

EXECUTIVE SUMMARY

The company and its mission. All Church Sound (ACS) is an Illinois-based company dedicated to providing high quality service of church sound systems, including Training, 88-Point System Service, Consulting, Insurance Inventory, and R.I.M. Service (Repair, Installation, and Modification). The mission of ACS is "All Church Sound exists to provide churches with low cost, high quality Christian service of their sound system." ACS is a sole-proprietorship owned by its founder, Blake Engel.

The industry and market. Approximately 90% of American churches have an electronically amplified sound system. Of these, 99.2% are NOT happy with their system; only .8% are completely satisfied. A large and diversified industry has grown to fill the need for church sound system installation and maintenance. ACS is considered a "local provider," in that it serves a local market, providing routine services needed by almost every church at some time. All Church Sound specifically targets churches in Northeastern Illinois, primarily Lake County and adjacent areas. This target area is growing rapidly, and is expected to continue to do so for the next 20 years. Churches will continue to grow in numbers, attendance, and sophistication, all of which will lead to greater demand for ACS services.

The competition. There is no competitor which has dedicated itself to the church sound market in the way All Church Sound has. There are a number of local providers which currently operate in the ACS market area, and several of them offer services similar to ACS's R.I.M. Service and Consulting Service. However, none of them have a well-developed maintenance program like the ACS 88-Point System Service; none have a focused training program or an insurance inventory program. ACS has the following advantages at launch: ACS is dedicated to churches; ACS focuses on long-term relationships and provides truly outstanding service; and ACS is home-based, giving it a significant cost advantage compared to the competition. Conversely, ACS is currently weak in its customer development, reputation, long term professional experience, and capital funding.

Services offered. All Church Sound provides services in five specific areas:

1. Training. On-site training of church personnel regarding system components, layout, capabilities, operation, troubleshooting, etc.

2. Consulting. Providing guidance for improving existing systems, interacting with system designers.

3. 88-Point System Service. Scheduled or on-call system maintenance.

4. Insurance Inventory. Physically check and log all equipment, including photos.

5. R.I.M. Service. Repair, Installation, Modification work done to specifications.

-4-

Marketing and sales strategy. ACS services are designed and priced to meet customer needs at a cost that is at or below that of the competition.

The company will use a number of marketing vehicles to drive attention and interest of potential customers: quality stationery and brochures, a series of mailings to target churches, a high quality newsletter, and Yellow Pages advertising.

All advertising will be developed to drive customers to contact ACS, after which Blake will finalize the sale. The position ACS seeks in the customer's mind is "All Church Sound — Dedicated to providing information, knowledge, and services to help your church sound its best."

Management. ACS will initially be a one-man operation. Blake Engel, company founder, has been involved in church sound system operation and maintenance for many years, and is currently the Director of Sound Reinforcement at Libertyville Evangelical Free Church of Libertyville, IL. He has completed extensive study of acoustics, sound system components, system design and configuration, and sound mixing and recording. Blake is intelligent, honest, fair, and compulsively thorough. All previous work and ministry experience has built in Blake the knowledge and skills necessary to lead ACS into profitability.

Status of operations. ACS was founded in January 1997 and plans to initiate marketing in June 1997.

Financials. The financial strategy for the company is focused directly on achieving sales goals. Achieving sufficient sales volume is the critical factor in the company's success. As a service business with low variable costs per unit sold and low fixed costs, ACS will enjoy high gross margins and high net margins (assuming fixed costs are adequately controlled). ACS projects 1997 sales to exceed $15,000, growing to $39,000 in 1998 and $47,000 in 1999. Net profit before taxes for the same three years is projected at $6,800, $13,400, and $14,900.

COMPANY SUMMARY

All Church Sound is a sole proprietorship founded and owned by Blake Engel.

Mission

All Church Sound exists to provide churches with low cost, high quality Christian service of their sound system.

ACS is a Christian business and will be operated with a Christ-centered focus. While we do not suggest that our competitors are un-Christian, ACS will work to distinguish itself in this area. We will always conduct ourselves in an honest and moral manner.

We count it a privilege to do business with our customers, and our intent is to help each church we serve enjoy the fullest and most complete sound possible. We have a goal to be profitable, and will work diligently to achieve that goal. However, profit is NOT our primary life motivation. Complete service and devotion to God is our primary life motivation, and all other priorities fall subject to this overarching value. We will not sell unneeded service or products, and we will always be fair in our pricing and billing.

Objectives

We have set the following objectives for calendar year 1997:

1. Achieve sales of $15,000.

2. Perform three insurance inventories per month beginning in June.

3. Conduct two training sessions per month beginning in July.

4. Have 30 contracts for ongoing maintenance by year-end.

5. End the year with a profit.

Keys to Success

In order to accomplish the company objectives, the following Keys to Success must be in place:

- Develop excellent product offerings that are meaningful and appealing to the target churches.

- Execute the marketing plan aggressively and successfully, adjusting quickly when necessary.

- Manage time wisely to always focus on generating business or doing business.

- Keep costs down. Never spend unnecessarily.

- Maintain cash flow to enable continued marketing.

- Mail at least six issues of "Sound Advice" per year.

- Have at least 10 letters of reference from churches by year-end.

Company Location and Facilities

All business will be conducted from the home of Blake Engel, 18841 W. Marian Dr., Lake Villa, IL. Notification has been received from Lake County approving the operation of this home-based business at this location.

Startup Summary

Startup costs are detailed in the following table. All costs are appropriate and necessary.

Table 1: Startup Costs	
Startup Expenses	*Amount*
One-Time Startup Expenses	
Brochures	$ 250
Consultants	$ 500
Expensed Equipment	$1,650
Insurance	$ 0
Legal	$ 60
Rent	$ 0
Research and Development	$ 500
Stationery, etc.	$ 150
Other	$ 0
Total Startup Expenses	$3,110
Short-Term Assets	
Cash Requirements	$ 500
Beginning Inventory	$ 0
Other Short-Term Assets	$ 0
Total Short-Term Assets	$ 500
Total Long-Term Assets	$ 0
Total Startup Requirements	$3,610

Table 2: Startup Funding Plan	
Funding Source	*Amount*
Investment	
Blake Engel	$3,610
Other	$ 0
Total Investment	$3,610
Short-Term Borrowing	
Unpaid Expenses	$ 0
Short-Term Loans	$ 0
Interest-Free Short-Term Loans	$ 0
Total Short-Term Borrowing	$ 0
Long-Term Borrowing	
Long-Term Loans	$ 0
Total Borrowing	$ 0
Loss at Startup	($3,100)
Total Equity	$ 500
Total Debt and Equity	$ 500

INDUSTRY ANALYSIS

Technically, ACS falls in the industry category "Electrical Work," SIC Code #1731. This category is a broad one, including such diverse activities as burglar alarm installation, cable TV hookups, telecommunication equipment installation, and communications equipment installation. However, this view of the industry is much too broad to allow proper focus.

We first restrict our discussion to the business of live sound reinforcement systems in individual buildings. There are many types of public and private buildings which use professional sound equipment, such as theaters, schools, recording studios, sports facilities, etc. While there are undoubtedly opportunities in a variety of these building types, we view our true industry category to be the design, acquisition, installation, maintenance, and technical support of church sound reinforcement systems. By narrowing our recognition of the industry, we are able to maintain a sharper focus on our specific market, competition, and company objectives. For the sake of brevity, we will refer to this as the "church sound system" industry.

ACS has chosen to specialize in church sound systems for several reasons:

1. Churches account for 60% of the entire industry. All other building types combined account for the remaining 40%, with no group of singular significance. By focusing on churches, ACS will develop name recognition, tremendous expertise, and economies of focus in the dominant need area.

2. Our founder has years of experience in church sound systems, a clear strength at launch.

3. We have a passion for churches, and feel strongly about the need for high quality church sound reinforcement.

The church sound system industry is driven by the ongoing vitality of churches in the nation. As congregations grow, mature, and multiply, their need for quality sound reinforcement grows as well.

A review of the "business of churches" shows that from 1980 to 1995, total U.S. religious building floor space steadily increased from 28 million square feet to 33 million square feet. This indicates current churches are expanding, and new churches are being built. Another source reports annual church construction spending has remained steady at roughly $3.5 billion per year. Additionally, the growing American love affair with "entertainment" is driving churches to significantly improve the "professionalism" of their worship services, including music, voice, and drama. This phenomenon will continue to cause upgrading of church sound systems.

There are 257,640 individual congregations currently organized in the U.S. We will assume that each has a dedicated building. Approximately 90% of current church buildings have some type of electrically amplified sound system. Clearly, the business of church sound systems is large and growing.

Industry Participants

The participants in this industry are, for the most part, clearly identifiable.

First, the churches themselves. Churches are the purchasers of sound components and service. Yet a "church" does not make a decision to buy; a person (or committee) does. In each situation, there are certain individuals who recognize the need for a new, upgraded, repaired, cleaned, maintained system, and drive the purchase process forward. These may be paid staff music ministers, or unpaid volunteers. These people are entrusted by the membership to be good stewards of church funds, and work hard to maintain that trust.

Second, the component manufacturers. These are the companies, large and small, which manufacture the individual parts which are combined to build sound equipment. Components include wire, transistors, switches, connectors, etc., the basic building blocks of all sound equipment. There are many component manufacturers in the country, none dominant. Supply of components is not, and will not be, a barrier to success in this market.

Third, the equipment manufacturers. These are the companies which use components to build sound equipment such as amplifiers, mixers, cords, speakers, and microphones. Again, there are many high quality manufacturers in the U.S., and supply of equipment will not be a restraining factor in the business.

Fourth, retail stores. There are times when a church buyer has the knowledge (or thinks that he or she has the knowledge) to make direct purchases and installations of sound equipment. In these instances, purchases can be made from manufacturers directly, or from retail outlets such as Radio Shack or professional sound equipment stores such as Gand Music & Sound or The Music Source.

Fifth, the premier professional system designers and installers. These are large service companies which work primarily in the design and installation of new systems in new churches. There is a handful of these companies in North America which service all of the U.S. and beyond.

Sixth, the local service providers. These are local businesses which focus on upgrading, repairing, cleaning, and maintaining systems in a defined geographical area. All Church Sound is a local service provider.

TARGET MARKET

All Church Sound specifically targets churches with sound reinforcement system needs in the geographic area within 30 miles of the intersection of U.S. Rt. 45 and Grand Avenue in Lake County, Illinois. This includes all of Lake County, the eastern two-thirds of McHenry County, northern Kane County, northern Cook County, northeastern DuPage County, and southern Walworth and Racine Counties in Wisconsin.

We believe, and survey data support the idea, that this target market will support the entry of ACS into the market.

Market Size and Trends

In reviewing the market size and trends, a number of positive indicators are revealed.

First, the potential customer base consists of roughly 1000 churches in the target market, a substantial target group.

Second, the area population is expanding rapidly. Forecasters call for a 50% population increase in Lake County from 1990 to 2020. Other projected growth figures during the same time period include:

-10-

Market	Growth Rate
DuPage County	28%
Kane County	70%
Cook County	11%
McHenry County	84%

As a church grows, matures, and develops program sophistication, the congregation often desires higher quality in all its systems, including sound reinforcement. Clearly, the anticipated population growth will bring with it the need for expanded sound system capabilities in growing churches.

Third, as the population grows, it is logical to assume that new churches will be built. If one assumes a new building rate one-half that of population growth, then a 25% population growth in the target area would result in 12.5% growth in new church buildings, or 125 new churches being built in the area over the next 30 years. Fifty percent population growth could spawn an additional 250 church buildings.

Purchase Patterns/Process

The primary purchase pattern in this market is church-driven. Typically, a church musician or leader recognizes a need for equipment or service and initiates some contact to correct the problem. The direction taken is dependent on the person's knowledge, experience with previous suppliers, personal contacts, or Yellow Pages searching.

Alternatively, service providers contact churches via direct mail, word-of-mouth, and Yellow Pages ads. Most providers do not use telemarketing to make initial contact with churches.

COMPETITION

As we examine the competitive situation in our target market, we find there are a number of sound system businesses in our primary geographic area.

Some are large, well-established, and not really direct competitors of ACS because they focus primarily on developing and installing new systems. Others are smaller companies that are more direct competition for ACS.

Overall, the church sound system local market appears to be solid, with growth occurring as the population grows. There does not seem to be any massive change occurring, positively or negatively, which would impact our entry into the market.

Primary Competitors

There are two area businesses at the high end of local service providers: Ancha Electronics of Rolling Meadows, and Wizdum Audio of Arlington Heights. They must be regarded in a class separate from the other local providers. Both focus primarily on design and installation of new systems in the $10,000 to $100,000 range. These two will probably maintain their positions and will not threaten, nor be threatened by, All Church Sound.

Others in the market include:

- Gand Music & Sound of Northfield

- Metro Sound of New Berlin, WI

- Berler Communications of Waukegan

- Burrows Sound of Skokie

- Chicago Sound of Morton Grove

- Esdale Commercial Sound Systems of Highland Park

- Sound Planning Associates of Wheaton

These businesses vary in their market offerings, but all are somewhat connected to the church sound system industry. Most have done church systems, although only Metro Sound stated that they do "mainly church sound." It is interesting to note that none of them include "church" in their name. None of them have established a significant maintenance program, although several will perform maintenance for a fee on an as-needed basis.

The final, and perhaps primary, competitor is the local church volunteer. This is the individual with time and some expertise who is willing to pitch in and help maintain and operate the system. These are fine people who are a great help to the church. However, they are rarely professionals, and have truly limited capability. It can be safely said that most church systems are maintained in a state of tenuous functionality by these volunteers.

Barriers to Entry

The primary competitive barriers to entry will be:

1. Strong expertise required. Many of the competitors have many years of commercial experience to rely on. In addition, they have a long list of satisfied customers to present to potential clients.

Any newcomer to the market will need to show great ability to develop and demonstrate high level expertise, and relate that expertise via honesty, kindness, and outstanding service.

2. Market saturation. Since there are a number of qualified local suppliers of church sound reinforcement, a new entrant will be faced with the challenge of a well-served market. It will be necessary to be creative in developing a niche that can be effectively filled, and to be skilled enough in marketing and advertising to exploit that niche.

Future Competition

We see the potential for three likely future competitive challenges:

- New church volunteers. As church laity becomes more technically educated, church sound volunteers may become more aggressive in their effort to fulfill the needs of their churches. We expect that the new technology growth will continue to outpace most volunteers.

- Encroachment by the premier professional audio designers. These nationally and internationally dominant players may attempt to reach down further into the market and take business from the local service providers. This is unlikely, given the expected continued growth of the large, new buildings and systems that these players focus on.

- As ACS builds its niche and grows into a successful business, other local service providers will probably be alert enough to take note of the strategies and tactics used. We will need to be prepared to defend/protect our newly carved niche and/or move on to create an even newer niche.

SWOT ANALYSIS

An examination of the company's strengths and weaknesses, and the market opportunities and threats, helps to identify areas of concern and areas of additional potential.

Company Strengths

ACS brings these strengths to the marketplace at launch:

- Dedication to the church sound market. ACS is the only service focused solely on this market. This will allow an expertise and knowledge base unsurpassed in the target market.

-13-

- Honesty. Blake Engel is honest and fair in all dealings, personal and business.

- Knowledge of what is required to create quality church sound.

- Concern for each customer. Because of our focus on long-term relationships, ACS will always treat each customer as they want to be treated. No short-term "install it and disappear" acts at ACS.

- The ACS office is home-based, giving us extremely low overhead, which translates to lower customer costs and higher margins.

- Our company founder is highly intelligent and compulsively thorough.

Company Weaknesses

ACS enters the market with these weaknesses:

- Lack of commercial church sound experience. Although Blake has had a great deal of volunteer experience, and commands a detailed knowledge of the art and science of church music, prospective customers often wish to examine a list of previous customers. This weakness will be addressed via several means, including obtaining referral letters from as many sources as possible, assertive marketing to create early buyers, and focusing on "years of experience" overall. In addition, being new to the market can be a positive attribute as well: "As a new company, we can't afford to overlook any customer, any need, any problem", etc.

- Lack of references. This issue is partially addressed above. During the early phase of establishment, ACS will solicit letters of recommendation from a number of individuals who know the skill and care that Blake brings to the job. These will include pastors, music ministers, educators, musicians, and others. The letters will be written specifically to recommend Blake personally with regard to church sound system support and maintenance. All letters will be written on appropriate letterhead.

- Lack of unlimited launch capital. Equipment and supplies are easily provided by the startup capital available. However, limited funds will be an issue with regard to marketing. ACS will maintain a tight focus on the target market in the development of all marketing tools. We will not waste money by spending outside our targets. This will necessitate heavy use of mail, phone and personal selling.

- No formal acoustics/sound system education. Since there is very little available, this is not a competitive weakness.

-14-

Market Opportunities

Opportunities exist as follows:

- Only .8% of churches are completely satisfied with their current sound. This clearly establishes an unmet need for ACS services.

- None of the competitive local providers use the word "church" in their name. There is room in the market for a company devoted solely to churches.

- Most of the competition focuses on new installations, and views this as their primary business. This leaves many other opportunities open.

- There is no focused competition for the 88-Point System Service business in our target market. Local providers in other markets find this to be a profitable niche — it will be here as well.

- There is no focused competition in the "training" business. This can be exploited as well.

- There is no focused competition in the "insurance inventory" business. This can possibly be developed by calling on insurance agents.

- In addition to all of these need-based opportunities, there is also an opportunity to displace providers that are higher priced and offer a less personalized service. This will become clearer as we roll out.

Market Threats

We face the following marketplace threats:

- The primary market threat is target market indifference. 99.2% of churches know they have a sound problem, but they won't easily recognize how simple and inexpensive the solution may be. We must overcome this indifference and lack of knowledge.

- There are a number of well-established companies in the market which will compete strongly to maintain their niche. To the degree that ACS tries to displace them from that niche, they will do battle. Our strategy is to create a niche by meeting needs that have gone unmet to this point.

- As new, knowledgeable volunteers become active in certain churches, they may displace ACS in certain service areas.

-15-

NEEDS ANALYSIS

At launch, ACS competitors have met the need for design and installation of new systems in new and preexisting buildings. This niche is dominated and well served by Ancha, Wizdum, and others as detailed in the section on competition. ACS will not compete in this area at launch, but will observe the market and attempt to develop a customer base that will lead to potential opportunities for system design and installation.

Unmet and Incompletely Met Needs

Unmet and partially met needs abound in the target market.

- Almost all churches have a known need for better sound. They want and need to know what they've got, how it works, how to make it work better, and that it's going to work right THIS SUNDAY!

- There is an unmet need in the market for a high quality, highly responsive, customer need-driven, low cost local service provider.

- Training of all "need-to-know" personnel is not currently available in the market. This is an area that, when properly addressed, can greatly enhance the church sound quality for very low cost.

- Insurance inventory services are not currently available in the market.

- There may be a need in some target churches for a local, trusted consultant to work on behalf of the church as the church works with a premier professional system designer and installer. In this capacity, ACS would work to protect the church's interests and to allow the church to achieve an excellent system at a reasonable cost.

- The need for professional system maintenance is only partially met currently. Some local service providers will make service calls, but they do not make it easy or inexpensive.

SERVICES

Based on market needs, All Church Sound will provide service in five specific areas.

1. TRAINING. ACS will provide the following on-site training to church personnel:

    — System components

— System layout and design

— System capabilities

— System limits

— Basics of operation

— Advanced operation

— Troubleshooting

— Proper care

2. CONSULTING. ACS will work with target churches to work on behalf of the church as the church works with a premier professional system designer and installer. In this capacity, ACS would work to protect the church's interests and to allow the church to achieve an excellent system at a reasonable cost.

    — ACS will provide suggestions for improving/augmenting existing systems.

    — ACS will be available for "as needed" consultation in any sound area.

3. 88-POINT SYSTEM SERVICE. ACS will provide scheduled or on-call system maintenance to ensure quality performance. 88 specific points will be checked, including:

    — Checking each component individually

    — Cleaning each component.

    — Checking all wiring and cables, etc.

4. INSURANCE INVENTORY. ACS will physically check and log all equipment, including model number and serial number (when existing) and photos and/or video if requested.

5. R.I.M. SERVICE. ACS will repair, install, or modify a church's sound system as capabilities allow.

Competitive Comparison

All Church Sound will offer a different combination of services from those offered by other businesses currently in the market. Instead of focusing on high-priced systems installations, we offer a package of services designed to appeal to virtually every church in the target market. No other provider in the market is presenting a product group so clearly designed with customer needs in mind.

This distinction of service offerings, combined with an ever-present attention to high-quality, positive customer interaction, will separate ACS from the other local service providers in the market. Personal attention and personal service have always generated business, and we are confident they will in this case as well.

Sourcing

As noted in the discussion of industry participants, there is no shortage of suppliers for the supplies and repair and replacement products that will be needed in the course of doing business:

- Musician's Friend, Medford, OR — processing equipment, mixers, mics, cable.

- All Pro Sound, Pensacola, FL — mics, mixers, amps, etc.

- Conquest Sound, Monee, IL — cables and connectors.

- Gand Music, Northfield, IL — repairs.

- Rudy Zeifhammel, Zion, IL — Telex duplicator repair.

- MCM Electronics, Centerville, OH — cleaning supplies.

- Officemax, Gurnee, IL — office supplies, printing.

- Quill, Palatine, IL — office supplies.

- Nebs, Groton, MA — forms, etc.

Future Services

Our sole focus at launch will be the establishment of our beachhead with five key services: training, consulting, 88-point system service, insurance inventory, and R.I.M. We also look forward to the possibility of adding one or all of the following services in the future.

1. Sound system training book, for sale or gift to customers. 2 years.

2. Rental/loaner equipment. 5 years.

3. "Rent-a-Soundman" for special events. 5 years.

4. Audio tape. 5-10 minute cassette to be given by churches to their visitors. Would include welcome from pastor, information on service times and ministry areas, special music, drama, etc. 5 years.

5. Complete system installations. 10 years.

MARKETING PLAN

We will examine the marketing plan using McCarthy's "Four Ps" approach — Product, Price, Place (Distribution), and Promotion.

Product

The "Service Description" section of the plan defines and describes ACS services in detail. We will focus at launch on training, consulting, 88-point system service, insurance inventory, and R.I.M. The specific benefits that will accrue to churches employing ACS include:

- A relative in the sound business. Everyone knows the pleasure of having a relative who does what you need done. With ACS, a church has that relative in the sound business — someone they can trust to do what's right. Every time.

- Peace of mind. With ACS on board, a church is assured that its sound reinforcement system is fully functional, ready to perform flawlessly each and every time it is used.

- Smoother church services. With a system operating at peak performance, church services will run like clockwork. No bleeps, buzzes, or burps!

- Happier members. When churchgoers aren't distracted by lousy sound, they enjoy the service more. When they can hear and understand the music and sermons clearly, they learn and retain more.

- Greater attendance. Statistics demonstrate that churches which invest in high quality sound reinforcement systems enjoy corresponding growth in church attendance.

- Increased giving. Weekly giving also rises in churches with high quality sound systems. A church which pays attention to its sound system is really investing in the future. An investment which pays back in many ways.

Place

ACS will sell and deliver its services through mail, phone, and personal visits to churches. There is no reason for a customer to visit at our company office.

-19-

Price

Pricing the services of ACS requires an interesting combination of three forces: What customers are willing to pay; what will generate an acceptable profit margin; and what the competition is charging for similar services. Dealing with competitive pricing challenges should not be difficult at the outset, since none of our local service competitors currently focus on the service areas we will. If they offer the services at all, they are priced usually in the $90-110 per hour range. ACS can certainly fit within or below that competitive range.

Determining a pricing structure which generates an acceptable profit margin is more difficult to establish. Our approach here has been to develop tentative prices based roughly on those of the competition, then conduct a Breakeven Analysis to determine their viability. The Breakeven Analysis indicates, with currently stated prices, ACS will reach breakeven status at seven sales per month, a readily attainable and sustainable level.

The willingness of customers to pay has been evaluated in two ways. First, it is clear competitors in our target market are conducting business, indicating customers (at least many of them) are willing to pay their prices. If ACS prices are on the bottom side of the range, we should fare well. Second, we have verified, from similar businesses providing maintenance services in other markets, that they find many churches willing to pay prices similar to ours for similar service. In some cases, scheduled maintenance services represent these companies' foundation business. Based on each of these considerations, ACS will initiate operations using prices as indicated in Table 3.

Table 3: Pricing	
Service	**Price Schedule**
88-Point System Service	Trip and clean: $70, plus any repairs needed. Packages available: 3 trips: $190 one-time payment, a $20 savings, or 6 trips: $370 one-time payment, a $50 savings
R.I.M. Service	$70 per hour, plus $40 trip charge
Consulting	$70 per hour, plus $40 trip charge. Or, a package: 3 hours in two meetings or less*: $195, or 5 hours in two meetings or less*: $300, or 10 hours in three meetings or less*: $550, and Hours beyond 10: $50 per hour plus $40 trip charge *$40 trip charge for each meeting beyond maximum indicated

Training	In order to optimize training for the group as well as the individual, our training classes are limited to four operators, priced as follows**
	1-8 channels: $220; includes learning system and 3 hrs. training 9-16 channels: $290; includes learning system and 4 hrs. training 17 + channels: $350; includes learning system and 4 hrs. training
	Duplicate training sessions are available for additional operators (up to four operators per session), as follows:
	1-8 channels: $170; includes 3 hrs. training 9-16 channels: $220; includes 4 hrs. training 17 + channels: $290; includes 4 hrs. training
	**Systems with more than one console require a custom price quote based on the use and complexity of the system

Insurance Inventory	**No. of line items**	**2 text copies**	**Each additional**	**2 copies w/photos**	**Each additional**
	up to 20	$130	$15	$200	$35
	each add. 20	$40	—	$60	$10

Promotion

The initial marketing mix for ACS will be simple, inexpensive, and effective.

- A set of basic stationery will be designed and executed, including letterhead, envelopes, and business cards.

- A basic brochure will be designed and executed to include a company description, history, services offered, founder's biography, philosophy, etc.

- A series of topic-specific brochures will be designed and executed to address a number of church sound areas. The "What About..." series will include topics such as "Room Acoustics," "Strange Noises," and "Microphones," and will be used to promote the multiple facets of ACS services.

- A three-mailing series will be designed and executed to introduce ACS to the market and begin to generate attention and interest in the minds of potential customers. This initial three-wave program will be rolled out to multiple small segments of the target group, perhaps 50-100 churches per segment. This segmentation will help control mail overload, follow-up overload, and cost overload. These three mailings, over three successive weeks, will be targeted to the key person in each church who is responsible for the functioning and upkeep of the sound system.

The series will be designed to build on itself as we progress through each piece, adding interest and call-to-action as it grows. Immediately after the final mailing arrives at each church, we will phone to schedule an appointment to present a special introductory offer. An initial idea for the special offer is to present to the key person, at no charge, a custom-designed insurance inventory form for the church to use to protect itself against disaster. Other ideas will be considered, and we may use different offers in different segments to test the power of each.

- ACS will design and implement a newsletter, "Sound Advice," which will be sent to all target churches on a regular schedule, at least six times per year. Sound Advice will be a high quality 4-8 page newsletter with solid information of interest and value to those involved in church sound. Interspersed with the news in each issue will be offerings by ACS, news of new services, special pricing, etc.

- Yellow Pages advertising will be investigated for primary target geographic areas, including Shepherds Guide and/or other Christian phone directories.

- The purpose of each marketing tool is to get Blake in front of the church decision maker so he can move that customer from Awareness to Interest to Desire to Action, the classic AIDA selling principle.

Positioning Statement

After fully evaluating our services compared to those offered by the competition, and considering the user benefits described above, we have created the following positioning statement for ACS:

> **All Church Sound — Dedicated to providing information, knowledge, and services to help your church sound its best.**

Warranties/Guarantees

All Church Sound fully guarantees all services. If any customer is unsatisfied with ACS service, we will work with them until they are satisfied. If we still are not able to fulfill their needs, we will refund their money. All of it. Period.

SALES AND IMPLEMENTATION PLAN

All ACS selling will be done initially by Blake himself. Once the marketing activities have generated an interested potential client, Blake will visit the person-in-charge to complete the sale.

-22-

There is the potential to add sales staff as the company grows, but the first additions would likely be technicians, leaving the critical job of selling to the principal person in the company.

Additionally, we may find that insurance agents who focus on church policies will be able, willing sales agents for the insurance inventory segment of the business. This will be researched.

Sales Methods and Activities

Sales tools and methods will be very basic. The following sales aids are in development:

- Reference letters. These are being solicited from a variety of sources, and will initially be written to support Blake personally. Once satisfied customers have been generated, letters supporting ACS specifically will be solicited and procured.

- Brochures describing and defining what specifically is included in each type of service, training, maintenance, etc.

- Selling brochure to include basic statistics regarding the average church's dissatisfaction with its sound system, how a good system can boost attendance, giving, etc.

- Ad specialty items such as cord wraps, pens, etc. which will be left behind to carry the ACS name.

- Well-designed forms to be used for each type of service. These will create a quality image for the company.

These tools will be used to move a client through the four stages of the selling process: Awareness, Interest, Desire, and Action.

Sales Projections

Sales projections for three years follow, with detailed spreadsheets in the appendix.

-23-

Table 4: Sales Forecast			
Sales	**1997**	**1998**	**1999**
Training	$2,800	$7,000	$8,000
Consulting	$3,220	$7,280	$8,400
Maintenance	$2,450	$8,400	$10,500
Inventory	$3,600	$8,250	$9,750
Other	$2,625	$8,400	$10,500
Total Sales	$14,695	$39,330	$47,150
Cost of Sales	**1997**	**1998**	**1999**
Training	$280	$700	$800
Consulting	$322	$728	$840
Maintenance	$735	$2,520	$3,150
Inventory	$360	$825	$975
Other	$265	$840	$1,050
Total Cost of Sales	$1,962	$5,613	$6,815

Yearly Total Sales

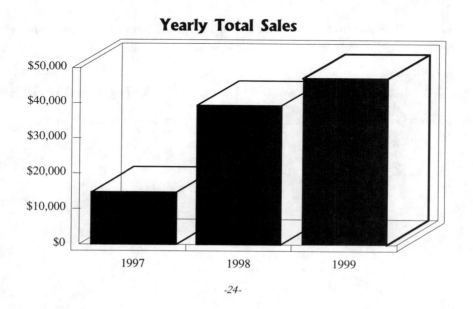

-24-

MANAGEMENT SUMMARY

Initially ACS is a one-man operation. Blake Engel is responsible for every aspect of the company's operation. Fortunately, he is capable and up to the job. Blake's resume is attached. *(Editor's note: resume has not been reproduced.)*

Management Team Gaps

The two areas where Blake will have to move up the learning curve very quickly are sales and accounting. Accounting is relatively simple since the advent of Quicken and similar accounting software. ACS will use Quicken initially. The art and science of selling is one that is not learned overnight, but since Blake is the only salesman ACS has, he's the man for the job. Blake has the ability to develop rapport, he's bright, quick, and easy to like. However, the rest of selling is more complicated than it looks. Evaluating Blake's situation using the KASE model, he has excellent product Knowledge, a tremendous Attitude, relatively undeveloped Skills, and will give exceptional Effort. The rapid development of high level selling skills will be very important to his ability to generate sales. This is an area he should begin working on immediately.

Personnel Plan

Currently, there is no plan to add staff. The first area to probably need additional people would be technical staff to complete the growing workload.

FINANCIAL PLAN

The financial strategy for the company is focused directly on achieving sales goals. Achieving sufficient sales volume is the critical factor in the company's success. As a service business with low variable costs per unit sold and low fixed costs, ACS will enjoy high gross margins and high net margins (assuming fixed costs are adequately controlled).

Important Assumptions

This plan is based on the following general and specific assumptions:

1. Population growth in the target market will continue as forecast.

2. The target market economy will continue to grow as forecast, with no significant recession.

3. There will be no major competitive threat from a currently unknown source.

4. At least 25% of the target market will have an interest in one or more ACS services.

Key Financial Indicators

There are a number of key financial indicators which will provide guidelines for ACS at launch. The company must focus on these 4 primary indicators in order to achieve its objectives.

1. Achieve or exceed sales projections. This is paramount.

2. Keep marketing costs at no more than 50% of sales in 1997, declining thereafter.

3. Achieve 50% repeat business in the system service area. This builds a profit base that keeps growing.

4. Sell to 10% of targets contacted.

Breakeven Analysis

At current assumptions of prices and direct costs, ACS will reach breakeven at roughly seven clients per month, as shown in the following table and chart.

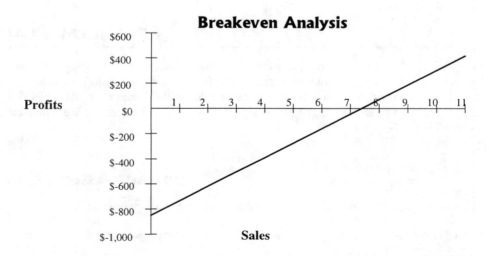

Breakeven Analysis

Table 5: Breakeven Analysis	
Monthly Units Breakeven	7
Monthly Sales Breakeven	$1,035
Assumptions	
Average Unit Sale	$140
Average Per-Unit Cost	$25
Fixed Cost	$850

Projected Profit and Loss

All Church Sound should be profitable from the beginning, with 1997 earnings of $6,000, rising to double that by 1999. Highlights are shown in the accompanying chart. Full details are in the appendix.

Table 6: Pro-forma Income Statement			
	FY1997	**FY1998**	**FY1999**
Sales	$14,695	$39,330	$47,150
Direct Cost of Sales	$1,962	$5,613	$6,815
Other	$0	$0	$0
Total Cost of Sales	$1,962	$5,613	$6,815
Gross Margin	$12,733	$33,717	$40,335
Gross Margin Percent	86.65%	85.73%	85.55%
Operating Expenses:			
Advertising/Promotion	$3,050	$12,000	$14,000
Travel	$510	$1,200	$1,300
Miscellaneous	$0	$0	$0
Payroll Expense	$1,700	$6,000	$9,000
Leased Equipment	$0	$0	$0
Utilities	$240	$500	$560
Insurance	$350	$600	$600
Rent	$0	$0	$0
Depreciation	$0	$0	$0
Contract/Consultants	$0	$0	$0
Other	$0	$0	$0
Total Operating Expenses	$5,850	$20,300	$25,460
Profit Before Interest and Taxes	$6,883	$13,417	$14,875
Interest Expense ST	$0	$0	$0
Interest Expense LT	$0	$0	$0
Taxes Incurred	$0	$0	$0
Net Profit	$6,883	$13,417	$14,875
Net Profit/Sales	46.84%	34.11%	31.55%

Business Plan Highlights

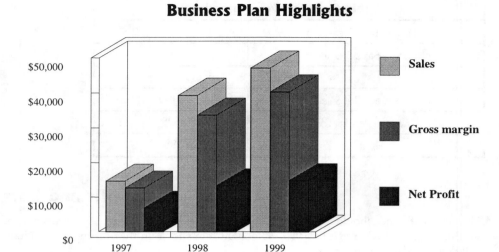

Projected Cash Flow

As noted in the following chart, cash flow will be positive from the outset, growing each month following. Details are found in the appendix.

Table 7: Projected Cash Flow			
	1997	**1998**	**1999**
Net Profit	$6,883	$13,417	$14,875
Plus:			
Depreciation	$0	$0	$0
Change in Accounts Payable	$0	$0	$0
Current Borrowing (Repayment)	$0	$0	$0
Increase (Decrease) Other Liabilities	$0	$0	$0
Long-Term Borrowing (Repayment)	$0	$0	$0
Capital Input	$0	$0	$0
Subtotal	$6,883	$13,417	$14,875
Less:			
Change in Accounts Receivable	$729	$1,222	$388
Change in Inventory	$0	$0	$0
Change in Other ST Assets	$0	$0	$0
Capital Expenditure	$0	$0	$0
Subtotal	$729	$1,222	$388
Net Cash Flow	$6,154	$12,195	$14,487
Cash balance	$6,654	$18,850	$33,337

-28-

Cash Analysis

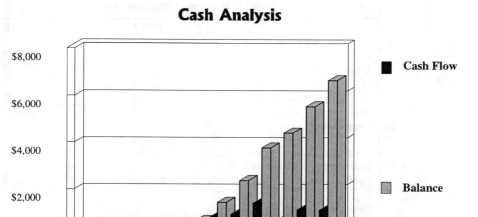

Projected Balance Sheet

Since the company has no significant plant and equipment and no inventory, assets will be primarily cash and receivables. These will accumulate gradually, achieving $8,000 in 1997; $21,000 by 1998; and $35,000 by 1999. Details may be found in the appendix.

-29-

Table 8: Projected Balance Sheet			
	1997	**1998**	**1999**
Short-Term Assets			
Cash	$6,654	$18,850	$33,337
Accounts Receivable	$729	$1,950	$2,338
Inventory	$0	$0	$0
Other Short-Term Assets	$0	$0	$0
Total Short-Term assets	$7,383	$20,800	$35,675
Long-Term Assets			
Capital Assets	$0	$0	$0
Accumulated Depreciation	$0	$0	$0
Total Long-Term Assets	$0	$0	$0
Total Assets	$7,383	$20,800	$35,675
Debt and Equity			
Accounts Payable	$0	$0	$0
Short-Term Notes	$0	$0	$0
Other Short-Term Liabilities	$0	$0	$0
Subtotal Short-Term Liabilities	$0	$0	$0
Long-Term Liabilities	$0	$0	$0
Total Liabilities	$0	$0	$0
Paid-in Capital	$3,610	$3,610	$3,610
Retained Earnings	($3,110)	$3,773	$17,190
Earnings	$6,883	$13,417	$14,875
Total Equity	$7,383	$20,800	$35,675
Total Debt and Equity	$7,383	$20,800	$35,675
Net Worth	$7,383	$20,800	$35,675

Appendix

Sales Forecast

Sales	Jan 97	Feb 97	Mar 97	Apr 97	May 97	Jun 97	Jul 97	Aug 97	Sep 97	Oct 97	Nov 97	Dec 97	1997	1998	1999
Training	$0	$0	$0	$0	$0	$200	$200	$400	$400	$400	$600	$600	$2,800	$7,000	$8,000
Consulting	$0	$0	$0	$0	$0	$280	$420	$560	$840	$280	$280	$560	$3,220	$7,280	$8,400
Maintenance	$0	$0	$0	$0	$0	$210	$350	$210	$280	$210	$560	$630	$2,450	$8,400	$10,500
Inventory	$0	$0	$0	$0	$0	$450	$450	$600	$450	$450	$600	$600	$3,600	$8,250	$9,750
Other	$0	$0	$0	$0	$0	$315	$315	$210	$525	$315	$420	$525	$2,625	$8,400	$10,500
Total Sales	$0	$0	$0	$0	$0	$1,455	$1,735	$1,980	$2,495	$1,655	$2,460	$2,915	$14,695	$39,330	$47,150
Cost of Sales															
Training	$0	$0	$0	$0	$0	$20	$20	$40	$40	$40	$60	$60	$280	$700	$800
Consulting	$0	$0	$0	$0	$0	$28	$42	$56	$84	$28	$28	$56	$322	$728	$840
Maintenance	$0	$0	$0	$0	$0	$63	$105	$63	$84	$63	$168	$189	$735	$2,520	$3,150
Inventory	$0	$0	$0	$0	$0	$45	$45	$60	$45	$45	$60	$60	$360	$825	$975
Other	$0	$0	$0	$0	$0	$32	$32	$21	$53	$32	$42	$53	$265	$840	$1,050
Total Cost of Sales	$0	$0	$0	$0	$0	$188	$244	$240	$306	$208	$358	$418	$1,962	$5,613	$6,815

Pro-forma Income Statement

	Jan 97	Feb 97	Mar 97	Apr 97	May 97	Jun 97	Jul 97	Aug 97	Sept 97	Oct 97	Nov 97	Dec 97	1997	1998	1999
Sales	$0	$0	$0	$0	$0	$1,455	$1,735	$1,980	$2,495	$1,655	$2,460	$2,915	$14,695	$39,330	$47,150
Direct Cost of Sales	$0	$0	$0	$0	$0	$188	$244	$240	$306	$208	$358	$418	$1,962	$5,613	$6,815
Other	$0	$0	$0	$0	$0	$0	$0	$0	$0	$0	$0	$0	$0	$0	$0
Total Cost of Sales	$0	$0	$0	$0	$0	$188	$244	$240	$306	$208	$358	$418	$1,962	$5,613	$6,815
Gross Margin	$0	$0	$0	$0	$0	$1,267	$1,491	$1,740	$2,189	$1,447	$2,102	$2,497	$12,733	$33,717	$40,335
Gross Margin Percent	0.00%	0.00%	0.00%	0.00%	0.00%	87.08%	85.94%	87.88%	87.74%	87.43%	85.45%	85.66%	86.65%	85.73%	85.55%
Operating Expenses:															
Advertising/Promotion	$0	$0	$0	$0	$0	$400	$300	$400	$300	$550	$300	$800	$3,050	$12,000	$14,000
Travel	$0	$0	$0	$0	$0	$60	$60	$70	$80	$80	$80	$80	$510	$1,200	$1,300
Miscellaneous	$0	$0	$0	$0	$0	$0	$0	$0	$0	$0	$0	$0	$0	$0	$0
Payroll Expense	$0	$0	$0	$0	$0	$200	$200	$200	$200	$300	$300	$300	$1,700	$6,000	$9,000
Leased Equipment	$0	$0	$0	$0	$0	$0	$0	$0	$0	$0	$0	$0	$0	$0	$0
Utilities	$0	$0	$0	$0	$0	$30	$30	$30	$30	$40	$40	$40	$240	$500	$560
Insurance	$0	$0	$0	$0	$0	$50	$50	$50	$50	$50	$50	$50	$350	$600	$600
Rent	$0	$0	$0	$0	$0	$0	$0	$0	$0	$0	$0	$0	$0	$0	$0
Depreciation	$0	$0	$0	$0	$0	$0	$0	$0	$0	$0	$0	$0	$0	$0	$0
Contract/Consultants	$0	$0	$0	$0	$0	$0	$0	$0	$0	$0	$0	$0	$0	$0	$0
Other	$0	$0	$0	$0	$0	$0	$0	$0	$0	$0	$0	$0	$0	$0	$0
Total Operating Expenses	$0	$0	$0	$0	$0	$740	$640	$750	$660	$1,020	$770	$1,270	$5,850	$20,300	$25,460
Profit Before Interest and Taxes	$0	$0	$0	$0	$0	$527	$851	$990	$1,529	$427	$1,332	$1,227	$6,883	$13,417	$14,875
Interest Expense ST		$0	$0	$0	$0	$0	$0	$0	$0	$0	$0	$0	$0	$0	$0
Interest Expense LT		$0	$0	$0	$0	$0	$0	$0	$0	$0	$0	$0	$0	$0	$0
Taxes Incurred		$0	$0	$0	$0	$0	$0	$0	$0	$0	$0	$0	$0	$0	$0
Net Profit	$0	$0	$0	$0	$0	$527	$851	$990	$1,529	$427	$1,332	$1,227	$6,883	$13,417	$14,875
Net Profit/Sales	0.00%	0.00%	0.00%	0.00%	0.00%	36.22%	49.05%	50.00%	61.28%	25.80%	54.15%	42.09%	46.84%	34.11%	31.55%

Pro-Forma Cash Flow

	Jan 97	Feb 97	Mar 97	Apr 97	May 97	Jun 97	Jul 97	Aug 97	Sep 97	Oct 97	Nov 97	Dec 97	1997	1998	1999
Net Profit	$0	$0	$0	$0	$0	$527	$851	$990	$1,529	$427	$1,332	$1,227	$6,883	$13,417	$14,875
Plus:															
Depreciation	$0	$0	$0	$0	$0	$0	$0	$0	$0	$0	$0	$0	$0	$0	$0
Change in Accounts Payable	$0	$0	$0	$0	$0	$0	$0	$0	$0	$0	$0	$0	$0	$0	$0
Current Borrowing (Repayment)	$0	$0	$0	$0	$0	$0	$0	$0	$0	$0	$0	$0	$0	$0	$0
Increase (Decrease) Other Liabilities	$0	$0	$0	$0	$0	$0	$0	$0	$0	$0	$0	$0	$0	$0	$0
Long-Term Borrowing (Repayment)	$0	$0	$0	$0	$0	$0	$0	$0	$0	$0	$0	$0	$0	$0	$0
Capital Input	$0	$0	$0	$0	$0	$0	$0	$0	$0	$0	$0	$0	$0	$0	$0
Subtotal	$0	$0	$0	$0	$0	$527	$851	$990	$1,529	$427	$1,332	$1,227	$6,883	$13,417	$14,875
Less:															
Change in Accounts Receivable	$0	$0	$0	$0	$0	$364	$70	$61	$129	($210)	$201	$114	$729	$1,222	$388
Change in Inventory															
Change in Other ST Assets	$0	$0	$0	$0	$0	$0	$0	$0	$0	$0	$0	$0	$0	$0	$0
Capital Expenditure	$0	$0	$0	$0	$0	$0	$0	$0	$0	$0	$0	$0	$0	$0	$0
Subtotal	$0	$0	$0	$0	$0	$364	$70	$61	$129	($210)	$201	$114	$729	$1,222	$388
Net Cash Flow	$0	$0	$0	$0	$0	$163	$781	$929	$1,400	$637	$1,131	$1,113	$6,154	$12,195	$14,487
Cash Balance	$500	$500	$500	$500	$500	$663	$1,444	$2,373	$3,773	$4,410	$5,541	$6,654	$6,654	$18,850	$33,337

Pro-forma Balance Sheet

	Jan-97	Feb-97	Mar-97	Apr-97	May-97	Jun-97	Jul-97	Aug-97	Sep-97	Oct-97	Nov-97	Dec-97	1997	1998	1999
Short-Term Assets															
Cash	$500	$500	$500	$500	$500	$663	$1,444	$2,373	$3,773	$4,410	$5,541	$6,654	$6,654	$18,850	$33,337
Accounts Receivable	$0	$0	$0	$0	$0	$364	$434	$495	$624	$414	$615	$729	$729	$1,950	$2,338
Other Short-Term Assets	$0	$0	$0	$0	$0	$0	$0	$0	$0	$0	$0	$0	$0	$0	$0
Total ST Assets	$500	$500	$500	$500	$500	$1,027	$1,878	$2,868	$4,397	$4,824	$6,156	$7,383	$7,383	$20,800	$35,675
Long-Term Assets															
Capital Assets	$0	$0	$0	$0	$0	$0	$0	$0	$0	$0	$0	$0	$0	$0	$0
Accumulated Depreciation	$0	$0	$0	$0	$0	$0	$0	$0	$0	$0	$0	$0	$0	$0	$0
Total Long-Term Assets	$0	$0	$0	$0	$0	$0	$0	$0	$0	$0	$0	$0	$0	$0	$0
Total Assets	$500	$500	$500	$500	$500	$1,027	$1,878	$2,868	$4,397	$4,824	$6,156	$7,383	$7,383	$20,800	$35,675
Debt and Equity															
Accounts Payable	$0	$0	$0	$0	$0	$0	$0	$0	$0	$0	$0	$0	$0	$0	$0
Short-Term Notes	$0	$0	$0	$0	$0	$0	$0	$0	$0	$0	$0	$0	$0	$0	$0
Other ST Liabilities	$0	$0	$0	$0	$0	$0	$0	$0	$0	$0	$0	$0	$0	$0	$0
Subtotal ST Liabilities	$0	$0	$0	$0	$0	$0	$0	$0	$0	$0	$0	$0	$0	$0	$0
Long-Term Liabilities	$0	$0	$0	$0	$0	$0	$0	$0	$0	$0	$0	$0	$0	$0	$0
Total Liabilities	$0	$0	$0	$0	$0	$0	$0	$0	$0	$0	$0	$0	$0	$0	$0
Paid-in Capital	$3,610	$3,610	$3,610	$3,610	$3,610	$3,610	$3,610	$3,610	$3,610	$3,610	$3,610	$3,610	$3,610	$3,610	$3,610
Retained Earnings	($3,110)	($3,110)	($3,110)	($3,110)	($3,110)	($3,110)	($3,110)	($3,110)	($3,110)	($3,110)	($3,110)	($3,110)	($3,110)	$3,773	$17,190
Earnings	$0	$0	$0	$0	$0	$527	$1,378	$2,368	$3,897	$4,324	$5,656	$6,883	$6,883	$13,417	$14,875
Total Equity	$500	$500	$500	$500	$500	$1,027	$1,878	$2,868	$4,397	$4,824	$6,156	$7,383	$7,383	$20,800	$35,675
Total Debt and Equity	$500	$500	$500	$500	$500	$1,027	$1,878	$2,868	$4,397	$4,824	$6,156	$7,383	$7,383	$20,800	$35,675
Net Worth	$500	$500	$500	$500	$500	$1,027	$1,878	$2,868	$4,397	$4,824	$6,156	$7,383	$7,383	$20,800	$35,675

The Plan For
Bob's Big Pencils

BOB HILLMAN

1848 East 27th St.

Hays, Kansas 67601

(913) 625-7056

Copy Number __ of Five.

THE PLAN FOR BOB'S BIG PENCILS

-2-

EXECUTIVE SUMMARY

Company summary. My name is Bob Hillman, owner of Bob's Big Pencils. This is a company that does just what the name implies — we make and sell giant, genuine pencils. The company was born in the small town of Hays, Kansas, in 1984. From that original location, we currently make and sell an assortment of products, all with the giant pencil theme. Our best-selling item is a pencil desk set, which includes a 12-inch pencil laying sideways in a notched stand. Bob's Big Pencils has no debt, operates profitably, and has little direct competition from other producers of giant pencils. Our mission is to be the best maker of genuine giant pencils in the country, have fun, and make money. I have set the following objectives for 1998:

1. Achieve 1998 sales of $175,000.

2. Achieve a distribution of sales as follows: Promotional Products Distributors, 40%; Educators, 20%; Catalog Merchants, 20%; Retail Stores, 10%; Other, 10%.

3. Maintain cost of goods sold at 17%.

4. Achieve a net profit before taxes of $80,000.

Industry analysis. Although there are a few other manufacturers of giant pencils across the country, I don't view my company as just a part of the "giant pencil" industry. I believe that my "industry" spans two broad categories — Gifts, a $100 billion market; and Promotional Products, a $7 billion market. These industries are both huge, complicated, and growing. And there is room in both of them for me to find a growing and profitable niche.

Target market. Historically, we have built our business primarily (about 70%) through direct sales to school teachers at teacher conventions. This has been good, profitable business. However, the excitement of selling directly to customers at conventions and other public events is wearing off quickly. It just isn't as much fun or as interesting as it used to be. We need to make some changes in the customers we target, and we need to make them now. Beginning in 1998, we will target the following four specific market groups:

1. Educators. This includes teachers and administrators working in Kindergarten through 12th Grade, both public and private.

2. Promotional Products Distributors. These are the retail companies which act as intermediaries between business customers and promotional products producers.

3. Catalog Merchants. These are the producers and distributors of catalogs which carry items complementary to big pencils.

-4-

4. Retail Stores. There are many of these stores for which big pencils would be a natural fit.

Products. Almost all of our products are a variation on the theme of the original giant pencil. All of our pencils are solid wood, with a real lead and a real rubber eraser. Everything we produce and sell is top quality and hand-finished. Computerized vinyl-transfer lettering machines yield lettering that is beautiful, professional, and durable.

Operations. There are currently parts of three buildings involved in the business: Raw Materials Storage and Rough Cut Room, Shop and Paint Rooms, and Office and Shipping Center. The company's production plan has been developed over the years to reduce costs as much as possible. We carefully manage inventory based on my knowledge of anticipated demand (based on historical demand and orders in negotiation) and our production capacity. One-hundred percent on-time order fulfillment and customer satisfaction are of vital importance to me, and are points of great pride for the company.

Marketing plan. I have rewritten the marketing plan based on our new mix of target customers. Promotional Products distributors will be targeted through aggressive multiple-level interaction in the Promotional Products Association International (PPAI), the dominant industry trade group. We will continue to promote to Educators primarily through direct sales at teacher conventions. One hundred and twenty high-potential Catalog Merchants will be targeted through sampling, personal selling, and trade shows. Retail Stores will be reached via multiple trade shows.

Financial projections. Sales should total $175,000 in 1998, growing to $252,000 by 2000. Before tax profit should reach $80,000 in 1998, and grow to $130,000 by 2000.

COMPANY SUMMARY

Bob's Big Pencils is a sole proprietorship founded and owned by me, Bob Hillman.

The company was born in a small town in the heartland of America: Hays, Kansas. During a road trip in Colorado, my wife Rose and I made a gasoline stop at an out-of-the-way General Store. I noticed for sale a roughly-made giant pencil, about 3 feet long. Although the pencil wasn't "real", and was poorly made, I really believed that there just might be a market for giant pencils.

As soon as we got home, I went to work figuring out how to make and sell them, and Bob's Big Pencils was born! I built about 80 three-foot-long samples and took them to the first big gathering of people I could find, a computer convention, to see how people would react. Since we didn't have a booth at the convention, I just walked around the convention floor with a pencil over my shoulder. Attendees began to stop me in the aisles to ask about the pencil, and by the end of the first day, I'd sold all 80 pencils! Not bad!

Since then, it's been a long and exciting road, with lots of ups and downs along the way. We currently make and sell an assortment of products, all with the giant pencil theme. Our best-selling item is a pencil desk set, which includes a 12-inch pencil laying sideways in a notched stand.

Bob's Big Pencils has no debt, operates profitably, and has little direct competition from other producers of giant pencils. From the beginning, Rose and I have had to wrestle with two major business issues in order to make the business profitable — production and marketing. I believe that I have the production side of the equation reasonably under control, but I've got a lot more work to do with regard to marketing. Evaluating the marketing plan and developing new marketing strategies is the primary reason for the development of this business plan.

Company Location and Facilities

Bob's Big Pencils has always been housed in a cluster of buildings on our property at 1848 East 27th St., Hays, Kansas. We own about 10 acres; five buildings, including our home, occupy three acres, with the remaining seven acres farmed. There are currently parts of three buildings involved in the business, as follows:

- Raw Materials Storage and Rough Cut Room.

- Assembly Shop and Paint Room.

- Office and Shipping Center.

These facilities will be described more fully in later chapters.

Mission

Bob's Big Pencils exists to be the best maker of genuine giant pencils in the country, have fun, and make money.

Objectives

I have set the following objectives for 1998:

1. Achieve 1998 sales of $175,000.

2. Achieve a distribution of sales as follows:

   — Promotional Products Distributors, 40%.

   — Educators, 20%.

   — Catalog Merchants, 20%.

— Retail Stores, 10%.

— Other, 10%.

3. Maintain cost of goods sold at 17%.

4. Achieve a net profit before taxes of $80,000.

Keys to Success

The following are the Keys to Success which must be accomplished in order to achieve my 1998 objectives:

1. Successfully sell to at least five new promotional products distributors.

2. Achieve at least one sale to Norwood Promotional Products. Details are in the Promotional Products section of the Marketing Plan, below.

3. Achieve inclusion in at least five catalogs for Christmas '98.

4. Sell at least 50 items to each of ten retail stores for Christmas '98.

5. Continue to relentlessly hold costs down on every component, every supply item, everything.

INDUSTRY ANALYSIS

How does one analyze the "Giant Pencil Industry"? IS THERE a giant pencil industry? What industry am I really a part of? These are hard questions, but I think that there are a couple of ways to approach them. I've broken my analysis of the industry into two distinct views: the Global View and the Local View.

The Global View

In the global view, I've taken the widest look possible in order to identify the industry in which I compete. I don't know a lot about analyzing nationwide business trends, but I do know the customers that are the most likely to buy my giant pencils. The bulk of my sales are concentrated in two broad categories — Gifts and Promotional Products. So, let's take a look at these two industries.

The "Gift" industry is so massive that it almost defies description, but one statistic should help give it some perspective. It is estimated that the average American household spends at least $1,000 per year on gifts for friends and family ($750 on Christmas gifts alone). Since there are roughly 100 million U.S. households, simple math yields a total gift market of at least $100 billion per year.

One hundred billion dollars is a big market by any standard, and the "gift market" includes an extremely broad range of products — candy, flowers, toys, clothing, housewares, etc., etc., etc.

In addition, the distribution strategies used within the gift market vary widely, including traditional retail (with all its variations), public sales and exhibitions, catalog, Internet, direct selling using direct mail, and many others. There are no dominant players on either the manufacturing or distribution side of the business. There is no single manufacturing or distribution company which controls more than 1% of this market. Because of the incredibly broad range of products and distribution channels, competing in this market can sometimes make your head spin.

The "Promotional Products" market may in some ways be considered a part of the gift market, but for my purposes it is distinct. Let's take a minute to define the Promotional Products market. Businesses are always looking for ways to improve their image and visibility with customers, potential customers, employees, suppliers, investors, etc. The purposes include maintaining ongoing relationships, attracting new customers, a special promotional theme or event, employee and investor relations, etc. These businesses use gifts — small and large, inexpensive and expensive -- to accomplish their promotional goals. Anyone who has ever received a free "company-labeled" pen or calendar or mug or tote bag or cap or T-shirt or key-ring has been a part of the Promotional Products market. This is a big market. The Promotional Products Association International estimates total U.S. annual sales of $7 billion, generated by 2,600 suppliers and 13,000 distributors. Again, no single player has emerged to control this market.

The Local View

What I call the "local view" is really a look specifically at the giant pencil business. Believe it or not, there are other manufacturers who make and sell giant pencils, and therefore there is an "industry" comprised of big pencil makers.

Although there are other companies in the big pencil business, I believe that it would be very shortsighted for me to build my business and marketing plans based solely on what these other companies are doing. In my opinion, the only successful way for me to approach my planning is to view my business primarily as part of the gift industry and the business promotional products industry.

This plan includes a review of other big pencil makers as part of my competition, but the overall thrust of the plan will be toward penetrating the gift and business promotional products markets.

TARGET MARKET

As I examine the Gift and Promotional Products Industries, my challenge has been to identify which specific customer groups represent my best opportunity to optimize sales and profit. That may sound simple, but it continues to be a challenge for Rose and me.

The issue of properly selecting the targeted markets is vitally important in any business, and it has become especially important at this stage in the evolution of Bob's Big Pencils. Over the past several years, we have built our business primarily (about 70%) through direct sales to school teachers at teacher conventions. This has been good, profitable business. However, the excitement of selling directly to customers at conventions and other public events is wearing off quickly. Actually, it's not the selling part that's getting old, but all that goes with it — scheduling shows, paying sometimes exorbitant fees to exhibit, packing the van for long trips, days of road travel, hauling merchandise and equipment into the exhibit hall, setting up, staying in motels (or in our motor home), tearing down, reloading the van, etc. It just isn't as much fun or as interesting as it used to be. We need to make some changes in the customers we target, and we need to make them now.

As I've built my sales to teachers, I've had to focus my time and energy on that market, to the detriment of other markets that I believe have additional sales potential. Beginning in 1998, we will target the following four specific market groups:

1. Educators. This includes teachers and administrators working in Kindergarten through 12th Grade, both public and private. This will remain a target group for Bob's Big Pencils, although it will not be the dominant group.

2. Promotional Products Distributors. These are the retail companies which act as intermediaries between business customers and promotional products producers.

3. Catalog Merchants. These are the producers and distributors of catalogs which carry items complementary to big pencils.

4. Retail Stores. There are many of these stores for which big pencils would be a natural fit.

Market Size and Trends

I view each of the four target groups individually:

Educators. In 1995, there were about 2.8 million elementary and secondary school teachers in the country, with roughly 100,000 new teachers coming into the system each year. All of these are included in my target market.

Teachers, especially female teachers, like to use our giant pencils as a nameplate on their desks. I've included a copy of our current brochure to illustrate what a pencil desk set looks like. *(Editor's note: brochure has not been reproduced.)* Although we've sold THOUSANDS of pencils to teachers across the country, we haven't even scratched the surface of the potential that is still out there.

Promotional products distributors. Total sales in the promotional products market grew to $7 billion in 1995, an increase of 13% over 1994. There are roughly 13,000 promotional products distributors in the United States. These distributors work on behalf of their business customers to locate, negotiate, and purchase the desired promotional products. Distributors are often in a position to recommend new ideas to their customers, and can easily suggest giant pencils in appropriate situations.

Catalog merchants. Catalog retailing has exploded across the country in recent years. There are now more than 10,000 different retail catalogs distributed throughout the United States each year. We have identified 120 different catalog retailers whose catalogs may be appropriate for Bob's Big Pencils. These will be our specific targets within this group.

Retail stores. There are over 1.5 million single-unit retailers and roughly 500,000 multi-unit retailers in the nation. We specifically target gift and general merchandise stores which cater to teachers or school-aged children, and stores specializing in hand-made gift and craft items.

Purchase Patterns/Process

Each targeted group has its own purchase pattern:

- Educators. Teachers locate and purchase personal classroom supplies and decorations through three major means: 1) catalogs and flyers delivered to home or school, 2) local teacher's supply stores, and 3) teacher convention exhibits.

- Promotional Products Distributors. This market features the Distributor working on behalf of the "end-use" company, and displays two primary patterns:

  — Specific promotional product need. In this situation, the end-use company has decided the specific type of promotional item they want, based on their company's products, their customers, and their customer's decision-making process. Companies in this situation will often contact a number of promotional products distributors to try to find the best supplier at the lowest cost. I have gotten pencil orders in this way, but not often — most company marketers don't sit down to strategize and conclude that what they need for their promotion is giant pencils.

-10-

— Specific marketing need; looking for promotional tools to help accomplish goal. This is the most common situation through which I receive orders for promotional products. Here, the end-use company marketers have a special event planned, a new product launch, etc., and are looking for a promotional product to use for that specific need. They will contact a promotional products distributor (or several) and present the situation. The distributors then use their expertise and access to sources, especially familiar vendors, to come up with ideas and sources for the client. In either case, once the right product has been located, the distributor negotiates the purchase, monitors completion of the order, arranges delivery of the product to the customer, collects from the end-user, and pays the producer.

- Catalog Merchants and Retail Stores. These retailers buy primarily in two ways: the manufacturer (or his intermediary) makes a direct sales call at the retailer's location, or the retail buyer sees the product at one of the numerous product exhibitions across the country. Of course, there are many variations on these themes, but these are the basics.

COMPETITION

As stated earlier, I view Bob's Big Pencils as part of the entire gift market and the entire promotional products market. Therefore, any company selling its products in these markets may be considered a competitor. However, it serves very little purpose for me to say that I'm competing with Mattel Toys, Russell Stover Candy, and 1-800-Flowers. A practical view of my "competition" should, however, include the other big pencil producers across the country.

Over the years, I have encountered a number of companies which have tried to make it in the big pencil business. It's very hard to make a profit though, and most of them have fallen by the wayside. There are two people that I know of who are apparently still in the business. Frank's Big Pencils (I wonder where he came up with that idea for a name!) is in Pennsylvania. He sells very few pencils, mainly at State and County Fairs. His prices are low, his quality OK, and his creativity limited. In addition, there is a company in Michigan which has for years made and sold 3-feet long pencils with the colors and logos of the University of Michigan and Michigan State University. It's never stepped beyond that arena.

SWOT ANALYSIS

An examination of my company's strengths and weaknesses, and the market opportunities and threats, will help to identify areas of concern and areas of additional potential.

Company Strengths

What are the current strengths of Bob's Big Pencils? There are several:

1. An unusual and attractive product. I'm not absolutely sure why people like giant pencils so much, but I think I've narrowed it down to these areas:

    — It's just the right size for a desk nameplate (this refers to the 12" pencil and holder).

    — It's a real pencil with a real lead and a real eraser. Very cool!

    — We personalize each pencil and stand with the recipient's name and individual message.

    — For educators, it really fits into the theme of school — pencils and books, bright yellow color, etc.

2. The giant size is very eye-catching and attracts a lot of attention (from kids and adults as well).

3. A strong, positive reputation. Over the years, I have worked hard to build a reputation for quality products, fair dealing with customers, a friendly and fun company to patronize, and timely delivery of orders. This may sound easy, but it requires constant work. There is no question that this is a strength for the company.

4. An efficient, cost-controlled production process. I have continuously worked to control production costs. I've spent hundreds of hours negotiating with suppliers to get the absolute lowest prices on materials. I've spent hundreds of hours developing systems and processes to cut costs while maintaining top quality. It has paid off by giving me the lowest possible unit cost. And I continue to fight the cost battle every day.

5. An excellent knowledge of the education market. This knowledge allows me to operate in this market with a "comfort zone" that a newcomer wouldn't have. I've made a lot of mistakes over the years that I shouldn't have to make again.

Company Weaknesses

Weaknesses are more difficult to admit, but here goes:

1. Location. Our location is a weakness because we are very far away from the population centers of the country. If we were located in the northeast U.S., for instance, I would have much greater access to the bulk of our markets than I

do from Hays, Kansas. In addition, a location in a more populated area would give us better access to suppliers, and might help get our costs down even further.

2. New product development. Although I have worked hard to develop new products over the years, and to update and improve our basic pencil product, I feel as though there should be more that I could do in this area. I've introduced many new ideas, but the customers seem to drive me back to the standard 12-inch pencil and stand, just as it's been for the past 10 years.

3. Limited knowledge of how to penetrate the catalog retail market, the retail store market, and the promotional products market.

Market Opportunities

1. The marketplace continues to be infatuated with the novelty of giant pencils. Each time we exhibit and sell our product at a "virgin" teacher's convention, the response is overwhelming — the teachers who come to the booth are thrilled to see such a unique item, and we can barely keep up with the orders. This interest in and enjoyment of our product represents a great opportunity. If we can find new and better ways of getting our pencils into the marketplace, there is business to be had.

2. Our competition is uninspired. Their lack of pressure is an opportunity for us.

3. Continuing U.S. economic growth. This growth in jobs and income stimulates growth in gift and promotional spending.

Market Threats

The threat that I have feared for many years is the entry into the market of a company selling imported giant pencils (probably from Asia) at half of my price. This is possible, and may happen. However, the current total sales volume is not sufficient to justify the time and expense necessary to establish a foreign production system.

PRODUCTS

They say a picture is worth a thousand words, so I've included a copy of the front of my current brochure on the next page. *(Editor's note: brochure have not reproduced.)* After our initial foray into the market with three-foot long pencils had been so successful, I just kept making and selling the initial model, working to make it better and better with each new batch I made.

-13-

However, Rose suggested that if I made them the same diameter (about one and one-half inches) but only about 12 inches long, people might use them on their desks as a display item or nameplate. I thought that was a silly idea and dismissed it immediately. But after about three nights sleeping in the barn, I began to think that her idea might have some merit after all. We began to experiment with 12-inch models, including a stand for the pencil to lay in, and before long, the 12-inchers became our best-sellers.

As you can see in the brochure, almost all of our products are a variation on the theme of the original giant pencil, and I don't see that changing in the near future. All of our pencils are solid wood, with a real lead and a real rubber eraser. Everything we produce and sell is top quality and hand-finished. For the lettering, we use two computerized vinyl-transfer lettering machines made by Gerber, Inc. These machines are the same type used by sign shops to create vinyl-lettered posters, signs, and banners for indoor and outdoor use. The lettering is beautiful, professional and durable.

Competitive Comparison

As noted earlier, there are some competitors in the market. Generally, our big pencils are of higher quality — better sanding, smoother paint, better erasers, much better lettering system. We have seen giant pencils from an unknown maker which include a metal ferrule (the piece that connects the eraser to the pencil). We have investigated metal ferrules, but moved away from them for two reasons: 1) while the metal looks great new, it quickly tarnishes and looks dark and old, and 2) metal ferrules are very expensive and would add significantly to our cost and raise the retail price. We use a ferrule made of material which fits perfectly, looks great, and never tarnishes.

Sourcing

In the manufacturing of giant pencils, there are four primary components that must be sourced correctly in order to manage costs and quality.

1. Wood. This represents a vital piece of the process. Cost is the primary consideration, but not the only one. The wood selected must be a light color so that the sharpened end is attractive and "normal looking," and the unpainted, varnished model looks light and pleasant. The wood must be soft enough to be easily shaped and worked, but not too soft. The wood must not be too wet or sticky, which would slow or stop the sharpening process. Over the years, we have used many wood sources, but I have found that there are a small number of lumber mills in Oregon and Washington which will provide us with 10-foot sections pre-cut to the finished hexagonal pencil shape, 10-foot sections pre-cut to the V-shape for the stands, and 10-foot sections pre-cut to 3.5" x 3.5" for the caddies.

-14-

I have traveled to the Pacific Northwest to visit these mills, and these visits have helped in the negotiations. I currently have two or three suppliers which I can depend on to provide the lumber I need.

2. Eraser. This may sound simple, but it's a lot more complicated than it sounds. First, erasers are not just rubber, they are a complicated composite of rubber and fillers. So I've found it necessary to limit my search to companies who know how to make erasers, not just rubber. I have searched for eraser producers throughout the United States, and even searched Asia via a government-sponsored business development program. Nothing in Asia worked out, and I have developed a relationship with Jones Rubber Products in Gothan, Alabama, to produce and supply my erasers. They require a special manufacturing run, so I need to give them about a month lead time. Each order is enough to last about three or four months. I'm a little uncomfortable with just one supplier for this important component, so I continue to work to locate other suppliers at better prices, or at least a secondary source.

3. Lead. Again, what looks like a simple component is not quite so simple. I buy my lead in three-sixteenths inch diameter rods. Since lead is not really lead, but a graphite composite, I've found that the best place to get our #2 graphite is from a pencil graphite company. There are a number of companies available, but Gustafson Graphite Company in Patterson, New Jersey has given us excellent service and reasonable pricing over the years.

4. Ferrule. The ferrule is the band that helps connect the eraser to the pencil. I source the material from a local oilfield supplier.

OPERATIONS

The company's production facilities, equipment, and production plan have been selected and developed over the years to reduce costs as much as possible.

Plant and Facilities

There are currently parts of three buildings involved in the business, as follows:

-   Raw Materials Storage and Rough Cut Room. This is a 30-foot x 30-foot metal building used to store all the raw wood stock used for product. This building also houses the space and machinery necessary to make the initial cut-downs from raw stock to product-sized pieces.

-   Shop and Paint Rooms. These are actually two separate rooms in one building. The 20-foot x 20-foot Shop is used for final cutting and shaping, and the 20-foot x 20-foot Paint Room is used for final assembly, finishing, bulk packing, and finished-goods storage.

-15-

- Office and Shipping Center. This 30-foot x 30-foot building is used for all order-taking, accounting and bookkeeping, lettering, and packing and shipping.

Equipment and Technology

There is a great deal of equipment needed to make this operation run. The following listing includes the primary pieces of equipment and is identified by its location.

1. Rough Cut Room. This room contains:

    — Twelve-inch radial arm saw.

    — Eight-foot long-armed belt sander.

    — Ten-inch table saw.

    — Twelve-inch drill press.

    — Table-mounted router.

    — Heavy-duty clothes washer.

2. Shop.

    — Modified twelve-inch drill press for conical shaping.

    — Upright two-inch belt sander.

    — Lead insertion press.

    — Ten-inch radial arm saw.

    — Twelve-inch disk sander.

    — Three cordless power drills.

    — Air compressor.

    — Central vacuum system w/attachments to necessary tools.

3. Paint Room.

    — Painting equipment and racks.

    — Motorized paint striper.

    — Point-protector punch.

-16-

4. Office and Shipping Center.

— Two Gerber vinyl-transfer lettering machines.

— Copier.

— Fax.

— Typewriter.

— Credit card modem.

— Phones and answering system.

Production Plan

All production work is done in a batch process. To demonstrate, I have included below a basic description of the process we use to produce about 50 twelve-inch pencils per batch.

1. Rough Cut Room.

— Hexagonal stock pulled from storage rack.

— Stock cut to twelve-inch size and loaded into wheeled cart. (As each step is performed, each piece is taken from one waist-high wheeled cart, worked, and then placed into a second wheeled cart, which then moves to the next station.)

— All six sides of each piece sanded smooth.

2. Shop.

— All pieces shaped at end to accept ferrule.

— All pieces shaped to point and bored for lead insertion (single step).

— Ferrule end sanded to finish quality.

— Lead insertion.

— Final finish sanding of point.

3. Paint Room.

— Light hand sanding as required.

— First coat paint, hand-brushed.

— Second coat paint, hand-brushed.

— Varnish coat, hand-brushed.

— Ferrule attached and secured. (The ferrules have been previously cut, sanded, washed, painted, and striped.)

— Eraser glued in place.

— Ferrule wrapped in paper for packing.

— Plastic point-protector added and taped.

— Two boxes of 25 pencils boxed, taped, labeled, and stored.

Inventory Management

We manage inventory based on my knowledge of anticipated future demand (based on historical demand and orders in negotiation) and our production capacity.

1. The bulk of our sales can be anticipated within a reasonable error factor. For instance, phone orders are a small part of our total sales, and are generally predictable. Sales at Teacher Conventions can be fairly well forecasted based on which shows we have booked and historical sales data from the same or similar shows. Most direct orders from promotional products distributors are small and readily handled from normal stock levels. And large direct orders (several hundred to over 1,000 pencils) from promotional products distributors usually have a fairly long lead time which gives us the opportunity to "gear up" to meet the customer's time line.

2. We have developed our production capacity to be sufficiently expandable to meet any foreseeable order. We maintain about six months of raw material stock on hand at all times (enough to produce about 4,000 pencils) so that we can begin immediate production on any order. Although our normal production schedule will produce about 600-700 pencils per month, we have the capacity to produce up to 1,000 pencils in two weeks. This can be accomplished with in-house equipment by expanding work schedules and bringing in temporary workers. One thousand pencils in two weeks is a "sprint" speed, and can not be maintained indefinitely. As sales grow, we will make the necessary adjustments to the production schedule.

Based on these factors, we maintain a finished-product inventory of about one month's supply of primary products. This includes 12" pencil desk sets in five colors; a stock of 22", 36" and 43" pencils; and a supply of pencil caddies, bookends, and plaque sets.

Order Fulfillment and Customer Service

Our orders are fulfilled in one of two ways:

First, when we are exhibiting at a convention or public show, we take orders at the booth, print the item(s) on site per the customer's order, and have the order available for customer pickup within 30 minutes.

-18-

The ability to make immediate delivery is vital to this part of our business. Taking orders on site for future delivery decreases show sales by 50-80%.

Second, any orders which come to us via phone, mail, or fax are shipped from the office. One of the primary ways we have developed such a good reputation is that we take customer service very seriously. All orders for ten items or less are shipped within 24 hours. Most larger orders for 10-100 items are shipped within 24-72 hours, depending on the printing required. Delivery terms for orders for more than 100 items are negotiated as part of the sale. I am proud that we have never lost an order because of an inability to meet delivery requirements.

Finally, with regard to customer service, I never want one of our customers to be unhappy with our people or our products. We go out of our way to be sure that all of our customers are happy with their decision to do business with Bob's Big Pencils. After all, my name's on the sign! And that commitment to 100% satisfaction pays off — every Christmas we get a number of cards from customers with whom we've developed friendships over the years. That feels really good.

MARKETING PLAN

We will examine the marketing plan using McCarthy's "Four P's" approach — Product, Price, Place (Distribution), and Promotion.

Product

I believe that the first part of good marketing is knowing what product your customers want, and giving it to them. We have worked diligently over the years to refine our product to meet the desires of our customers. We've gone through dozens of different product ideas, shapes, colors, sizes, paint types, lettering systems, etc., etc., etc. We could probably set up a "Giant Pencil Museum" to display all the ideas we've tried, most of which failed. But each failure brought us closer to, or back to, the point where we are now — the nation's top producer of giant genuine wood pencils. We have a well developed product that our customers tell us is right on the money. We continue to ask our customers about our products, and as their desires change, we want to change with them. But for right now, I believe that we have the right product for the market.

Price

Retail pricing is an area where we have had the unusual luxury of conducting routine pricing tests. Every time we set up at a teacher convention, we have a closed audience which we can use to test price.

In the early years of the business, we sold 18" pencils for just $6.95, and 45-inchers for only $15.50. We sold a lot. In fact we often had more business than we could handle. As time went on, we began to find that the 12-inch pencil was most popular, and we could raise the price significantly. Although we sold somewhat fewer pencils, the lower unit volume was more than offset by the higher price, and total profit increased. I continued to raise prices until there was moderate price resistance.

We currently retail the 12-inch pencil and stand for $15.95, including ten letters of printing at no charge. Additional lettering is $.20 per letter. This is viewed by the majority of our potential customers as a reasonable price, although there is some price resistance at this level. At this time, I feel comfortable with our pricing, and feel that we have our prices in place to optimize profit. If we see the amount of price resistance increase or decrease, or if costs change significantly, we will reconsider our pricing structure.

Pricing to resellers has been a much more challenging area. The resellers we target are separated into three groups: 1) retail stores, 2) catalog merchants, and 3) promotional products distributors. Each of these groups has their own set of challenges, but one that they have in common is their desire for a full 100% markup, also known as "keystone." In other words, if they are to maintain our retail price of $15.95 for a 12-inch pencil and stand, they would need to pay us only half the retail price, or about $8. An $8 selling price is not adequate to give me the margin that I need to make the sale worthwhile. In lieu of a "wholesale price list," I have designed a quantity price schedule that gives the large buyer a discount on increasing quantities, and includes a price on 1,000 or more 12-inch pencil sets of $10.38. This equates to a markup of roughly 55% — not what the retailers want — but what I am willing to live with.

Because of this conflict between our need to maintain gross margin and the retailer's desire for a full keystone markup, I have developed a strategy that will hopefully generate a win-win for the retailers and Bob's Big Pencils. The strategy is to target retail stores, catalog merchants, and promotional products distributors whose customers are able and willing to pay premium prices for premium products. This allows me to maintain my wholesale price at $11.92 for orders of 100 or more of the 12-inch pencil and stand, and the retailer can sell at $24.95, earning slightly above full keystone.

Place (Distribution)

As noted earlier, we distribute our products through two primary channels. The first is direct delivery to the end user either at a teacher convention or through a direct order to our factory. The second is selling to a reseller: a promotional products distributor, a catalog merchant, or a retail store. I am comfortable with these channels, and do not anticipate expanding to other channels.

-20-

Promotion

Promotion brings together the other "P's" — Product, Price, and Place (Distribution) — and moves them into direct contact with customers. A successful promotional strategy is absolutely vital to the success of this plan.

I have segmented the promotional plan into four subsets addressing each of our four target customer groups. However, there are promotional tools which will be used in our promotion to all four target customer groups:

1. Professional, glossy, four-color brochure. The front has photographs and descriptions, and the back has quantity prices and ordering information.

2. Toll-free phone number.

3. "Bob's Stickers." These are clear 1" by 1.5" stickers with the company's name, address, and toll-free phone number.

4. Business cards.

5. Exhibit booth. This is designed to fit in a standard 10' x 10' space, and has historically been used at teacher's conventions for on-site sales. Some modifications will be necessary in order to make it optimal for use at non-selling trade shows.

6. Publicity Notebook. This is a looseleaf notebook with plastic page liners. We have filled it with all of the newspaper stories, politician photos (including Bob Dole as Senate Minority Leader), crowded booth photos, awards, etc. that we've accumulated over the years. Our publicity notebook is a great ice-breaker in selling situations, and helps establish Bob's Big Pencils as a substantial business.

Promotional Products Distributors

Since there are about 13,000 promotional products distributors nationwide, it would be cost-prohibitive, time-prohibitive, and inefficient to attempt to locate and make personal calls on all of them. In recognition of this industry inefficiency, a trade group was formed in 1904 which is now named Promotional Products Association International (PPAI). PPAI boasts 5,700 members, suppliers, and distributors of promotional products. PPAI publishes annually a Membership Directory and Reference Guide, and conducts two trade shows (including exhibits) each year. PPAI is THE entry point for us to begin building our sales to promotional products distributors. We will join PPAI, exhibit at the trade shows, and consider advertising in their monthly magazine "Promotional Products Business."

In addition to targeting promotional products distributors universally through PPAI, there is one specific distributor which I will attempt to sell directly. Norwood Promotional Products, Inc., based in San Antonio, Texas, is the largest promotional products distributor in the country, and has 3% of the entire $7 Billion promotional products market. That's $210 million a year. Norwood buys products from all over the world, and performs the "logo-ization" at its plant in San Antonio. Norwood is a big challenge, and I like big challenges. I want to have Bob's Big Pencils carried by Norwood by the end of 1998.

Educators

We will sell to teachers and other educators primarily through direct selling at teacher conventions. We know which conventions are best for our product, and will attend mostly national association meetings, such as:

- American Education Association

- National Council of Teachers of Biology

- American Science Association

- National Education Federation

- Council for Gifted Children

- National Elementary Teachers' Association

- International Learning Association

- National Headstart Association

- National Christian Educators Association

- National Junior High School Association

At each convention, we will purchase a 10-foot by 10-foot exhibit space and sell directly to the attendees. We will also distribute our four-color brochure to generate future sales.

Catalog Merchants

We have identified 120 catalog merchants which we believe are appropriate vehicles for Bob's Big Pencils. In order to penetrate these targets, we have divided the 120 into two groups. The first group includes those merchants located where we can visit them personally as part of one of our teacher convention trips in 1998. We call these "Level One Targets." Level Two Targets are those that we will target by mail and phone in 1998.

- Level One Targets. By phone, I will determine the key contact person. Two weeks prior to our trip into their area, we will send a 12-inch pencil set to the key contact, personalized with his or her name and company name. No sales information will be included. After the contact receives the pencil, about a week before our trip to the company's locale, I will phone him or her and schedule an appointment to discuss how Bob's Big Pencils may be of benefit to his or her catalog. The rest depends on my selling skills.

- Level Two Targets. By phone, I will determine the key contact person. We will send a 12-inch pencil set to the key contact, personalized with his or her name and company name. No sales information will be included. After he or she receives the pencil, I will phone to discuss how Bob's Big Pencils may be of benefit to his or her catalog. The rest depends on my selling skills.

Retail Stores

There are over 2 million retail outlets in the U.S., most of them single-store companies. We specifically target gift and general merchandise stores which cater to teachers or school-aged children, and stores specializing in hand-made gift and craft items. Even with this specification, there is no efficient way to directly contact each potential customer. Fortunately, there are other ways.

I have identified three major trade show opportunities attended by retail store buyers. These trade shows are within a reasonable traveling distance, and include buyers from the types of stores that we are targeting. We will exhibit at each of the following shows at least once in 1998.

1. Beckman's Handcrafted Gift Show. Twice per year in Dallas (and other locations throughout the U.S.). Only handmade gifts and crafts are allowed. 16,000 attendees.

2. Dallas National Gift and Accessories Market. Held in January, June, and September in Dallas. 35,000 attendees.

3. Denver Merchandise Mart Gift and Jewelry Show. February and August in Denver. 7,500 attendees.

There are many more trade shows of this type throughout the country. As sales build, we will select which shows to attend.

HUMAN RESOURCES

The primary human resources we use at Bob's Big Pencils are Rose and me. We work full time at this business, and plan to do so for a long time to come.

We also have two part-time employees: Sharon Behrman works about 25 hours per week on painting and final assembly, and Terri Fisher works approximately seven hours per week on bookkeeping and correspondence, and she is also quite capable in painting, assembling, and lettering. Both of them are great workers, dedicated to helping the company succeed. I'm very fortunate to have these ladies as part of the team. When we get large orders, they are both willing to work overtime to get the job done.

FINANCIAL PLAN

Since this is an ongoing business, the projections for the four key financial statements are reasonably firm.

Projected Sales

By actively changing our target market to increase sales to resellers and decreasing our sales directly to teachers, I estimate that our average selling price for the 12" pencil and stand will drop from $18 (including lettering charges) to $14. This will increase our marginal cost to 17% from 14%, and reduce our gross margin to 83% from 86%. However, I also realize that direct sales at teacher conventions have other costs: exhibit fees, electricity fees, parking fees, hotel and meal costs, travel costs. Therefore, I believe that our net profit margin will not be hurt by this shift in sales, and may actually increase because of the shift.

Sales projections are shown below in Table 1 and the chart below. Complete details are presented in the Appendix. Seasonality trends are based on 1) Spring and Fall teacher convention seasons, and 2) Christmas sales in the second half.

Table 1: Sales Forecast			
	1998	**1999**	**2000**
Sales	$175,000	$210,500	$252,000
Direct cost of sales	$29,750	$35,700	$42,840

Total Sales by Month in Year 1

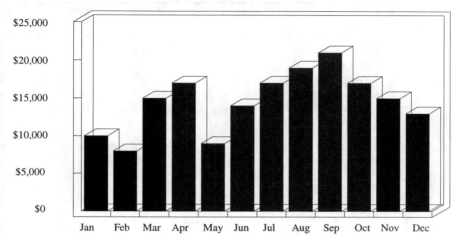

Projected Profit and Loss

Projected profit is shown in Table 2, and the chart below. Twelve teacher conventions are planned for the year, along with three gift trade shows and two PPAI exhibits. For each convention and trade show, I have included $500 in travel expense (hotel, auto, and meals).

Business Plan Highlights

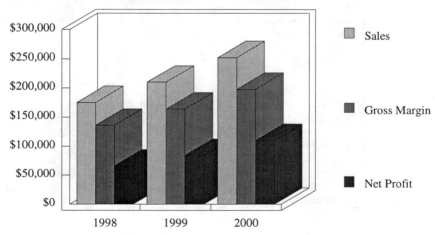

-25-

Table 2: Pro-forma Income Statement

	1998	1999	2000
Sales	$175,000	$210,000	$252,000
Direct Cost of Sales	$29,750	$35,700	$42,840
Production Payroll	$9,330	$10,300	$11,300
Other	$0	$0	$0
Total Cost of Sales	$39,080	$46,000	$54,140
Gross Margin	$135,920	$164,000	$197,860
Gross Margin Percent	77.67%	78.10%	78.52%
Operating Expenses:			
Sales and Marketing Expenses:			
Sales/Marketing Salaries	$0	$0	$0
Advertising/Promotion	$600	$700	$700
Travel (Hotel, Auto, Meals)	$8,500	$8,500	$8,500
Teacher Convention Fees	$12,000	$12,000	$12,000
Trade Show Exhibit Fees	$5,600	$9,200	$9,200
Other	$0	$0	$0
Total Sales/Marketing Expenses	$26,700	$30,400	$30,400
Sales and Marketing Percent	15.26%	14.48%	12.06%
General and Administrative Expenses:			
G&A Salaries	$2,025	$2,230	$2,450
Leased Equipment	$0	$0	$0
Utilities	$2,400	$2,600	$2,800
Insurance	$720	$720	$720
Depreciation	$2,400	$2,400	$2,400
Payroll Burden	$1,136	$1,253	$1,375
Legal/Accounting Fees	$3,600	$3,600	$3,600
Office Expense & Supplies	$3,600	$3,600	$3,600
Credit Card and Bank Fees	$1,200	$1,200	$1,200
Freight	$8,000	$8,800	$9,700
Telephone	$1,500	$1,600	$1,800
Other	$0	$0	$0
Total General and Administrative Expense	$26,581	$28,003	$29,645
General and Administrative Percent	15.19%	13.33%	11.76%
Other Operating Expenses:			
Other Salaries	$0	$0	$0
Contract/Consultants	$0	$0	$0
Other	$0	$0	$0
Total Other Operating Expenses	$0	$0	$0
Percent of Sales	0.00%	0.00%	0.00%
Total Operating Expenses	$53,281	$58,403	$60,045
Profit Before Interest and Taxes	$82,640	$105,597	$137,815
Interest Expense ST	$0	$0	$0
Interest Expense LT	$0	$0	$0
Taxes Incurred	$16,528	$21,119	$27,563
Net Profit	$66,112	$84,478	$110,252
Net Profit/Sales	37.78%	40.23%	43.75%

Projected Cash Flow

The cash flow projections are shown in Table 3 and the chart below. Complete details may be found in the Appendix.

Table 3: Projected Cash Flow			
	1998	**1999**	**2000**
Net Profit	$66,112	$84,478	$110,252
Plus:			
Depreciation	$2,400	$2,400	$2,400
Change in Accounts Payable	$4,088	$550	$432
Current Borrowing (Repayment)	$0	$0	$0
Increase (Decrease) Other Liabilities	$0	$0	$0
Long-Term Borrowing (Repayment)	$0	$0	$0
Capital Input	$0	$0	$0
Subtotal	$72,600	$87,428	$113,084
Less:			
Change in Accounts Receivable	($1,495)	($530)	($624)
Change in Inventory	$0	$0	$0
Change in Other ST Assets	$0	$0	$0
Capital Expenditure	$0	$0	$0
Subtotal	($1,495)	($530)	($624)
Net Cash Flow	$71,105	$86,898	$112,460
Cash Balance	$81,105	$168,002	$280,463

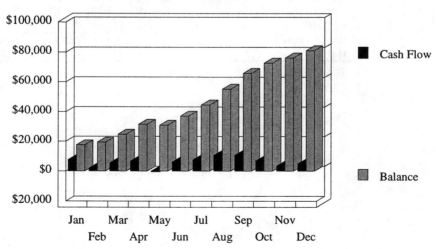

Cash Analysis

-27-

Projected Balance Sheet

The projected balance sheet is shown in Table 4, below. The complete balance sheet may be located in the Appendix.

Table 4: Projected Balance Sheet			
	1998	**1999**	**2000**
Short-Term Assets			
Cash	$81,105	$168,003	$280,463
Accounts Receivable	$0	$0	$0
Inventory	$2,995	$3,525	$4,149
Other Short-Term Assets	$0	$0	$0
Total Short-Term Assets	$84,100	$171,528	$284,612
Long-Term Assets			
Capital Assets	$25,000	$25,000	$25,000
Accumulated Depreciation	$12,400	$14,800	$17,200
Total Long-Term Assets	$12,600	$10,200	$7,800
Total Assets	$96,700	$181,728	$292,412
Debt and Equity			
Accounts Payable	$4,088	$4,638	$5,070
Short-Term Notes	$0	$0	$0
Other Short-Term Liabilities	$0	$0	$0
Subtotal Short-Term Liabilities	$4,088	$4,638	$5,070
Long-Term Liabilities	$0	$0	$0
Total Liabilities	$4,088	$4,638	$5,070
Paid-in Capital	$0	$0	$0
Retained Earnings	$26,500	$92,612	$177,089
Earnings	$66,112	$84,478	$110,252
Total equity	$92,612	$177,089	$287,341
Total Debt and Equity	$96,700	$181,728	$292,412
Net Worth	$92,612	$177,089	$287,341

Appendix

	Jan 98	Feb 98	Mar 98	Apr 98	May 98	Jun 98	Jul 98	Aug 98	Sep 98	Oct 98	Nov 98	Dec 98	1998	1999	2000
Sales	$10,000	$8,000	$15,000	$17,000	$9,000	$14,000	$17,000	$19,000	$21,000	$17,000	$15,000	$13,000	$175,000	$210,000	$252,000
Direct Cost of Sales	$1,700	$1,360	$2,550	$2,890	$1,530	$2,380	$2,890	$3,230	$3,570	$2,890	$2,550	$2,210	$29,750	$35,700	$42,840

Sales Forecast

Projected Profit and Loss

	Jan 98	Feb 98	Mar 98	Apr 98	May 98	Jun 98	Jul 98	Aug 98	Sep 98	Oct 98	Nov 98	Dec 98	1998	1999	2000
Sales	$10,000	$8,000	$15,000	$17,000	$9,000	$14,000	$17,000	$19,000	$21,000	$17,000	$15,000	$13,000	$175,000	$210,000	$252,000
Direct Cost of Sales	$1,700	$1,360	$2,550	$2,890	$1,530	$2,380	$2,890	$3,230	$3,570	$2,890	$2,550	$2,210	$29,750	$35,700	$42,840
Production Payroll	$715	$715	$715	$785	$785	$785	$825	$825	$825	$785	$785	$785	$9,330	$10,300	$11,300
Total Cost of Sales	$2,415	$2,075	$3,265	$3,675	$2,315	$3,165	$3,715	$4,055	$4,395	$3,675	$3,335	$2,995	$39,080	$46,000	$54,140
Gross Margin	$7,585	$5,925	$11,735	$13,325	$6,685	$10,835	$13,285	$14,945	$16,605	$13,325	$11,665	$10,005	$135,920	$164,000	$197,860
Gross Margin Percent	75.85%	74.06%	78.23%	78.38%	74.28%	77.39%	78.15%	78.66%	79.07%	78.38%	77.77%	76.96%	77.67%	78.10%	78.52%
Operating Expenses:															
Sales and Marketing Expenses:															
Sales/Marketing Salaries	$0	$0	$0	$0	$0	$0	$0	$0	$0	$0	$0	$0	$0	$0	$0
Advertising/Promotion	$50	$50	$50	$50	$50	$50	$50	$50	$50	$50	$50	$50	$600	$700	$700
Travel (Hotel, Auto, Meals)	$500	$1,000	$1,000	$1,500	$500	$500	$0	$500	$1,000	$1,500	$500	$0	$8,500	$8,500	$8,500
Teacher Convention Fees	$0	$1,000	$1,000	$3,000	$0	$1,000	$0	$1,000	$2,000	$3,000	$0	$0	$12,000	$12,000	$12,000
Trade Show Exhibit Fees	$1,400	$1,100	$1,100	$0	$1,000	$0	$0	$0	$0	$0	$1,000	$0	$5,600	$9,200	$9,200
Total Sales and Marketing Expense	$1,950	$3,150	$3,150	$4,550	$1,550	$1,550	$50	$1,550	$3,050	$4,550	$1,550	$50	$26,700	$30,400	$30,400
Sales and Marketing Percent	19.50%	39.38%	21.00%	26.76%	17.22%	11.07%	0.29%	8.16%	14.52%	26.76%	10.33%	0.38%	15.26%	14.48%	12.06%
General and Administrative Expenses:															
G&A salaries	$155	$155	$155	$170	$170	$170	$180	$180	$180	$170	$170	$170	$2,025	$2,230	$2,450
Leased Equipment	$0	$0	$0	$0	$0	$0	$0	$0	$0	$0	$0	$0	$0	$0	$0
Utilities	$200	$200	$200	$200	$200	$200	$200	$200	$200	$200	$200	$200	$2,400	$2,600	$2,800
Insurance	$60	$60	$60	$60	$60	$60	$60	$60	$60	$60	$60	$60	$720	$720	$720
Depreciation	$200	$200	$200	$200	$200	$200	$200	$200	$200	$200	$200	$200	$2,400	$2,400	$2,400
Payroll Burden	$87	$87	$87	$96	$96	$96	$101	$101	$101	$96	$96	$96	$1,136	$1,253	$1,375
Legal and Accounting Fees	$300	$300	$300	$300	$300	$300	$300	$300	$300	$300	$300	$300	$3,600	$3,600	$3,600
Office Expense & Supplies	$300	$300	$300	$300	$300	$300	$300	$300	$300	$300	$300	$300	$3,600	$3,600	$3,600
Credit Card & Bank Fees	$100	$100	$100	$100	$100	$100	$100	$100	$100	$100	$100	$100	$1,200	$1,200	$1,200
Freight	$650	$550	$700	$750	$400	$650	$700	$750	$800	$750	$700	$600	$8,000	$8,800	$9,700
Telephone	$125	$125	$125	$125	$125	$125	$125	$125	$125	$125	$125	$125	$1,500	$1,600	$1,800
Total General and Administrative Expense	$2,177	$2,077	$2,227	$2,301	$1,951	$2,201	$2,266	$2,316	$2,366	$2,301	$2,251	$2,151	$26,581	$28,003	$29,645
General and Administrative Percent	21.77%	25.96%	14.85%	13.53%	21.67%	15.72%	13.33%	12.19%	11.26%	13.53%	15.00%	16.54%	15.19%	13.33%	11.76%

Other Operating Expenses:															
Other Salaries	$0	$0	$0	$0	$0	$0	$0	$0	$0	$0	$0	$0	$0	$0	$0
Contract/Consultants	$0	$0	$0	$0	$0	$0	$0	$0	$0	$0	$0	$0	$0	$0	$0
Total Other Operating Expenses	$0	$0	$0	$0	$0	$0	$0	$0	$0	$0	$0	$0	$0	$0	$0
Percent of Sales	0.00%	0.00%	0.00%	0.00%	0.00%	0.00%	0.00%	0.00%	0.00%	0.00%	0.00%	0.00%	0.00%	0.00%	0.00%
Total Operating Expenses	$4,127	$5,227	$5,377	$6,851	$3,501	$3,751	$2,316	$3,866	$5,416	$6,851	$3,801	$2,201	$53,281	$58,403	$60,045
Profit Before Interest and Taxes	$3,458	$698	$6,358	$6,475	$3,185	$7,085	$10,970	$11,080	$11,190	$6,475	$7,865	$7,805	$82,640	$105,597	$137,815
Interest Expense ST	$0	$0	$0	$0	$0	$0	$0	$0	$0	$0	$0	$0	$0	$0	$0
Interest Expense LT	$0	$0	$0	$0	$0	$0	$0	$0	$0	$0	$0	$0	$0	$0	$0
Taxes Incurred	$692	$140	$1,272	$1,295	$637	$1,417	$2,194	$2,216	$2,238	$1,295	$1,573	$1,561	$16,528	$21,119	$27,563
Net Profit	$2,766	$558	$5,086	$5,180	$2,548	$5,668	$8,776	$8,864	$8,952	$5,180	$6,292	$6,244	$66,112	$84,478	$110,252
Net Profit/Sales	27.66%	6.98%	33.91%	30.47%	28.31%	40.48%	51.62%	46.65%	42.63%	30.47%	41.94%	48.03%	37.78%	40.23%	43.75%

Pro-Forma Cash Flow

	Jan 98	Feb 98	Mar 98	Apr 98	May 98	Jun 98	Jul-98	Aug-98	Sep 98	Oct 98	Nov 98	Dec 98	1998	1999	2000
Net Profit:	$2,766	$558	$5,086	$5,180	$2,548	$5,668	$8,776	$8,864	$8,952	$5,180	$6,292	$6,244	$66,112	$84,478	$110,252
Plus:															
Depreciation	$200	$200	$200	$200	$200	$200	$200	$200	$200	$200	$200	$200	$2,400	$2,400	$2,400
Change in Accounts Payable	$5,508	$750	$1,322	$1,765	($4,645)	$1,085	($927)	$1,864	$1,864	$759	($3,344)	($1,913)	$4,088	$550	$432
Current Borrowing (Repayment)	$0	$0	$0	$0	$0	$0	$0	$0	$0	$0	$0	$0	$0	$0	$0
Increase (Decrease) Other Liabilities	$0	$0	$0	$0	$0	$0	$0	$0	$0	$0	$0	$0	$0	$0	$0
Long-Term Borrowing (Repayment)	$0	$0	$0	$0	$0	$0	$0	$0	$0	$0	$0	$0	$0	$0	$0
Capital Input	$0	$0	$0	$0	$0	$0	$0	$0	$0	$0	$0	$0	$0	$0	$0
Subtotal	$8,475	$1,508	$6,608	$7,145	($1,898)	$6,953	$8,048	$10,928	$11,016	$6,139	$3,148	$4,530	$72,600	$87,428	$113,084
Less:															
Change in Accounts receivable	$0	$0	$0	$0	$0	$0	$0	$0	$0	$0	$0	$0	$0	$0	$0
Change in Inventory	$915	($340)	$1,190	$410	($1,360)	$850	$550	$340	$340	($720)	($340)	($340)	($1,495)	$530	$624
Change in Other ST Assets	$0	$0	$0	$0	$0	$0	$0	$0	$0	$0	$0	$0	$0	$0	$0
Capital Expenditure	$0	$0	$0	$0	$0	$0	$0	$0	$0	$0	$0	$0	$0	$0	$0
Subtotal	$915	($340)	$1,190	$410	($1,360)	$850	$550	$340	$340	($720)	($340)	($340)	($1,495)	$530	$624
Net Cash Flow	$7,560	$1,848	$5,418	$6,735	($538)	$6,103	$7,498	$10,588	$10,676	$6,859	$3,488	$4,870	$71,105	$86,898	$112,460
Cash Balance	$17,560	$19,408	$24,826	$31,561	$31,023	$37,126	$44,624	$55,212	$65,888	$72,747	$76,235	$81,105	$81,105	$168,002	$280,463

Pro-forma Balance Sheet

	Jan-98	Feb-98	Mar-98	Apr-98	May-98	Jun-98	Jul-98	Aug-98	Sep-98	Oct-98	Nov-98	Dec-98	1998	1999	2000
Short-Term Assets															
Cash	$17,560	$19,408	$24,826	$31,561	$31,023	$37,126	$44,624	$55,212	$65,888	$72,747	$76,235	$81,105	$81,105	$168,003	$280,463
Accounts Receivable	$0	$0	$0	$0	$0	$0	$0	$0	$0	$0	$0	$0	$0	$0	$0
Inventory	$2,415	$2,075	$3,265	$3,675	$2,315	$3,165	$3,715	$4,055	$4,395	$3,675	$3,335	$2,995	$2,995	$3,525	$4,149
Other Short-Term Assets	$0	$0	$0	$0	$0	$0	$0	$0	$0	$0	$0	$0	$0	$0	$0
Total Short-Term Assets	$19,975	$21,483	$28,091	$35,236	$33,338	$40,291	$48,339	$59,267	$70,283	$76,422	$79,570	$84,100	$84,100	$171,528	$284,612
Long-Term Assets															
Capital Assets	$25,000	$25,000	$25,000	$25,000	$25,000	$25,000	$25,000	$25,000	$25,000	$25,000	$25,000	$25,000	$25,000	$25,000	$25,000
Accumulated Depreciation	$10,200	$10,400	$10,600	$10,800	$11,000	$11,200	$11,400	$11,600	$11,800	$12,000	$12,200	$12,400	$12,400	$14,800	$17,200
Total Long-Term Assets	$14,800	$14,600	$14,400	$14,200	$14,000	$13,800	$13,600	$13,400	$13,200	$13,000	$12,800	$12,600	$12,600	$10,200	$7,800
Total Assets	$34,775	$36,083	$42,491	$49,436	$47,338	$54,091	$61,939	$72,667	$83,483	$89,422	$92,370	$96,700	$96,700	$181,728	$292,412
Debt and Equity															
Short-Term Liabilities															
Accounts Payable	$5,508	$6,258	$7,580	$9,345	$4,700	$5,785	$4,858	$6,722	$8,586	$9,345	$6,002	$4,088	$4,088	$4,638	$5,070
Short-Term Notes	$0	$0	$0	$0	$0	$0	$0	$0	$0	$0	$0	$0	$0	$0	$0
Other ST liabilities	$0	$0	$0	$0	$0	$0	$0	$0	$0	$0	$0	$0	$0	$0	$0
Subtotal ST Liabilities	$5,508	$6,258	$7,580	$9,345	$4,700	$5,785	$4,858	$6,722	$8,586	$9,345	$6,002	$4,088	$4,088	$4,638	$5,070
Long-Term Liabilities	$0	$0	$0	$0	$0	$0	$0	$0	$0	$0	$0	$0	$0	$0	$0
Total Liabilities	$5,508	$6,258	$7,580	$9,345	$4,700	$5,785	$4,858	$6,722	$8,586	$9,345	$6,002	$4,088	$4,088	$4,638	$5,070
Paid-In Capital	$0	$0	$0	$0	$0	$0	$0	$0	$0	$0	$0	$0	$0	$0	$0
Retained Earnings	$26,500	$26,500	$26,500	$26,500	$26,500	$26,500	$26,500	$26,500	$26,500	$26,500	$26,500	$26,500	$26,500	$92,612	$177,089
Earnings	$2,766	$3,325	$8,411	$13,591	$16,138	$21,806	$30,582	$39,445	$48,397	$53,576	$59,868	$66,112	$66,112	$84,478	$110,252
Total Equity	$29,266	$29,825	$34,911	$40,091	$42,638	$48,306	$57,082	$65,945	$74,897	$80,076	$86,368	$92,612	$92,612	$177,089	$287,341
Total Debt and Equity	$34,775	$36,083	$42,491	$49,436	$47,338	$54,091	$61,939	$72,667	$83,483	$89,422	$92,370	$96,700	$96,700	$181,728	$292,412
Net Worth	$29,266	$29,825	$34,911	$40,091	$42,638	$48,306	$57,082	$65,945	$74,897	$80,076	$86,368	$92,612	$92,612	$177,089	$287,341

The Plan for
Computer Solutions, Inc.

LINDA SARVER

2750 Northeast Highway

Puyallup, Washington 98373

(206) 775-0523

Copy Number ____ of Five

THE PLAN FOR COMPUTER SOLUTIONS, INC.

EXECUTIVE SUMMARY

The company. In the late 1980's, a young entrepreneur by the name of Linda Sarver saw that there was room in the Pierce County, Washington marketplace for a different kind of computer retailer. Linda envisioned a company that would do more than just sell a computer-in-a-box to customers that would be "seen, sold, and forgotten" all within the space of less than an hour.

Armed with a knowledge of computers and computer retailing honed since her college days, Linda founded Computer Solutions, Inc., opening a storefront retail location in Puyallup. The experts might not have given this venture much of a chance — after all, Linda was trying to open a new computer store in a "saturated market." Well, that first store did just fine. Better than fine, in fact. Soon, there was a larger location, then a second store, and then a third. And within a scant three years, Linda's startup computer retailing storefront business grew to be the largest computer retailer in Pierce County.

How did she do it? Well, it was a combination of several things — Linda's great vision of "what could be," a well-developed understanding of what customers want and need, good personnel decisions, solid financial footing, and continuing strong demand for computers. Put them all together, and you've got a winning combination — Computer Solutions, Inc.

The industry. The U.S. computer retailing industry includes over 2,900 companies, and generated over $52 billion in sales in 1996. While the industry is best known for the giant national players such as CompUSA, Best Buy, and Computer City, the business is really dominated by the small retailers — almost 2,300 of the 2,900 different companies operate with only one retail outlet. Revenue growth is robust; 1997 industry growth is forecast at 13%, with much of this growth coming from repeat computer buyers.

The target market. Computer Solutions, Inc. specifically targets households, businesses, government agencies, and schools in all of Pierce County, Washington. The target-area population matches perfectly with the demographic profile of "computer buyer" — young, well-educated, upper-middle income. What's more, various planning agencies predict continuing rapid growth in target-area population, jobs, income, and businesses through at least 2020. Computer Solutions focuses a great deal of energy on developing "outside sales" in the business, government, and education sectors.

The competition. Computer Solutions, Inc. is the only multi-location computer retailer in the target area, and is the dominant player in this market. Competitors are primarily divided into two main categories: the national chain retailers and direct marketers; and other local retailers, dealers, and value-added resellers.

As the market leader in sales (over $1.8 million projected 1997 revenues) and retail presence (three stores in the target area), Computer Solutions has built significant advantages over the competition — name recognition, visibility, distribution, management and personnel strength, cash flow, economies of scale in purchasing, etc.

-4-

The products and services. Computer Solutions has designed all of its product and service offerings around specific customer needs. The products and services are grouped into seven broad categories, as follows: 1) custom computer systems, 2) networking, 3) computer accessories, 4) service and repair, 5) upgrades and reconfiguration, 6) training, and 7) public connectivity. Custom computer systems are the heart of the business, and represent 60% of revenue.

The marketing plan. Computer Solutions uses an effective mix of marketing tools, with Personal Selling as the dominant vehicle used to generate sales. The company maintains two types of sales staff — Key Account Managers and Floor Sales Associates — and uses performance-based pay for all sales staff.

The management team. As President of Computer Solutions, Inc., Linda Sarver has been a vital contributor to the success of the company to date, and her vision is the moving force behind anticipated future growth. Linda has an exceptional background in the establishment and growth of new businesses. In her college days at the University of Washington, she grew a dorm-room-based computer retailing business into a multi-million dollar enterprise, and she's grown Computer Solutions to the number one position in computer sales in Pierce County.

Mark Sarver, Linda's husband, has taken on the responsibilities of District Manager, coming to Computer Solutions with a solid computer retailing background. Mark has 10 years of business management experience, including personnel management, training, inventory control, Accounts Payable/Accounts Receivable management, trade show management, and sales force management.

Each of the three Computer Solutions stores is managed by a capable and trained professional manager. Chuck Meyer, Puyallup, developed his management skills by founding and running his own computer assembly business. Melissa Chang, Lakewood Center, joined CS in 1996 in the Technology area, moved quickly through several mid-management positions, and accepted the Store Manager position at Lakewood Center in 1997. Rob Patton, Parkland, began his computer career in 1991 as a customer service representative at X-Tech, a computer manufacturer and retailer. Rob came to CS in 1996 as a Key Account Manager, and he accepted the position of Store Manager in 1997.

The financials. The year 1997 is shaping up to be an outstanding year in revenue growth for Computer Solutions, Inc. The company anticipates sales of $1,822,000, with a gross margin of 40%. Although net profit will be just 1% of sales in 1997, we anticipate net profit growing to over 9% in 1998 and beyond.

COMPANY SUMMARY

Computer Solutions, Inc. is an S-Corporation registered in the State of Washington. All company stock is owned by the founders, Linda and Mark Sarver.

Background and Current Situation

The business of selling computers at retail has been growing and evolving for several decades, and by the late 1980's, a solid group of retail dealers had developed in Pierce County. However, a young entrepreneur by the name of Linda Sarver saw that there was room in the marketplace for a different kind of computer company. Linda envisioned a company that would do more than just sell a computer-in-a-box to customers that would be "seen, sold, and forgotten" all within the space of less than one hour.

Armed with a knowledge of computers and computer retailing honed since her college days, Linda founded Computer Solutions, Inc., opening a storefront retail location in Puyallup. The experts might not have given this venture much of a chance — after all, Linda was trying to open a new computer store where there were already several (some growing, some slowly failing). That first store did just fine. Better than fine, in fact. Soon, there was a larger location, then a second store, and then a third. And within a scant three years, Linda's startup computer retailing storefront business grew to be the largest computer retailer in Pierce County.

How did she do it? Well, it was a combination of several things — Linda's great vision of "what could be", a well-developed understanding of what customers want and need, good personnel decisions, solid financial footing, and continuing strong demand for computers. Put them all together, and you've got a winning combination — Computer Solutions, Inc.

Mission

The mission of Computer Solutions, Inc. is to provide the households, businesses, governments, and schools of Pierce County with computer systems designed to their specific needs. Within this mission, we pledge to provide the training, service, knowledge, and assistance that customers want and need from their computer supplier.

Objectives

The following are the company's objectives for 1997:

1. Achieve sales of $1,822,000.

-6-

2. Maintain a gross margin of at least 40%.

3. Achieve an operating profit.

4. Achieve an inventory turnover rate of 10.

5. Establish an effective sales training program.

6. Publish an employee handbook.

7. Establish a new-employee training program.

Keys to Success

In order to achieve the company's objectives, there are a number of important steps that must be taken. These include the following keys to success:

1. Successfully recruit and fill new management and "key account" sales staff positions.

2. Increase store walk-in traffic.

3. Increase the success rate of competitive bids.

4. Increase effectiveness of sales staff.

5. Continuously, consciously, control costs.

6. Aggressively pursue the "employee maintenance" issues, including a time-line for completion.

Company Locations and Facilities

Computer Solutions, Inc. occupies three retail storefront locations, as follows:

1. **Puyallup. 2750 Northeast Highway.** The company's flagship store occupies a premier location near the Beyerly's Food Store in "The Commons" shopping center, a primary anchor of the Northeast Highway Puyallup "retail strip." Of the 5040 sq.ft. total, roughly 3000 are devoted to front end sales floor, with 1400 sq.ft. allocated for sales office space, and almost 700 sq. ft. designated for tech/assembly space. Hours of operation are: Monday-Friday, 10 am-9 pm; Saturday-Sunday, 10 am-6 pm.

2. **Lakewood Center. 4230 Lakewood Rd.** This storefront is in a prime exterior corner of the County Faire shopping center, a well-executed property, anchored by McDonalds and Walgreens, at the intersection of Rt. 127 and Lakewood Rd. in Lakewood Center. This location totals 1800 sq. ft.; 1300 as sales floor, 100

office, and 400 tech/assembly. Hours are: Monday-Friday, 10 am-9 pm; Saturday, 10 am-6 pm.

3. **Parkland. 979 South Roberts Blvd.** The Parkland location is a stand-alone building site on the southwest side of Roberts Blvd., one-eighth mile south of Walmart. This location splits its 2750 sq. ft. between a 1150 ft. sales floor, 350 ft. office space, and 1250 sq. ft. of tech/assembly space. Hours are: Monday-Friday, 8:30 am-8 pm; Saturday, 9 am-6 pm.

INDUSTRY ANALYSIS

Computer Solutions, Inc. is part of SIC Code 5734, "Computer and Computer Software Stores." The business of selling computers at the retail level has grown into a large and diverse industry, as demonstrated in a brief statistical review.

Industry Overview

The 1997 Directory of Computer Retailers, Dealers and Distributors (CRD&D) recognizes 2,904 companies operating 31,372 individual outlets in the "Computer Retailing" industry (USA and Canada).

The following is the breakdown of companies by type of business:

No. of Companies	Type of Business	No. of Outlets
1,170	Computer Retailer*	3,219
1,493	Computer Dealer**	2,433
61	Consumer Electronics	9,996
78	Office Supply	1,689
28	Mass Merchandiser	10,567
4	Membership Warehouse	765
18	Bookstores	2,651
52	100% Mail Order	52
*Retailers include storefront operations in which walk-in retail trade is at least 30% of sales. **Dealers sell primarily via a sales force, with walk-in retail trade less than 30% of sales.		

The following is a breakdown of companies by number of outlets:

No. of Companies	No. of Outlets
52	100% mail order
2,297	One
253	Two
81	Three
49	Four
23	Five
42	Six-Ten
46	11-50
34	51-200
27	201+

These 2,904 companies generated 1996 sales of $52,295,659,270, as follows:

Type of Business	Sales
Computer Retailers	$12,948,861,528
Computer Dealers	$21,890,551,562
Consumer Electronics Computer Sales	$6,737,764,560
Office Supply Computer Sales	$2,995,899,700
Mass Merchandise Computer Sales	$2,417,550,000
Membership Warehouse Computer Sales	$1,093,800,000
Bookstore Computer Sales	$65,960,000
100% Mail Order	$4,145,271,920

The ten largest retailers, ranked by computer sales are:

Rank	Name	Type	Sales
1	CompUSA, Dallas, TX	Computer Retailer	$3,829 M
2	Best Buy Co., Eden Prairie, MN	Consumer Electronics	$2,771 M
3	Computer City, Fort Worth, TX	Computer Retailer	$1,764 M
4	Office Depot, Delray Beach, FL	Office Supply Store	$1,600 M
5	Circuit City, Richmond, VA	Consumer Electronics	$1,575 M
6	Micro Electronics, Hilliard, OH	Computer Retailer	$930 M
7	Sears, Hoffman Estates, IL	Mass Merchandiser	$700 M
8	Future Shop, Burnaby, BC	Consumer Electronics	$678 M
9	OfficeMax, Shaker Heights, OH	Office Supply Store	$670 M
10	CDW, Buffalo Grove, IL	Computer Retailer	$629 M

The computer retailing industry continues to experience double digit annual growth, with experts forecasting 1997 U.S. growth at 13% (*Business Week*, 1/13/97). *Business Week* analysts also remain bullish on the long-term growth prospects for this business, with worldwide shipments of personal computers growing from an estimated 85 million units in 1997 to 132 million in 2000, 55% growth over the three-year period.

While few would question the continued expansion of this industry, the business is changing, and there have been casualties. Savage price wars have been waged, straining gross margins to the limit. These price pressures, combined with consumer shifts, has left certain distribution channels, namely consumer electronics stores, scrambling to maintain market share. In many cases, they're losing the battle. As reported in *PC Week*, Feb. 24, 1997, December '96 same-store sales at Circuit City and Best Buy were off about 13%. Nobody Beats the Wiz had trouble paying its bills, and Sun TV and Appliances said it would close 20% of its stores. In January '97, Tandy took the biggest fall — it announced that it would close all of its Incredible Universe stores. Finally, Egghead moved to close half of its 156 retail stores and reduce its number of geographical markets to 24 from 54 (*Computerworld*, Feb. 17, 1997). Many are asking the obvious questions — why is this happening, and what are the strategies for continued growth and profitability?

Part of the answer to the first question lies in changes occurring in the customers themselves. The year 1997 marks the crossing of a threshold into uncharted territory — for the first time, repeat buyers now account for more than half of all PC purchases (*PC Week*, 2/24/97). In fact, a mid-April 1997 survey of 2,450 households conducted by The Verity Group and reported in *Computer Retail Week*, found that 40% of recent PC-purchasing households described themselves as "repeat buyers," another 32% described their purchases as "additional PCs," and only 8% said they were "first time" buyers.

-10-

In other words, computer shoppers are fast-forwarding in their knowledge and comfort level regarding how they use computers, what features they need, and the service level that they expect from the retail channels they use. This is a monumental shift in the evolution of computer retailing, and it is having a major impact on how purchasing decisions are made. *PC Week* (2/24/97) says it best: "The confused neophyte who once drove to the familiar surroundings of a consumer electronics or department store is now a savvy, value-conscious veteran, ready to order by phone or to patronize the local screwdriver shop."

Another aspect of the "new buyer/repeat buyer" phenomenon is the level of penetration of PCs into American homes. About one third of U.S. homes now have a PC, leaving a monstrous two-thirds left to penetrate, right? Well, it may not be quite that easy. It turns out that half of homes with an income of more than $50,000 own computers, and a full 65% of households with incomes over $75,000 own at least one PC (*The Economist*, Mar. 23, 1996). The intention to buy a computer — and the likelihood that the purchase will actually be made — declines sharply with income. If the "easy" customers have already bought, the smart retailer must look for new growth in the lower-income levels, repeat buyers, or a different customer pool.

The business buyer is changing as well. Consider this excerpt from *PC Week*, Feb. 17, 1997:

> The PC price wars are over. Desktop hardware has become virtually indistinguishable in terms of price and performance. So how do IT (Information Technology) managers decide which brand to buy? Across corporate America, IT departments are basing purchase decisions on the quality of service and support PC manufacturers provide. That shift is dramatically reshaping the PC market. The support, simplicity, and consistency of PCs have become vital targets for IT managers. But who has the answer? The bottom line is that no vendor has the perfect solution. And that means there's likely to be more shake-up in the year ahead, as vendors continue to tinker with their strategies to address ever-changing IT needs.

The journal *Purchasing*, Dec. 12, 1996, notes that the two largest purchase channels for business PCs are: 1) the direct model, buying direct from manufacturers such as Gateway and Dell; and 2) the reseller/dealer model, buying a usually branded product from a local or national reseller or dealer. The challenge for the direct sellers is to find a way to provide the service and support that business customers now demand, in a market where margins on PC sales don't leave them much room to maneuver. "Another option gaining favor with buyers is sort of a combination of the other two — assembly of nonbranded PCs by local vendors." These value-added resellers (VARs), including Computer Solutions, Inc., offer the one-stop-shopping experience of a direct seller, plus the local on-site support provided by the brand name reseller/dealer.

What are the strategies for success now? The answer is quite simple, yet very difficult to accomplish. In order to continue to grow sales and profit in this new era of computer retailing, a company must find ways to provide customers, both personal and business, the high quality products they demand, and give them the highest level of service, support, advice, training, return policy, etc., all at prices no higher than the store down the street or at the other end of the toll-free line.

The company currently leading the pack in pursuit of this goal is CompUSA, based in Dallas, Texas. Corporate sales, training and technical services now account for 40% of the company's revenue (*PC Week*, 2/24/97). Their fastest-growing revenue line, although still small, is technical services, which ranges from repair to upgrade to custom configuration for a whole company. James Halpin, CEO, projects that "within two years, retailing won't be a majority of our business." CompUSA represents a good model to follow in the development of company strategy, and Computer Solutions has utilized CompUSA-like strategies in the development of its business.

Industry Participants

The players in this industry include four basic classes of participants, as follows:

1.   Customers:

— Household customers.

— Business customers.

— Government customers.

— Education customers.

2.   Retail sellers, including all channels which sell directly to the end users.

3.   Brand name manufacturers: Compaq, IBM, Dell, etc.

4.   Component manufacturers: Intel, Western Digital, etc.

Although there are hundreds of variations and mixtures of these four groups, they represent the primary foundational groups.

First, the component manufacturers. These are the high-tech companies that produce the chips, circuits, memory, hard drives, cases, monitors, keyboards, etc. that are the basic pieces of every PC of every brand. These companies are vital to the industry, and their ability to push forward to better, faster, and cheaper technology is the factor that, in many respects, drives the growth in this business. Clearly, for CS to continue to thrive, it must create and maintain excellent supply relationships with the key players in this group.

Second, the brand name manufacturers. Approximately 70-80% of the PCs sold in the U.S. are made by branded manufacturers (Dataquest, from *USA Today*, June 27, 1996). The top five brands are Compaq, Packard Bell, Apple, IBM, and Gateway 2000.

-12-

These manufacturers distribute their products in a variety of ways, mostly through the retail/dealer channel. Gateway markets and distributes directly to customers. These companies and their distributors are primary competition for Computer Solutions.

Third, the retail sellers. This is the arena in which CS operates. The players in this group have been described in detail in the Industry Overview, above. The dominant retailers sell primarily brand name machines, while the independent assemblers, or VARs, including Computer Solutions, purchase components directly from component manufacturers and assemble custom systems to customer specifications.

Fourth, the customers. Each of the four primary customer groups has its own set of needs and wants. Each will be examined in detail in the next section, Target Market.

TARGET MARKET

Computer Solutions, Inc. specifically targets households, businesses, government agencies, and schools in Pierce County, Washington, especially the suburban areas outside the city of Tacoma. The principal cities included in the target market are: Tacoma, Puyallup, Lakewood Center, Milton, Parkland, Spanaway, and Steilacoom.

The four individual customer groups that CS targets are households, businesses, government, and education.

1. Households. Demographics demonstrate that the "average" household computer owner is between the ages of 31 and 42, has graduated from college, and earns $40,000 to $60,000 per year. Conversely, the average non-PC owner is 28 to 40 years old, has completed high school, and makes less than $30,000 per year (*Computer Retail Week,* as presented April 18, 1997). Although there is a distinct gap between the two groups with regard to education and income, those lines of distinction may be blurring a bit. When asked why they don't own a computer, most people will give two answers: price and relevance. CS believes that as usefulness, daily application, and internet value become more commonplace, non-college-educated households will find PC ownership more relevant to their lives. In addition, as prices fall — there are systems available now for under $1,000 — lower income households will increasingly join the market.

   While the "first-time buyers" are still in the market, there is significant growth in the repeat buyers as well. As noted in the Industry Analysis, a recent survey showed that 72% of recent PC buyers described themselves as "repeat buyers" or were purchasing "additional PCs." This data would lead the sharp retailers to build their future marketing to households increasingly around the wants and needs of the repeat/multiple buyer. CS will continue to provide products and services for the novice buyer, but intends to build future household market growth by focusing on the needs of the repeat/multiple buyer.

-13-

2. Businesses. Businesses of all types and sizes use computer technology. Computer Solutions targets all businesses in the target market. As the number of businesses in the target area grows, and as those businesses grow in size, they will have a greater and greater need for high quality technology. The fastest growing group of business PC buyers are SOHO, Small Office/Home Office, buyers (*Purchasing*, Oct. 19, 1995). These SOHO buyers are a new phenomenon that is changing the look of American business. In the face of decreased corporate job security, a growing number of individuals nationwide are striking out on their own, starting new businesses at a breakneck pace. The Entrepreneurial Research Consortium conducted a study which reveals that of the roughly 95 million households in the U.S., 18 million of them (19% of the total) include someone currently running a business; and another 6.8 million (7% of the total) include someone trying to start a business. Taken together, an impressive 26% of American households have a member directly and personally involved in the SOHO marketplace, and this number may be expected to grow as the flight from corporate jobs continues.

3. Government. City, county, state, federal — each level of government needs current technology in order to accomplish its tasks efficiently. CS targets the government entity headquarters within its target area: villages, towns, cities, and Pierce County.

4. Education. Like businesses and government, the educational community has a large and growing need for technology products. Public schools, private schools, Pacific Lutheran University, and University of Puget Sound are all active targets for CS.

Market Size and Trends

The geographic target market of Pierce County represents a large and rapidly growing area of the outlying Seattle suburbs. Roughly 25 miles from downtown Seattle, this area was historically rural land well distant from the rigors of the Big City. Suburbanization has set in, however, and the entire target market area is now one of the fastest growing in the metro region.

The population of the target market area in the 1990 census totalled 498,232. Demographers anticipate that by 2020, the area population will have grown to 843,663, an increase of 69% over the 30-year period. This growth rate dwarfs that projected for King County (11%), Kitsap County (28%), and Thurston County (32%) over the same period. The growth is pervasive, persistent, and exciting (all data from Puget Sound Planning Commission, Feb. 7, 1997).

The income level of the target market is high. Calendar year 1995 tax returns indicate an average adjusted gross income (AGI) in Pierce County of almost $50,000, among the top 3% of counties nationwide (all data from Transactional Records Access Clearinghouse, Apr. 12, 1997).

-14-

The households in the CS target market are clearly within the income range capable of continuing to grow PC demand into the future.

Where there are people, there are businesses and jobs, and the CS target market will reap the rewards of rapid growth in its job base. The Puget Sound Planning Commission predicts that between 1990 and 2020, the number of jobs in Pierce County will grow by 106% to over 471,000 total jobs. This rate compares to suburban King County at 46% growth, Kitsap County at 53% growth, and Thurston County at 81% growth.

Recent data report over 25,000 businesses located in Pierce County. New business growth and expansion may reasonably be expected to mirror growth in population and jobs. In fact, a recent independent survey of new business filings in Pierce County showed a rate of DBA filings of roughly 1000 annually, confirming the rapid growth which should coincide with jobs and population growth.

Purchase Patterns/Process

Purchase patterns vary with the customer group, and between individual customers within a group. However, some generalities may be made:

1. Households. The decision process usually follows a pattern like this:

    — Friends and family have computers, or there are computers at work.

    — The desire and/or need for a PC begins to grow.

    — Storefront and catalog "window-shopping" begins.

    — Advice is sought from friends, family and work colleagues.

    — Serious shopping begins.

    — The purchase is made based on features, price, availability, payment terms, service, and support.

2. Businesses. As a business recognizes its need for initial computer technology, or an upgrade, overhaul, or replacement of its system, someone in the organization is given the responsibility to research the market and make a recommendation to upper management. Increasingly, businesses are seeking higher levels of service, support, training, and system consistency as they choose PC vendors.

3. Government. A process similar to that in businesses occurs, with the usual addition of a bidding or contract procedure superimposed on top of the basic decision-making operation.

4. Education. Most schools are governmental bodies, and they generally follow the same processes as government entities.

COMPETITION

The business of PC retailing is extremely competitive on a national scale, as seen in the statistics in our Industry Overview. There is a handful of national retailers which dominate the market, led by CompUSA. While there is a strong contingent of national players, there is also room for local providers as well. In fact, local assemblers such as Computer Solutions, Inc. may be in a strong position to gain market share as consumers' needs change.

Although it has gone through tremendous growing pains over the last 30 years, the computer industry is still viewed as a young industry, certainly not yet in mid-life. While the unbridled growth of the last decade may have subsided, there are technological advances as yet unseen which will surprise even the most jaded observer. These advances will continue to stimulate wave after wave of new excitement and demand for upgraded and expanded computer capabilities at home, work, government, and school.

Computer Solutions, Inc. is the only multi-location computer retailer in the target area, and is the dominant player in this market. Competitors are primarily divided into two main categories: the national chain retailers and direct marketers, and other local retailers, dealers, and value-added resellers.

Primary Competitors

While we recognize that any computer retailer in the Seattle metro area could be considered a competitor, and that all mail-order sellers are indirect competition, Computer Solutions believes that its primary competitors are businesses offering local storefront retail sales and/or an outside sales force.

With this understanding, Computer Solutions has several local competitors.

1. Computer Hut, Tacoma. With 11 years in Pierce County, Computer Hut is the oldest and perhaps the strongest competitor, although it is quite different in its approach to the business and in its offerings to customers. Computer Hut is a retailer of high-end boxed systems from IBM, Compaq, etc. It does not custom-build systems. They do offer service, at a higher price than CS. A basic system from Computer Hut would be $500-$1,000 more expensive than a similar system from CS. Computer Hut is believed to have an estimated sales volume of approximately $1 million annually.

2. Custom Built Computers, Milton. CBC is an assembler of non-branded PCs. It reports between one and four employees, and annual sales between $500,000 and $1 million. This is a small operation with limited impact on the market.

3. Computer Consultants, Puyallup. A non-branded assembler and used computer dealer, CC is also a small player who claims to have lower prices than CS. No data is available on annual sales.

4. The Data Center, Parkland. TDC is primarily an upgrade/service/networking operation. It does not sell branded systems, nor do they custom build. Instead, it takes custom orders, and contracts the manufacturing. No sales data available.

5. Access All, Inc., Lakewood Center. This is a small assembler and networker. They reports one to four employees, and annual sales of $500,000 to $1 million.

6. Pinnacle Computers, Tacoma. Pinnacle is also a small assembler. Service is its stated point of differentiation. Annual sales unknown.

7. Applied Computer Technologies, Tacoma. After eight years in a retail setting, ACT moved in 1996 to an office setting, changed its name from Midas Computers to ACT, and shifted its business to a dealer style, serving primarily government and education. It sells mainly assembled machines with branded components, and all machines have a 3-year warranty.

8. Stan's Business Machines, Spanaway. Stan's is an office machine retailer with total sales of $5-10 million annually, including a small amount in computers.

9. Best Buy, Tacoma. As a national consumer electronics retailer, Best Buy has made an apparent commitment to the PC retailing business. It relies on low prices to sell preboxed systems to retail customers. It makes an attempt at service, although it finds it difficult to offer any significant service when working from very slim gross margins on branded systems.

10. Circuit City, Puyallup. A new store opened in May of 1997, Circuit City is similar to Best Buy in its product mix and customer profile.

Barriers to Entry

The examination of barriers to entry must be made at two levels — national and local.

There are formidable barriers to entry at the national level: capital, staffing, inventory, distribution, marketing and advertising, etc. In addition, there is intense competition among the major retailers, with several dominant participants, which would create a considerable barrier to any new national scale entrant.

At the local level, the barriers to entry are not as great, but exist nonetheless.

Through hard work, Computer Solutions, Inc. has established itself as the computer retailing leader in the target market area. As the market leader in sales (over $1.8 million per year), and retail presence (three stores in the target area), CS has created significant hurdles that any new entrant must overcome — name recognition, visibility, distribution, management and personnel strength, cash flow, economies of scale in purchasing, etc. Specifically, the most important barriers that a serious new local retail competitor would be forced to overcome are high start-up costs and high expertise requirements.

Future Competition

It is likely that there will be new local entrants in this market over the next five years. Many individuals see the "computer" field as highly profitable, easy to penetrate, and with limitless growth potential. They will find that it will not be easy to take market share away from the established providers, especially CS. There is no way to know at this point who these new competitors will be, or when they will make their entrance. Nevertheless, CS is prepared to defend its dominant position.

The most likely real threat to the leadership position of Computer Solutions would be in one of two ways:

First, the opening of a CompUSA in Puyallup, Lakewood Center, or Parkland would obviously pose a significant threat to CS's position. Discussions with local managers at CompUSA's Tacoma location reveal the following competitive information on CompUSA's current plans for the Seattle market. The Tacoma store is being moved to a new and larger location next door to the current location. The new store is under construction now, and should open October '97. There is a new downtown Seattle store under construction which should open this fall as well. Finally, a new store is being built in Renton, south of Seattle proper. These are all in addition to the company's other Seattle locations. The realistic view of potential competition from a CompUSA store in the target area is that it is unlikely to happen in the next three to five years. The typical expansion location for CompUSA is a large, established "hub" suburb, and the CS target area does not fit that prototype. However, CompUSA has opened two "small market" stores in Colorado Springs and Boise. Whether these would be possibilities in the CS target area remains to be seen. In the event of direct competition from CompUSA or a similar national competitor, CS will continue to focus on its strengths, and implement strategies to defend its business.

Second, national mail-order retailers will be making every effort to expand their business without regard to geography or zip code. While these have not been a hindrance to profitable operation to date, there are a few of these operators which need watching: Gateway 2000, Computer Discount Warehouse, Elektek, and PCs Compleat, a unit of CompUSA. If these mailers begin to grow into a dominant market share nationwide, they would be expected to grow in the CS target area as well.

-18-

Of course, CS is working to build such overwhelming value into every product and service it sells that a shopper in the target market would make the wiser choice — Computer Solutions, Inc.

SWOT ANALYSIS

An examination of my company's strengths and weaknesses, and the market opportunities and threats, will help to identify areas of concern and areas of additional potential.

Company Strengths

Computer Solutions, Inc. enjoys a number of strengths which give it marketplace advantage:

1. Market Leadership. As the leading computer retailer in the target area, CS has the highest visibility, the greatest number of new systems being installed, and the cash flow and profit to sustain and grow the business to higher levels.

2. Visionary Ownership. Linda Sarver has proven herself to be an uncharacteristically strong leader who has the ability to recognize and seize opportunities well ahead of the rest of the pack. This vision has enabled Computer Solutions to achieve great success where others have failed.

3. Excellent Technical Support and Design. CS has developed a team of technical wizards who work together to develop the solutions needed by the customers it serves. This expertise has been painstakingly built over a number of years, and is a large contributor to the market dominance that CS enjoys today.

4. Strong and Dedicated Management Team. Throughout its three stores, CS has put in place a team of strong managers who share the vision of the company and have the ability and autonomy to truly be "intrapreneurs" within Computer Solutions.

5. Strong Outside Sales Focus. We know that business customers, government customers, and education customers drive sales and profit, and we are strongly developing that portion of the business.

Company Weaknesses

While CS is strong in many areas, there are places where the company needs to improve its operation.

1. Staffing. Even with an aggressive recruitment effort, the company still has difficulty locating enough qualified sales and technical staff. This is an area

which has been a major focus, and will continue to be an issue as the grows into the future.

2. Consistency between stores. As new products and/or prices are introduced, there have been occasional instances of disparate pricing of the same item at two different locations. This has been a focus of attention, and is being remedied by the establishment of the position of Administrative Assistant.

3. Employee training and assimilation. Because of the company's rapid growth, CS has not developed optimal employee assimilation and training systems. These are primary objectives for 1997, and will be aggressively pursued.

Market Opportunities

The marketplace offers Computer Solutions a number of opportunities.

1. The primary market opportunity is the continuing population and job growth in the target market. This growth fuels demand for technology in all four customer sectors (household, business, government, and education). As the area expands, CS has the opportunity to continue to build its franchise in each customer sector, solidifying its position as the premier computer retailer in the target area. A number of specific growth opportunities are occurring now:

    — A major road widening project is scheduled for Northeast Highway, the major road passing by the Puyallup store. This road project will increase the number of lanes on Northeast Highway to five lanes from two lanes. Traffic flow will improve, and traffic volume will increase.

    — In Lakewood Center, a new Walmart mega-center prototype store will be built on nearby undeveloped land, and a new craft/specialty store will replace an empty Home Center store. All of this activity is occurring within 400 feet of the Computer Solutions store. Substantial traffic increases are anticipated.

    — As a part of the stores "shift" in Lakewood Center, new street-front signage options will be created for Computer Solutions.

2. Business customers need a single-source computer resource — a place where they can talk to knowledgeable salespeople, buy the system they need, get training in how to use the system efficiently, get service and support when it's needed, and be able to upgrade when desired.

3. The rapid expansion of internet technology gives CS the opportunity to provide a unique service to its customers: a high speed T-1 line internet connection via on-site workstation pods in each of the three CS stores. This is a service for area computer users who value high speed internet access.

-20-

4. The geographic setting of Computer Solutions in a recently rural, and still relatively underdeveloped, suburban setting creates the opportunity to grow the business with very little encroachment from the national players. Our current strategy is to avoid over-developed communities such as Tacoma, due to their inherent higher competition and lower margins. This is an opportunity that may not last, and the company will make definite and positive use of it while it exists.

Market Threats

The most direct competitive threat would be the arrival of a national retailer such as CompUSA in one of our primary cities. As noted in our Future Competition section, we do not anticipate this as a reality in the foreseeable future.

The second threat of note is simply the threat of rapidly expanding technology. The entire computer industry is changing and evolving so quickly that it is truly impossible to know what the business will look like in five years. Most industries can predict with relative certainty what the mid-length future holds for them. Not the technology field. The computer retailing sector is not as susceptible to the rapid shifts in technology as the software, internet, or chip manufacturing companies. Retailers, including CS, must be able to move with the technology, or risk being left in the wake of this giant change wave rolling across the last part of the 20th century.

NEEDS ANALYSIS

Because the entire field of technology is changing so quickly, it would be hard to visualize a great number of "met" needs in computer retailing. As soon as a new technology hits the shelves, it is being antiquated by the next generation. Still, there are some areas in retailing specifically where it can be said that the needs have been primarily met. There certainly is no shortage of places and ways to buy computers. A computer shopper can walk into Walmart, Sam's Club, OfficeMax, Best Buy, Sears, etc., and see computers in all of them. For the shopper who wants to walk into a familiar shopping environment, shop for a few minutes, and walk out with a computer-in-a-box, things couldn't be easier! The need for easy accessibility to computer hardware and software has been fully met.

Unmet Needs

There are a great many unmet needs in the world of computer retailing.

1. There is an unmet need for one-stop computer shopping — a place where a customer can talk to knowledgeable salespeople, buy the system they need, get training in how to use the system efficiently, get service and support when it's

needed, and be able to upgrade when desired. This shouldn't be too much to ask from computer sellers, but it is a need that very few retailers can fulfill. (CS does this better than anyone in the market.)

2. There is a need for business systems that have consistency from one generation to the next. In other words, if a business buys ten desktop stations this year, and buys ten additional stations next year, the twenty stations should be able to operate the same software and network together without much reconfiguration or upgrading. This is an inadequately addressed issue.

3. There is a need in the retail market for high-speed internet accessibility services for on-site customer use. These customers know the latest technology, and they want it now. Retailers that can fill this need will establish themselves as the technical leaders in their geographical area.

PRODUCTS AND SERVICES

Computer Solutions, Inc. has designed all of its product and service offerings around the customer needs previously identified. The products and services are grouped into seven broad categories, as follows:

1. Custom Computer Systems. This is the heart of the business, and represents 52% of current revenue. CS designs systems to match the present and future needs of its customers: household, business, government, and education. CS is the premier builder of custom hardware in the target area, and has grown into that position by providing the excellent sales staff needed to determine what the customer really needs, using the highest quality components, and getting the product built and delivered on time and on budget. Sharp customers demand sharp and attentive service, and that's what CS provides — every time, for every customer. In addition to the typical on-demand customized systems, CS also develops "suggested" or "pre-designed" systems which are advertised as special offers. These systems, as are all CS hardware systems, are built only after purchase. This strategy allows CS to genuinely meet the exact customer desire and to minimize inventory carrying costs. The average turn-around time from system order to delivery is 4 working days. Maintainence Agreements are available with each computer system sold — these are customer — oriented and profitable. Price lists for components and pre-designed systems are included in the Supporting Documents.

2. Computer Accessories. CS stocks and sells a broad array of parts and accessories for computer users. In fact, CS boasts the largest assortment of cables and gender changers in the Pierce County area. This business sector provides 10% of current revenue, and allows the three stores to achieve the appearance desired — large, stocked, complete. A partial floor-product list is included in the Supporting Documents. *(Editor's note: supporting documents have not been reproduced.)*

-22-

3. Service. As noted in the Industry Analysis, service is becoming more and more important to customers as they select a computer retailer. Every computer ever built will eventually need service. As a customer-focused retailer, CS has developed the most complete diagnostic and repair department of any computer seller in the target market. This has been accomplished intentionally to create the one-stop computer shopping experience that buyers increasingly demand of their hardware supplier. In fact, service can be performed at the customer's location using the Computer Solutions SST Van (Special Services Transport), a new van designed for delivery, pickup, repair, etc. Service currently accounts for 10% of revenue. Service rates are in the Supporting Documents. *(Editor's note: supporting documents have not been reproduced.)*

3. Upgrades and Reconfiguration. Differentiated from "service," which is basically the process of fixing something that's wrong or broken, the Computer Solutions Upgrade and Reconfiguration department focuses on making something good even better. Due to the industry standard components used in every CS system, upgrading is simple and inexpensive. As technology moves continuously forward, the ability to upgrade a customer's system is an important part of being a full-service computer retailer. Upgrades represent 10% of current revenue.

4. Networking. A growing subsegment of the business is networking, the interconnecting of two or more PCs in a business or any multi-computer system. Networking involves in-depth consulting, proper development of the hardware, installation, and system setup, testing and troubleshooting. Networking currently generates 8% of revenues.

5. Training. All of the CS customer groups have need for training services. Many retailers, especially the consumer electronics superstores and direct mailers, make only a feeble effort to provide customer training on how to optimize the usefulness and enjoyment of the systems they sell. Computer Solutions, on the other hand, believes that customer training is a responsibility and an opportunity for additional profit. Training can also be done at the customer's location, using the SST Van. Training generates 5% of revenue currently, and is expected to grow quickly to as much as 12-15%.

6. Public Connectivity. This is an area of retailing which has exploded over the last several years, with different players taking a different approach to the idea. Kinko's, for example, offers services aimed at document production — hardware and software designed for word processing and some graphics, laser printers, copiers, etc. CS has designed its public connectivity business to highlight the forward edge of technology — the latest and best computer gaming, individual and networked, and internet access using the highest speed lines available, the T-1 line. While creating revenue in its own right (5% currently), using the public connectivity arena to showcase the latest technology helps drive demand for new systems and system upgrades.

-23-

Some customers are curious as to why CS does not sell printers, scanners, and software. The reason is a reflection of the company's mission — to meet customer needs, including low prices. CS has determined that the consumer electronics superstores can virtually always sell printers and scanners for less than the lowest prices we could offer. In fact, they often sell these items for less than our cost. In the best interest of the customers, CS suggests that they purchase printers and scanners from these competitors. While this sounds as if it may drive customers to the competition for other items as well, in reality the policy has helped to strengthen customer relations and generate additional business. When asked to provide these items for a specific customer, we do so gladly. In the case of software, CS has determined that software is not a company strength, that software is too inventory-intensive, and that some competitors do it better. Therefore, Computer Solutions has decided to eliminate software from the retail floor.

Strategic Alliances

Computer Solutions has developed a number of alliances which allow better customer service and peaceful coexistence with competitors.

1. Microcomputer Works. This Parkland company acts as a subcontractor on some networking projects, providing expertise in the areas of software and consulting. John Brenkman is a quality provider who shares the CS philosophy of high-level service to meet customer needs.

2. Computer Hut. This Tacoma retail competitor is also a valued ally. Computer Hut sells IBM and Compaq brand systems, while CS sells custom-designed clones. When CS has customers looking for brand systems, they are sent to Computer Hut, and Computer Hut reciprocates by referring clone customers to CS. The relationship is strong and amicable.

3. CPS. This service company focuses on cabling operations and network installations. CPS assists CS in the setup and installation of new multi-terminal systems.

4. USA Net. This is another company which works with CS to assist in the installation of new network systems.

5. DataClimb. This is an internet provider company. DataClimb and CS are joint venture partners in an agreement to sell and provide T-1 line service to retail customers.

Competitive Comparison

There are two ways of establishing a competitive comparison of Computer Solutions to its competitors.

First, one may examine the "computer," the actual hardware, produced and/or delivered by each retailer. In many respects, there are few differences between the offerings of CS and the different companies listed in the section entitled Primary Competitors. Each company sells a good quality product, and many of the components are identifiable by brand and model number. For example, the Intel Pentium 200 Mhz processor CS uses is exactly the same as the Intel Pentium 200 Mhz processor used in a machine from Computer Hut or Best Buy or Applied Computer Technologies. While there are differences in some components, each company produces a functional computer.

Second, one may compare the different companies based on shopper perspective. What do computer buyers see, feel and hear as they shop the various retail establishments in the CS target area? It is in this comparison that Computer Solutions stands head and shoulders above all of the competition. No other retailer in the target area can match the CS combination of selection, pricing, delivery, warranty, training, service, and upgrade facilities. No other retailer in the target area can match the dedication, training, and professionalism of the CS sales staff and technical staff. When it comes to one-stop computer shopping, Computer Solutions is the undisputed leader in Pierce County.

Sourcing

Computer Solutions has developed a functional and safety-conscious approach to component sourcing. While some value-added-resellers develop very close relationships with only a few key suppliers, CS believes that an "all your eggs in one basket" strategy leaves the VAR at a significant competitive disadvantage during times of market shortages, or if a supplier fails for any reason. Therefore, CS strives to develop a three-layer supply line for each component needed for normal operations. Specifically, we work to develop a local supplier, a national supplier, and an international supplier (usually Chinese), for each primary component. With this strategy in place, CS is prepared to weather almost any supply problem likely to occur.

CS uses Synnex, Nemco, Globelle, Wintergreen Systems, Merisel, SED International, Tripp Lite, and Tech Data for various components. In addition, CS is negotiating to become primary Northwest distributor of Shamrock Monitors.

There are a great number of component suppliers in the market place, none of them dominant, and none with undue influence or power with regard to Computer Solutions.

Future Products and Services

Computer Solutions, Inc. has established two specific future expansion goals.

-25-

1. Internet conferencing within one year.

2. Within five years, beginning in 2000, CS will double the number of stores to six. Locations under consideration include the current target market, along with additional locations in the Olympia market.

MARKETING PLAN

Marketing is the process of bringing together the buyer and the seller into a mutually beneficial agreement. Classically, this process is broken into the "Four Ps of Marketing": Product, Price, Place, and Promotion. This plan addresses these four areas specifically.

Product

The connection of "product" to "marketing" is very important and often overlooked. Many companies make the mistake of designing and building a product, then trying to find someone who might want to buy it. The effective and profitable way to view product design is to see it as a function of marketing — find out what the customer wants, then find a way to make it. This is the view of Computer Solutions. CS designs every "product" — computers, training, service, upgrades, etc. — with the customer's needs and wants in mind. CS truly views the product to be sold as part of the marketing mix, and constantly works to adjust the company's offerings to reflect the market needs.

With this overarching view, CS has taken the lead in the target market by providing a "one-stop" computer shopping experience. Examine the offerings made by CS to those of any competitor in the target market: No other computer retailer can match the complete Computer Solutions mix of products and services. While one retailer may try to sell on "quality", their quality is no better than CS, and their prices are usually substantially higher. Another competitor might sell on "low price", and may actually be able to beat CS prices on some items at some times — but just try to get training, or set-up assistance, or repair or troubleshooting assistance from the low-baller. Only Computer Solutions offers the total package of products and services needed, even demanded, by the computer buyers of 1997 and beyond.

CS stands firmly behind everything sold, offering a one-year Computer Solutions, Inc. warranty on parts and labor. If there is a longer warranty from a component manufacturer, CS will process the defective component return at no charge to the customer. Additionally, CS offers longer optional warranties.

Price

As noted in the Industry Overview, price wars have plagued the computer retailing industry in the past. While CS has joined in these battles to a degree, the company's diversification into other products and services has allowed it to weather the price wars well.

CS uses two basic methods for establishing prices: Cost-based pricing and competitor-based pricing. The final prices charged are established using a combination of these two parameters. Generally, tangible products are priced using a 40% gross margin. This enables the company to use 60% of the selling price to cover its direct cost of components and production payroll, while reserving 40% of the selling price to cover all other costs. In the current market, this pricing structure generally puts CS products well within the acceptable range of competitive pricing, and often lower than many, even Best Buy. There are times when a competitor uses a low price as a loss-leader or near loss-leader. Standard operating procedure in this situation is to reduce a bid price as necessary, while still retaining a positive gross margin. Only in a case in which we were trying to capture a very large long-term account would CS price a bid below cost, and then only if there were reason to believe that substantial future business would be profitable.

In addition, CS occasionally uses price discounting to move floor merchandise and older components, and in seasonal promotions.

Place (Distribution)

The distribution of products and services is a strength for Computer Solutions. Three stores in the target market make CS the dominant computer retailer in the area, and give the company a profile that no other retailer can match. This three-store strength also gives CS an advantage in inventory control, since components can be shifted as required.

The product distribution plan for Computer Solutions, Inc. is as follows:

1. Components for use in building custom systems are ordered from primary and secondary suppliers every two or three days. (Out-of-stocks are easily covered by alternate suppliers.) Very little component inventory is maintained on an ongoing basis, greatly reducing inventory carrying costs. Approximately five to seven demonstrator systems are on display at all times in each store. These can be cannibalized for orders if absolutely necessary. When a sale is made, a component list is generated, and the components for that machine are ordered the same day. Component delivery to CS usually occurs within two days. The system is assembled and put through a pre-delivery series of diagnostic checks to confirm operational integrity.

-27-

2. A small stock of repair parts is maintained in each store for ongoing repair work.

3. A selection of accessories is maintained in each store to accomplish the "look" of a full retail store. Sales of accessory items are taken from store stock. Bar code tracking manages inventory on these items and flags reorder decisions.

Promotion

We will address the promotion plans of Computer Solutions in four subsegments. Each subsegment is a vital part of the overall promotional plan for the company, and each is developed to merge with and supplement the others.

Before reviewing the four parts of the promotional plan, it is necessary to establish the "positioning statement" for CS. The positioning statement is a definitive description of how the company wishes to be viewed by the customer base within the target market. In other words, if random people from the customer base were asked, "What is your first thought when you hear the name, Computer Solutions, Inc.?" what would the ideal response be? Some companies want to be known as the low price leader, others want to have the position of "Only the best and wealthiest shop here." Computer Solutions has established its positioning statement as:

"Computer Solutions, Inc.: the only true one-stop computer shop in Pierce County."

A special operations team called S.P.A.R.K. (Sales Programs Accelerate Real Kash) has been established to create new sales programs for all CS locations. The SPARK Team is a voluntary group which meets every two weeks. This group consists of management and non-management personnel, and has the sole purpose of generating specific sales-growth ideas and programs in the areas of Personal Selling, Advertising, Sales Promotion, and Public Relations. Meetings are held before normal store hours; team members are not paid for the meeting time, but the company provides a light breakfast. The "payoff" for the SPARK Team is real and measurable — when the ideas work, then sales and commissions are higher, and Accelerated Real Kash is the result.

Personal Selling

Personal Selling is the dominant promotional vehicle used by Computer Solutions to generate sales. Since inception, it has been clear that the personal presentation of information to a potential customer has been the most effective and efficient form of marketing. CS believes in performance-based pay for all sales staff, and has designed its salary and commission structure to reflect that belief. CS maintains two types of sales staff — Key Account Managers and Floor Sales Associates.

1. Key Account Managers (KAMs). These eight sales people are dedicated to generating outside sales to Business, Government, and Education customers, and generally have no responsibility to cover retail walk-in customers.

KAMs are paid a moderate monthly salary, plus a variable commission on sales. The commission is calculated as a percentage of the gross margin on each sale, ranging from a low 2% of the gross margin on sales up to $5,000, up to a full 25% of the gross margin on sales over $100,000. The sales responsibilities for the eight KAMs are currently not divided by boundaries of geography, product line, or customer type. All potential customers are available targets for all eight KAMs. KAMs have office space provided at the three stores, and most of their selling is done via phone with mail follow-up. In fact, many sales are initiated, finalized, and delivered without any face-to-face contact. However, KAMs are reimbursed for mileage and limited customer entertainment. KAMs receive special Key Account sales training from experienced management personnel.

2. Floor Sales Associates. These individuals are responsible to convert walk-in prospects into paying customers. They are paid an hourly wage, plus 5% of the gross margin of all products sold. All Floor Sales Associates receive product training and sales training from their store managers.

In order to ensure that all Key Account Managers and Floor Sales Associates have the proper "tools" to accomplish their sales objectives, Computer Solutions has established a simple four-level post-training assessment vehicle. Using the letters K.A.S.E., this program allows the appropriate manager to make an objective assessment for each sales person in each of four vital areas: Knowledge, Attitude, Skills, and Effort. For each area, an individual may be rated as low as a "1", indicating a very low level of achievement, or as high as a "5", indicating a very high level of achievement. All sales people receive a semi-annual evaluation including their K.A.S.E. status and their actual sales performance compared to 1) their previous year's performance, 2) this year's sales goals, and 3) other sales people in the same position. When deficiencies are observed in K.A.S.E. areas, they are dealt with in a reasonable, respectful, and straightforward manner. For deficiencies in the areas of knowledge and skills, remedial training and role-playing are called for. Deficiencies in attitude and effort are not as easily dealt with, but are often solvable via open discussion.

Advertising

As CS has grown, print advertising has been used, dominated by Yellow Pages space advertisements in each of the books covering the target area. In addition, CS has used The Advertiser, a local free-distribution weekly newspaper, for seasonal promotional ads.

In July and August, CS will initiate a special advertising blitz using 60,000 flyers per month per store — that's 120,000 flyers per store — inserted into local newspapers, including the Northwest Bugle, the Market Journal, the Advertiser, the Lakefield Papers, and the Pioneer Patrol.

Fall of 1997 represents a new beginning for Computer Solutions advertising. As noted in the Objectives section of the Company Summary, increasing walk-in store traffic is one of the Keys to Success that CS needs to accomplish in order to exceed the 1997 sales and profit objectives. Therefore, the company will be embarking on a major advertising campaign beginning in September designed to take advantage of the back-to-school selling period. The Computer Solutions "Colossal Computer Conniption" kicks off on Friday, August 29 — the beginning of Labor Day Weekend — and extends for one full week, through Thursday, September 4. Check out the complete details of the Conniption and its advertising in the section just ahead.

The Conniption will initiate a new era in the advertising plans for CS, and will set the stage for a series of print and broadcast advertisements which will drive new customers into the three stores throughout the Fall season, right up to the Christmas selling period. In addition, this campaign will include radio, cable television, coupon mailers, newspaper inserts, and direct mail. The post-Conniption Fall advertising series runs from September 7 through October 31. The objectives for this series include:

- Introduce Computer Solutions to the listener/reader.

- Establish the "one-stop" features and benefits.

- Establish the three locations of CS stores.

- Give a reason to visit NOW.

A new and different series of print, broadcast, and alternative advertisements will begin on November 1 and carry through the Christmas selling season. This promotional blitz is being designed to build on the knowledge established during the Conniption and the post-Conniption ad series, and to reap the sales rewards during the peak retail buying time of the year.

Sales Promotion

Sales Promotion includes a diverse group of short-term incentive tools designed to stimulate quicker and/or greater purchases of a product or service by customers. CS has used a number of sales promotion vehicles to date. These include premiums such as pens, candy, etc.; exhibits at trade shows; low-interest financing; discount coupons; and trade-in allowances.

Beginning with the Conniption, Computer Solutions will utilize several new and unique sales promotion tools, such as The Computer Solutions Card (a private label credit card which rewards users with discounts and special offers) and Computer Solutions Customer Appreciation Week (a special week dedicated to honor previous customers, offering free system check-ups, free refreshments, special future-purchase discount coupons, etc.

-30-

Public Relations

Marketing Public Relations is an often misunderstood part of the marketing mix. Marketing PR involves securing editorial space, as differentiated from paid space, in all media read, viewed, or heard by a company's customers or prospects, for the specific purpose of assisting in the achievement of sales goals.

Computer Solutions uses a number of PR tools, including press releases, Chamber of Commerce interaction, and extensive personal networking by Linda Sarver. In addition, all management staff and Key Account Managers are invited and encouraged to participate in PR opportunities.

A new PR tool in development is a program called "Solutions in the Schoolhouse," modeled after the wildly successful "Market Day" food buying program currently in use in many public schools. This initiative is being designed to allow Computer Solutions to team with the PTOs (Parent/Teacher Organizations) in all target-area public schools. The plan is to offer home computer systems (loaded with child-friendly software) to the parents of public school children at a slightly discounted price. The PTO receives 5% of all revenue. This program has tremendous potential to generate sales and long-term customers, and is very appealing to the key players in this arena. In fact, in its first test presentation, the concept of Solutions in the Schoolhouse was warmly embraced by a technology specialist in a target-area public school district.

The "Colossal Computer Conniption"

The Computer Solutions "Colossal Computer Conniption" kicks off on Friday, August 29 — the beginning of Labor Day Weekend — and extends for one full week, through Thursday, September 4.

The intention is to introduce Computer Solutions to those target customers who don't know us yet, to reintroduce CS to those who already know us, and to sell a truckload of merchandise. This will be accomplished by:

- Special print advertising in The Advertiser, Market Journal, Lakefield Papers, and Val-Pak.

- Special radio broadcasts on Star 101, KXLS, and KQRS.

- Super blow-out prices on special-purchase merchandise.

- Free refreshments every day.

- Live component manufacturer's rep demonstrations.

- One-year-same-as-cash offer on all systems purchased during the Conniption.

-31-

- Deep discounts on service, repair, and upgrades.

- Special offers to all Key Account Manager customers -- discounts, add-ons, free training, extended terms, etc.

- Special incentives paid to all Key Account Managers and Floor Sales Associates.

- Registration for prizes.

HUMAN RESOURCES

Computer Solutions, Inc. has built a productive and dedicated management team, as demonstrated in the following subchapters.

Current Management Team

President, Linda Sarver. As President of Computer Solutions, Inc., Linda Sarver has been a vital part of the success of CS to date, and her vision is the moving force behind the future growth of the company. Linda has an exceptional background in the establishment and growth of new businesses. In her college days at the University of Washington, she grew a dorm-room-based computer retailing business into a multi-million dollar enterprise. And she's grown Computer Solutions to the number one position in computer sales in Pierce County.

District Manager, Mark Sarver. Computer Solutions has established the position of District Manager in order to provide guidance and daily leadership to the three stores. The responsibilities include oversight of the three stores, company-wide human resource development, and assisting the President with planning and implementation of sales and marketing plans.

Mark Sarver, Linda's husband, has taken on the responsibilities of District Manager, coming to CS with a solid computer retailing background. Mark has 10 years of business management experience, including personnel management, training, inventory control, Accounts Payable/Accounts Receivable management, trade show management, and sales force management.

Store managers. Each of the three Computer Solutions stores is managed by a capable and trained professional manager.

1. Chuck Meyer, Puyallup. Chuck has developed his management skills throughout his career, including founding and running his own computer assembly business. After joining CS at the opening of the first store, his management abilities quickly became apparent, and he accepted the position of Puyallup Store Manger in 1996.

2. Melissa Chang, Lakewood Center. Melissa's military experience has built on her inherent discipline and determination, and she has grown those attributes to a high level of leadership skill. Melissa joined CS in 1996 after three years at Computer Hut. In May 1997, she accepted the Lakewood Center Store Manager position.

3. Rob Patton, Parkland. Rob began his computer career in 1991 as a customer service representative at Custom Built Computers, a local computer manufacturer and retailer. Rob held numerous positions at CBC, including telemarketing (inbound and outbound), sales specialist, and Assistant Manager. Rob came to Computer Solutions in 1996 as a Key Account Manager with primary responsibility for Government Accounts. His background and performance at CS have prepared him well for management, and he accepted the position of Store Manager in 1997.

Management Team Gaps

Computer Solutions has grown to the point where the administration of daily activities for the company as a whole is more than can be handled by Linda alone. Therefore, an Accounting/Administrative Assistant position has been created, and recruitment has begun. This job should be filled by August 1.

Personnel Plan

In addition to the management position described above, CS is currently planning for the following additions to staff before year-end 1997:

- Three additional technical services personnel.

- Two more Key Account Managers. This will bring the total KAM staff to ten from eight.

Personnel Plan			
	1997	**1998**	**1999**
Production			
Total Direct Labor	$114,232	$131,102	$146,057
Other	$0	$0	$0
Subtotal	$114,232	$131,102	$146,057
Sales and Marketing			
Total S&M Salaries	$228,473	$262,204	$292,114
Other	$0	$0	$0
Subtotal	$228,473	$262,204	$292,114

Administration			
Total Administrative Salaries	$125,236	$131,500	$138,072
Other	$0	$0	$0
Subtotal	$125,236	$131,500	$138,072
Total Payroll	$467,941	$524,806	$576,243
Payroll Burden	$70,191	$78,721	$86,436
Total Payroll Expenditures	$538,132	$603,527	$662,679

FINANCIAL PLAN

The pages following include brief information and graphic presentations of key financial data. Complete spreadsheets are located in the appendix. Three-year historical data on sales, profit, cash flow and balance sheet is included in the Supporting Documents. *(Editor's note: historical information is not reproduced.)*

Sales Forecast

The chart below presents the monthly sales forecast for 1997. You will note the seasonality which has occurred each year since launch, with stronger sales in the second half of the year. The table shows projected sales for the three plan years.

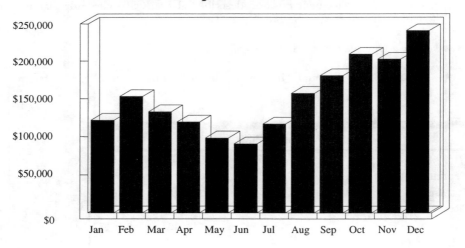

Total Sales by Month in Year 1

Sales Forecast			
	1997	**1998**	**1999**
Sales	$1,822,109	$2,432,600	$3,147,380
Direct Cost of Sales	$1,000,151	$1,310,430	$1,703,559

Profit Forecast

The chart below depicts sales, gross margin, and net profit for the three years of the plan. Further details are included in the table that follows.

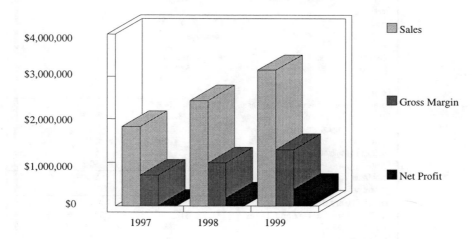

Projected Profit and Loss			
	1997	**1998**	**1999**
Sales	$1,822,109	$2,432,600	$3,147,380
Direct Cost of Sales	$1,000,151	$1,310,430	$1,703,559
Production Payroll	$114,232	$131,102	$146,057
Total Cost of Sales	$1,114,383	$1,441,532	$1,849,616
Gross Margin	$707,726	$991,068	$1,297,764
Gross Margin Percent	38.84%	40.74%	41.23%
Operating Expenses:			
Sales and Marketing Expenses:			
Sales/Marketing Salaries	$228,473	$262,204	$292,114
Advertising/Promotion	$33,236	$38,000	$42,000
Miscellaneous	$0	$0	$0
Other	$0	$0	$0
Total Sales/Marketing Expenses	$261,709	$300,204	$334,114
Sales and Marketing Percent	14.36%	12.34%	10.62%
General and Administrative Expenses:			
G&A Salaries	$125,236	$131,500	$138,072
Leased Equipment	$0	$0	$0
Utilities	$26,219	$28,840	$31,724
Insurance	$11,652	$12,817	$14,098
Rent	$120,132	$120,132	$120,132
Legal & Accounting	$9,300	$9,765	$10,253
Office	$10,061	$14,500	$15,225
Postage	$7,514	$13,800	$15,180
Telephone & Communication	$27,090	$33,862	$40,635
Depreciation	$20,352	$17,000	$13,000
Payroll Burden	$70,191	$78,721	$86,436
Other	$0	$0	$0
Total General and Administrative Expense	$427,747	$460,937	$484,755
General and Administrative Percent	23.48%	18.95%	15.40%
Other Operating Expenses:			
Other Salaries	$0	$0	$0
Contract/Consultants	$0	$0	$0
Other	$0	$0	$0
Total Other Operating Expenses	$0	$0	$0
Percent of Sales	0.00%	0.00%	0.00%
Total Operating Expenses	$689,456	$761,141	$818,869
Profit Before Interest and Taxes	$18,270	$229,927	$478,895
Interest Expense ST	$0	$0	$0
Interest Expense LT	$0	$0	$0
Taxes Incurred	$3,654	$45,985	$95,779
Net Profit	$14,616	$183,942	$383,116
Net Profit/Sales	0.80%	7.56%	12.17%

Cash Flow Forecast

Projected cash flow for 1997 is detailed in the chart that follows, with annual totals included in the table.

Cash Analysis

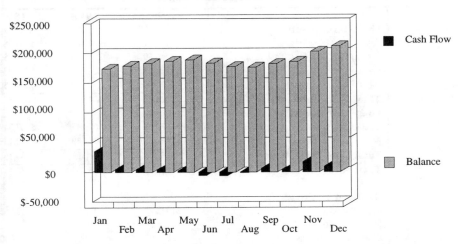

Projected Cash Flow			
	1997	**1998**	**1999**
Net Profit	$14,616	$183,942	$383,116
Plus:			
Depreciation	$20,352	$17,000	$13,000
Change in Accounts Payable	($132,859)	$40,405	$49,277
Curent Borrowing (Repayment)	$0	$0	$0
Increase (Decrease) Other Liabilities	$0	$0	$0
Long-Term Borrowing (Repayment)	$0	$0	$0
Capital Input	$0	$0	$0
Subtotal	($97,891)	$241,346	$445,393
Less:			
Change in Accounts Receivable	($135,000)	$0	$0
Change in Inventory	($35,702)	$50,530	$63,031
Change in Other ST Assets	$0	$0	$0
Capital Expenditure	$0	$0	$0
Dividends	$0	$0	$0
Subtotal	($170,702)	$50,530	$63,031
Net Cash Flow	$72,811	$190,816	$382,362
Cash Balance	$211,511	$402,327	$784,689

Balance Sheet Forecast

The next table presents the projected balance sheet data for the three years of the plan.

Projected Balance Sheet			
	1997	**1998**	**1999**
Short-Term Assets			
Cash	$211,511	$402,327	$784,689
Accounts Receivable	$0	$0	$0
Inventory	$172,123	$222,653	$285,684
Other Short-Term Assets	$0	$0	$0
Total Short-Term Assets	$383,634	$624,980	$1,070,373
Long-Term Assets			
Capital Assets	$107,547	$107,547	$107,547
Accumulated Depreciation	$69,189	$86,189	$99,189
Total Long-Term Assets	$38,358	$21,358	$8,358
Total Assets	$421,992	$646,338	$1,078,731
Debt and Equity			
Accounts Payable	$153,373	$193,777	$243,055
Short-Term Notes	$0	$0	$0
Other Short-Term Liabilities	$23,000	$23,000	$23,000
Subtotal Short-Term Liabilities	$176,373	$216,777	$266,055
Long-Term Liabilities	$0	$0	$0
Total Liabilities	$176,373	$216,777	$266,055
Paid-In Capital	$90,000	$90,000	$90,000
Retained Earnings	$141,003	$155,619	$339,561
Earnings	$14,616	$183,942	$383,116
Total Equity	$245,619	$429,561	$812,676
Total Debt and Equity	$421,992	$646,338	$1,078,731
Net Worth	$245,619	$429,561	$812,676

Appendix

Sales Forecast

	Jan 97	Feb 97	Mar 97	Apr 97	May 97	Jun 97	Jul 97	Aug 97	Sep 97	Oct 97	Nov 97	Dec 97	1997	1998	1999
Sales	$121,536	$153,006	$132,752	$119,147	$98,318	$90,500	$116,500	$157,200	$180,300	$209,350	$202,500	$241,000	$1,822,109	$2,432,600	$3,147,380
Direct Cost of Sales	$83,676	$89,849	$68,425	$63,645	$51,629	$47,360	$61,875	$84,260	$96,965	$112,942	$109,175	$130,350	$1,000,151	$1,310,430	$1,703,559

Personnel Plan

	Jan 97	Feb 97	Mar 97	Apr 97	May 97	Jun 97	Jul 97	Aug 97	Sep 97	Oct 97	Nov 97	Dec 97	1997	1998	1999
Production															
Total Direct Labor	$8,375	$8,746	$10,483	$8,742	$7,410	$6,984	$7,983	$9,575	$10,671	$11,322	$10,855	$13,086	$114,232	$131,102	$146,057
Other	$0	$0	$0	$0	$0	$0	$0	$0	$0	$0	$0	$0	$0	$0	$0
Subtotal	$8,375	$8,746	$10,483	$8,742	$7,410	$6,984	$7,983	$9,575	$10,671	$11,322	$10,855	$13,086	$114,232	$131,102	$146,057
Sales and Marketing															
Total S&M Salaries	$16,751	$17,493	$20,967	$17,484	$14,821	$13,969	$15,967	$19,151	$21,342	$22,644	$21,711	$26,173	$228,473	$262,204	$292,114
Other	$0	$0	$0	$0	$0	$0	$0	$0	$0	$0	$0	$0	$0	$0	$0
Subtotal	$16,751	$17,493	$20,967	$17,484	$14,821	$13,969	$15,967	$19,151	$21,342	$22,644	$21,711	$26,173	$228,473	$262,204	$292,114
Administration															
Total Administrative Salaries	$6,700	$6,900	$7,950	$6,550	$5,973	$8,850	$11,150	$13,650	$12,563	$11,600	$12,600	$20,750	$125,236	$131,500	$138,072
Other	$0	$0	$0	$0	$0	$0	$0	$0	$0	$0	$0	$0	$0	$0	$0
Subtotal	$6,700	$6,900	$7,950	$6,550	$5,973	$8,850	$11,150	$13,650	$12,563	$11,600	$12,600	$20,750	$125,236	$131,500	$138,072
Total Payroll	$31,826	$33,139	$39,400	$32,776	$28,204	$29,803	$35,100	$42,376	$44,576	$45,566	$45,166	$60,009	$467,941	$524,806	$576,243
Payroll Burden	$4,774	$4,971	$5,910	$4,916	$4,231	$4,470	$5,265	$6,356	$6,686	$6,835	$6,775	$9,001	$70,191	$78,721	$86,436
Total Payroll Expenditures	$36,600	$38,110	$45,310	$37,692	$32,435	$34,273	$40,365	$48,732	$51,262	$52,401	$51,941	$69,010	$538,132	$603,527	$662,679

Pro-forma Income Statement

	Jan 97	Feb 97	Mar 97	Apr 97	May 97	Jun 97	Jul 97	Aug 97	Sep 97	Oct 97	Nov 97	Dec 97	1997	1998	1999
Sales	$121,536	$153,006	$132,752	$119,147	$98,318	$90,500	$116,500	$157,200	$180,300	$209,350	$202,500	$241,000	$1,822,109	$2,432,600	$3,147,380
Direct Cost of Sales	$83,676	$89,849	$68,425	$63,645	$51,629	$47,360	$61,875	$84,260	$96,965	$112,942	$109,175	$130,350	$1,000,151	$1,310,430	$1,703,559
Production Payroll	$8,375	$8,746	$10,483	$8,742	$7,410	$6,984	$7,983	$9,575	$10,671	$11,322	$10,855	$13,086	$114,232	$131,102	$146,057
Total Cost of Sales	$92,051	$98,595	$78,908	$72,387	$59,039	$54,344	$69,858	$93,835	$107,636	$124,264	$120,030	$143,436	$1,114,383	$1,441,532	$1,849,616
Gross Margin	$29,485	$54,411	$53,844	$46,760	$39,279	$36,156	$46,642	$63,365	$72,664	$85,086	$82,470	$97,564	$707,726	$991,068	$1,297,764
Gross Margin Percent	24.26%	35.56%	40.56%	39.25%	39.95%	39.95%	40.04%	40.31%	40.30%	40.64%	40.73%	40.48%	38.84%	40.74%	41.23%
Operating Expenses:															
Sales and Marketing Expenses															
Sales/Marketing Salaries	$16,751	$17,493	$20,967	$17,484	$14,821	$13,969	$15,967	$19,151	$21,342	$22,644	$21,711	$26,173	$228,473	$262,204	$292,114
Advertising/Promotion	$321	$313	$344	$347	$361	$400	$650	$4,000	$14,000	$4,000	$3,500	$5,000	$33,236	$38,000	$42,000
Miscellaneous	$0	$0	$0	$0	$0	$0	$0	$0	$0	$0	$0	$0	$0	$0	$0
Other	$0	$0	$0	$0	$0	$0	$0	$0	$0	$0	$0	$0	$0	$0	$0
Total Sales and Marketing Expenses	$17,072	$17,806	$21,311	$17,831	$15,182	$14,369	$16,617	$23,151	$35,342	$26,644	$25,211	$31,173	$261,709	$300,204	$334,114
Sales and Marketing Percent	14.05%	11.64%	16.05%	14.97%	15.44%	15.88%	14.26%	14.73%	19.60%	12.73%	12.45%	12.93%	14.36%	12.34%	10.62%
General and Administrative Expenses															
G&A Salaries	$6,700	$6,900	$7,950	$6,550	$5,973	$8,850	$11,150	$13,650	$12,563	$11,600	$12,600	$20,750	$125,236	$131,500	$138,072
Leased Equipment	$0	$0	$0	$0	$0	$0	$0	$0	$0	$0	$0	$0	$0	$0	$0
Utilities	$2,197	$2,046	$2,202	$2,242	$2,202	$2,190	$2,190	$2,190	$2,190	$2,190	$2,190	$2,190	$26,219	$28,840	$31,724
Insurance	$971	$971	$971	$971	$971	$971	$971	$971	$971	$971	$971	$971	$11,652	$12,817	$14,098
Rent	$10,011	$10,011	$10,011	$10,011	$10,011	$10,011	$10,011	$10,011	$10,011	$10,011	$10,011	$10,011	$120,132	$120,132	$120,132
Legal & Accounting	$775	$775	$775	$775	$775	$775	$775	$775	$775	$775	$775	$775	$9,300	$9,765	$10,253
Office	$371	$436	$665	$455	$684	$400	$1,175	$1,175	$1,175	$1,175	$1,175	$1,175	$10,061	$14,500	$15,225
Postage	$216	$309	$327	$376	$336	$250	$275	$1,085	$1,085	$1,085	$1,085	$1,085	$7,514	$13,800	$15,180
Telephone & Communication	$2,341	$2,307	$2,202	$2,151	$2,339	$2,250	$2,250	$2,250	$2,250	$2,250	$2,250	$2,250	$27,090	$33,862	$40,635
Depreciation	$1,696	$1,696	$1,696	$1,696	$1,696	$1,696	$1,696	$1,696	$1,696	$1,696	$1,696	$1,696	$20,352	$17,000	$13,000
Payroll Burden	$4,774	$4,971	$5,910	$4,916	$4,231	$4,470	$5,265	$6,356	$6,686	$6,835	$6,775	$9,001	$70,191	$78,721	$86,436
Other	$0	$0	$0	$0	$0	$0	$0	$0	$0	$0	$0	$0	$0	$0	$0
Total G&A Expenses	$30,052	$30,422	$32,709	$30,143	$29,218	$31,863	$35,758	$40,159	$39,402	$38,588	$39,528	$49,904	$427,747	$460,937	$484,755
G&A Percent	24.73%	19.88%	24.64%	25.30%	29.72%	35.21%	30.69%	25.55%	21.85%	18.43%	19.52%	20.71%	23.48%	18.95%	15.40%

Other Operating Expenses															
Other Salaries	$0	$0	$0	$0	$0	$0	$0	$0	$0	$0	$0	$0	$0	$0	$0
Contract/Consultants	$0	$0	$0	$0	$0	$0	$0	$0	$0	$0	$0	$0	$0	$0	$0
Other	$0	$0	$0	$0	$0	$0	$0	$0	$0	$0	$0	$0	$0	$0	$0
Total Other Operating Expenses	$0	$0	$0	$0	$0	$0	$0	$0	$0	$0	$0	$0	$0	$0	$0
Percent of Sales	0.00%	0.00%	0.00%	0.00%	0.00%	0.00%	0.00%	0.00%	0.00%	0.00%	0.00%	0.00%	0.00%	0.00%	0.00%
Total Operating Expenses	$47,124	$48,228	$54,020	$47,974	$44,400	$46,232	$52,375	$63,310	$74,744	$65,232	$64,739	$81,077	$689,456	$761,141	$818,869
Profit Before Interest and Taxes	($17,639)	$6,183	($176)	($1,214)	($5,121)	($10,076)	($5,733)	$55	($2,080)	$19,854	$17,731	$16,487	$18,270	$229,927	$478,895
Interest Expense ST	$0	$0	$0	$0	$0	$0	$0	$0	$0	$0	$0	$0	$0	$0	$0
Interest Expense LT	$0	$0	$0	$0	$0	$0	$0	$0	$0	$0	$0	$0	$0	$0	$0
Taxes Incurred	($3,528)	$1,237	($35)	($243)	($1,024)	($2,015)	($1,147)	$11	($416)	$3,971	$3,546	$3,297	$3,654	$45,985	$95,779
Net Profit	($14,111)	$4,947	($141)	($972)	($4,096)	($8,061)	($4,586)	$44	($1,664)	$15,883	$14,185	$13,189	$14,616	$183,942	$383,116
Net Profit/Sales	-11.61%	3.23%	-0.11%	-0.82%	-4.17%	-8.91%	-3.94%	0.03%	-0.92%	7.59%	7.00%	5.47%	0.80%	7.56%	12.17%

Pro-Forma Cash Flow

	Jan 97	Feb 97	Mar 97	Apr 97	May 97	Jun 97	Jul 97	Aug 97	Sep 97	Oct 97	Nov 97	Dec 97	1997	1998	1999
Net Profit:	($14,111)	$4,947	($141)	($972)	($4,096)	($8,061)	($4,586)	$44	($1,664)	$15,883	$14,185	$13,189	$14,616	$183,942	$383,116
Plus:															
Depreciation	$1,696	$1,696	$1,696	$1,696	$1,696	$1,696	$1,696	$1,696	$1,696	$1,696	$1,696	$1,696	$20,352	$17,000	$13,000
Change in Accounts Payable	($185,062)	$6,054	($20,806)	($4,881)	($11,505)	($4,637)	$15,352	$26,181	$22,394	$5,895	($4,209)	$22,364	($132,859)	$40,405	$49,277
Current Borrowing (Repayment)	$0	$0	$0	$0	$0	$0	$0	$0	$0	$0	$0	$0	$0	$0	$0
Increase (Decrease) Other Liabilities	$0	$0	$0	$0	$0	$0	$0	$0	$0	$0	$0	$0	$0	$0	$0
Long-Term Borrowing (Repayment)	$0	$0	$0	$0	$0	$0	$0	$0	$0	$0	$0	$0	$0	$0	$0
Capital Input	$0	$0	$0	$0	$0	$0	$0	$0	$0	$0	$0	$0	$0	$0	$0
Subtotal	($197,477)	$12,696	($19,251)	($4,157)	($13,906)	($11,002)	$12,461	$27,921	$22,426	$23,474	$11,672	$37,250	($97,891)	$241,346	$445,393
Less:															
Change in Accounts Receivable	($135,000)	$0	$0	$0	$0	$0	$0	$0	$0	$0	$0	$0	($135,000)	$0	$0
Change in Inventory	($97,364)	$7,853	($23,624)	($7,825)	($16,018)	($5,634)	$18,617	$28,772	$16,561	$19,954	($5,081)	$28,087	($35,702)	$50,530	$63,031
Change in Other ST Assets	$0	$0	$0	$0	$0	$0	$0	$0	$0	$0	$0	$0	$0	$0	$0
Capital Expenditure	$0	$0	$0	$0	$0	$0	$0	$0	$0	$0	$0	$0	$0	$0	$0
Dividends	$0	$0	$0	$0	$0	$0	$0	$0	$0	$0	$0	$0	$0	$0	$0
Subtotal	($232,364)	$7,853	($23,624)	($7,825)	($16,018)	($5,634)	$18,617	$28,772	$16,561	$19,954	($5,081)	$28,087	($170,702)	$50,530	$63,031
Net Cash Flow	$34,887	$4,844	$4,374	$3,668	$2,112	($5,368)	($6,155)	($851)	$5,864	$3,521	$16,753	$9,163	$72,811	$190,816	$382,362
Cash Balance	$173,587	$178,430	$182,804	$186,472	$188,584	$183,216	$177,061	$176,210	$182,074	$185,595	$202,348	$211,511	$211,511	$402,327	$784,689

Pro-forma Balance Sheet

	Jan 97	Feb 97	Mar 97	Apr 97	May 97	Jun 97	Jul 97	Aug 97	Sep 97	Oct 97	Nov 97	Dec 97	1997	1998	1999
Short-Term Assets															
Cash	$173,587	$178,430	$182,804	$186,472	$188,584	$183,216	$177,061	$176,210	$182,074	$185,595	$202,348	$211,511	$211,511	$402,327	$784,689
Accounts Receivable	$0	$0	$0	$0	$0	$0	$0	$0	$0	$0	$0	$0	$0	$0	$0
Inventory	$110,461	$118,314	$94,690	$86,864	$70,847	$65,213	$83,830	$112,602	$129,163	$149,117	$144,036	$172,123	$172,123	$222,653	$285,684
Other Short-Term Assets	$0	$0	$0	$0	$0	$0	$0	$0	$0	$0	$0	$0	$0	$0	$0
Total Short-Term Assets	$284,048	$296,744	$277,493	$273,337	$259,431	$248,429	$260,891	$288,812	$311,237	$334,712	$346,384	$383,634	$383,634	$624,980	$1,070,373
Long-Term Assets															
Capital Assets	$107,547	$107,547	$107,547	$107,547	$107,547	$107,547	$107,547	$107,547	$107,547	$107,547	$107,547	$107,547	$107,547	$107,547	$107,547
Accumulated Depreciation	$50,533	$52,229	$53,925	$55,621	$57,317	$59,013	$60,709	$62,405	$64,101	$65,797	$67,493	$69,189	$69,189	$86,189	$99,189
Total Long-Term Assets	$57,014	$55,318	$53,622	$51,926	$50,230	$48,534	$46,838	$45,142	$43,446	$41,750	$40,054	$38,358	$38,358	$21,358	$8,358
Total Assets	$341,062	$352,062	$331,115	$325,263	$309,661	$296,963	$307,729	$333,954	$354,683	$376,462	$386,438	$421,992	$421,992	$646,338	$1,078,731
Debt and Equity															
Accounts Payable	$101,170	$107,224	$86,418	$81,537	$70,031	$65,395	$80,747	$106,928	$129,322	$135,217	$131,008	$153,373	$153,373	$193,777	$243,055
Short-Term Notes	$0	$0	$0	$0	$0	$0	$0	$0	$0	$0	$0	$0	$0	$0	$0
Other ST Liabilities	$23,000	$23,000	$23,000	$23,000	$23,000	$23,000	$23,000	$23,000	$23,000	$23,000	$23,000	$23,000	$23,000	$23,000	$23,000
Subtotal Short-Term Liabilities	$124,170	$130,224	$109,418	$104,537	$93,031	$88,395	$103,747	$129,928	$152,322	$158,217	$154,008	$176,373	$176,373	$216,777	$266,055
Long-Term Liabilities	$0	$0	$0	$0	$0	$0	$0	$0	$0	$0	$0	$0	$0	$0	$0
Total Liabilities	$124,170	$130,224	$109,418	$104,537	$93,031	$88,395	$103,747	$129,928	$152,322	$158,217	$154,008	$176,373	$176,373	$216,777	$266,055
Paid-in Capital	$90,000	$90,000	$90,000	$90,000	$90,000	$90,000	$90,000	$90,000	$90,000	$90,000	$90,000	$90,000	$90,000	$90,000	$90,000
Retained Earnings	$141,003	$141,003	$141,003	$141,003	$141,003	$141,003	$141,003	$141,003	$141,003	$141,003	$141,003	$141,003	$141,003	$155,619	$339,561
Earnings	($14,111)	($9,165)	($9,305)	($10,277)	($14,373)	($22,435)	($27,021)	($26,977)	($28,642)	($12,758)	$1,427	$14,616	$14,616	$183,942	$383,116
Total Equity	$216,892	$221,838	$221,698	$220,726	$216,630	$208,568	$203,982	$204,026	$202,361	$218,245	$232,430	$245,619	$245,619	$429,561	$812,676
Total Debt and Equity	$341,062	$352,062	$331,115	$325,263	$309,661	$296,963	$307,729	$333,954	$354,683	$376,462	$386,438	$421,992	$421,992	$646,338	$1,078,731
Net Worth	$216,892	$221,838	$221,698	$220,726	$216,630	$208,568	$203,982	$204,026	$202,361	$218,245	$232,430	$245,619	$245,619	$429,561	$812,676

The Plan for
Jumpin' Java Cybercafe

ETHAN STANLEY, President

DAN VICTOR, Executive Vice President

CAROLYN SCHWARTZ, Food Service Manager

3200 East Flying Cloud Drive

Eden Prairie, MN 55346

(612) 975-6262

Copy Number ____ of Ten

THE PLAN FOR JUMPIN' JAVA CYBERCAFE

-2

EXECUTIVE SUMMARY

The concept. What if it were possible to logically and profitably merge two of the fastest growing and least saturated businesses in the marketplace today? That's exactly the idea behind the "cybercafe," the latest development in the combined evolution of the booming specialty coffee industry and the new growth arena called public computer access. Traditional, or non-cyber, specialty coffeehouses are exploding in number, growing from a nationwide base of only 200 in 1989 to a projected 10,000 by 1999! That's a fifty-fold expansion in only ten years — already strong on the coasts, but just beginning to hit the Midwest! And computer technology continues to play a more and more prominent role in our lives, especially important in the lifestyle of today's youth. Combine the two, and what's been created is a business opportunity that is just waiting to be seized.

The background. Ethan Stanley, President of Jumpin' Java Cybercafe, in 1996 noticed several seemingly unrelated marketplace factors beginning to coalesce. First, as a computer major at the University of Minnesota, Ethan knew firsthand of the public's excitement over expanding technology. He especially took note of the number of high school and college students who were hyper-excited about the internet and high-tech computer gaming. Second, he began to see the success of specialty coffeehouses in the Minneapolis area, and he observed how popular they had become with upscale customers aged 50 years and below — exactly the same demographic customer as he saw in the computer world. And third, he realized there was no real "hang out" for young people anywhere near his Eden Prairie home. The seed for Jumpin' Java Cybercafe was planted, and we now stand ready to watch it break through to reality.

The company. Jumpin' Java Cybercafe will be the largest cybercafe in Minnesota, and one of the top ten in the entire United States. Located adjacent to the Eden Prairie Shopping Center in Eden Prairie, it will house 55 computer terminals, including five specialized super-fast computer gaming "pods" with four computers each; a fully-equipped state-of-the-art Technology Training Center with 25 complete PC systems for use in corporate and public computer training; a comfortable lounge area with a fireplace and separate audio system; an espresso bar serving the best specialty coffees and teas; and food service that includes fresh Rosati's Pizza from next door! Beginning the day it opens, Jumpin' Java Cybercafe will be a "destination" experience.

The market. Jumpin' Java has targeted six key groups of customers, each of which offer tremendous sales potential: 1) local Residents — 75,000 demographically perfect people live within a 5-mile radius; 2) Eden Prairie Shopping Center shoppers and employees; 3) Hennepin County Community College students and faculty, almost 15,000 strong; 4) high school students and faculty from schools within the 5-mile radius, over 10,000 total; 5) daytime commuters, nearly 300,000 per day; and 6) businesses in southwest Hennepin County with computer training needs.

Competitive position. There is little established competition from other cybercafes in Jumpin' Java's target area. In fact, there is little competition from any established specialty coffeehouses, with or without public computer access. Overall, we view the competition as poorly established and easily overtaken in light of the advantages which Jumpin' Java's has over its competitors:

- Visionary Ownership. Ethan Stanley has demonstrated his leadership and vision throughout his technology education and within his current position as Director of Information Systems at Datatech, Inc., a local PC Assembler.

- Low Cost Access to Technology. A firm long-term agreement with Datatech gives Jumpin' Java access to hardware and software at virtually manufacturer's cost.

- Strong Management Team. Jumpin' Java will begin operations with a cast of three strong, talented, and experienced managers.

- Knowledge of Computer Gaming. The Jumpin' Java management team has developed detailed knowledge of the computer gaming field.

- Location. Jumpin' Java is in a particularly advantageous location.

Management team. As President of Jumpin' Java Cybercafe, Ethan Stanley will take the leadership role in conceptual issues, strategy, and finance. Ethan comes to Jumpin' Java with an exceptional background in establishing and growing businesses. At the University of Minnesota School of Technology, Ethan led the Entrepreneurial Technology Team to a National Championship in the 1994 New Product Development category. His vision and leadership have been a vital contributor to the success of his current employer, Datatech, Inc.

Executive Vice President, Dan Victor, spent 10 years operating his own business as a computer systems builder and integrator. Throughout his career, Dan has demonstrated the ability to effectively manage in a retail setting, and has dealt expertly with sales, personnel selection and development, cash management, scheduling, cost control, merchandising and store appearance, etc. In his new assignment at Jumpin' Java, Dan will have day-to-day responsibility for ongoing operations and all technology.

Food Service Manager, Carolyn Schwartz, joins Jumpin' Java directly from a Chicago-area Starbucks Coffee, where she had been Store Manager for two years. Carolyn brings obvious expertise in the necessary food service arena — expertise that neither Ethan nor Dan has.

Financials. The company anticipates rapid acceptance of Jumpin' Java in the marketplace, with first year revenues of $744,000, growing to $900,000 in FY 2000. After-tax profit is expected to be $78,000 in the first year, growing to $114,000 in FY 2000.

Funds sought. The company is seeking $296,125 in a combination of long-term debt and short-term working capital. These funds will be utilized for startup expenses and to purchase fixtures, equipment, and computer hardware.

COMPANY SUMMARY

Jumpin' Java Cybercafe is a Minnesota S-Corporation. Company stock is owned by the management team, as follows:

- Ethan Stanley   51%

- Dan Victor   24.5%

- Carolyn Schwartz   24.5%

Mission

The mission of Jumpin' Java Cybercafe is to provide the adults and youth of Southwest Hennepin County, Minnesota with the ultimate cybercafe experience.

Objectives

The management team has established the following objectives for the launch phase of Jumpin' Java:

1. Obtain complete financing by July 31, 1997.

2. Celebrate the store's Grand Opening on Friday, Saturday and Sunday, September 5, 6, and 7.

3. Achieve first 12-month sales of $744,000.

4. Achieve profitable operation within three months of opening.

Keys to Success

In order to accomplish the goals from the previous section, the following keys to success must be realized:

1. Finalize the loan request package by June 30.

2. Achieve full staffing by August 15.

3. Have the store and all processes set and ready for "intro nights" on September 1, 2, 3, and 4.

-6-

4. Gain rapid and strong acceptance with high schools and HCCC students.

5. Develop adequate demand for Technology Training Center classes.

Startup Summary

The establishment of a cybercafe of the scope of Jumpin' Java is a substantial undertaking. Beyond the initial need recognition, the establishment of Jumpin' Java has required vision and planning, and now requires financial resources. Although complete details for each line item are available in the Supporting Documents *(editor's note: supporting documents are not reproduced)*, the following highlights may be useful:

- Store buildout. Total anticipated cost is $40,000. 25% is due on completion, with the remaining 75% amortized over five years at 10% annual interest.

- Expensed equipment. This includes miscellaneous supplies and equipment.

- Other short-term assets; plants.

- Long term assets. Computer hardware/software, $132,500; all other, (Furniture, Fixtures, etc.) $132,825.

Table 1 below details the startup plan, and assumes that the funding sought is achieved.

Table 1: Startup Costs	
Startup Expenses	*Amount*
Accounting	$ 3,000
Business Plan Prep.	$ 4,000
Expensed Equipment/Preopening Personnel	$ 25,000
Launch Advertising and Expenses	$ 20,000
Legal	$ 3,000
Stationary, Etc.	$ 500
Store Buildout	$ 10,000
Other	$ 0
Total Startup Expenses	$ 65,500
Cash Requirements	$ 60,000
Beginning Inventory	$ 5,000
Other Short-Term Assets	$ 300
Total Short-Term Assets	$ 65,300
Total Long-Term Assets	$265,325
Total Startup Requirements	$396,125
Left to Finance	$ 0

-7-

Table 2: Startup Funding Plan	
Funding Source	*Amount*
Investment	
Ethan Stanley	$ 50,000
Dan Victor	$ 25,000
Carolyn Schwartz	$ 25,000
Other	$ 0
Total investment	$100,000
Short-Term Borrowing	
Unpaid Expenses	$ 0
Short-Term Loans	$ 30,800
Interest-Free Short-Term Loans	$ 0
Total Short-Term Borrowing	$ 30,800
Long-Term Borrowing	$265,325
Total Borrowing	$296,125
Loss at Startup	($65,500)
Total Equity	$ 34,500
Total Debt and Equity	$330,625

INDUSTRY ANALYSIS

What if it were possible to logically and profitably merge two of the fastest growing and least saturated businesses in the market today? That is exactly the idea behind "cybercafes", the latest development in the combined evolution of the booming specialty coffee industry and the new growth arena called public computer access. The cybercafe (or internet cafe, as they are sometimes called), is the very appropriate combination of two businesses; one that is hundreds of years old, one that has existed for less than a decade.

The business of growing, roasting, brewing, and selling coffee is one of the oldest and largest industries in the world. In fact, the statistics regarding the coffee business are astounding. The Specialty Coffee Association of America (SCAA) reports that:

- Coffee is the world's most popular drink.

- The coffee industry is second in total dollars in worldwide trade only to the petroleum industry.

-8-

- More than 20 million people are employed in the global coffee industry.

- 400 billion cups per year are sold worldwide.

The National Coffee Association's statistics show that Americans drink 400 million cups of coffee PER DAY, one third of all the coffee grown in the world. This equals 1.87 cups per person over the age of 10. While total U.S. coffee sales remain at close to $5 billion annually, growth has come in a unique subset of the coffee trade, specialty coffee. Specialty coffee is differentiated from supermarket brand "commercial" coffee, and has grown in its share of the total coffee market from less than five percent in 1983 to an expected 28.9% in 1997. The SCAA projects that specialty coffee will control $3 billion of the entire $8 billion U.S. coffee trade by the end of the century, a 37.5% market share.

Specialty coffee is available through a variety of retail channels, but the fastest growing channel is the coffee cafe. A coffee cafe is a retail store focused on the brewing and selling of ready-to-drink specialty coffee. The coffees include brewed coffee, and espresso, coffee brewed one cup at a time through a high-pressure espresso machine. Coffee cafes usually sell other appropriate items as well, such as whole bean coffee, fresh ground coffee, pastries and other light food items, coffee giftware, etc. The best-known of the coffee cafes is Starbucks, with stores across the U.S. SCAA estimates that there were about 200 coffee cafes nationwide in 1989, but that by 1999, there will be over 10,000! This is phenomenal growth which began on the east and west coasts and is now moving to fill in the center of the country.

Reasons for the rapid growth of coffee cafes include:

1. Selling coffee by the cup offers a high gross margin.

2. Espresso-based coffees are difficult for consumers to prepare correctly at home.

3. Existing food service locations will be slow to upgrade their product quality to the level of specialty coffees.

The message is clear — the specialty coffee industry, and coffee cafes, are here to stay. And their popularity is growing at a caffeine-induced high rate of speed.

Now for the other half of the combination — public computer access. As the use and the utility of computer technology continue to expand at breakneck speed, the inevitable has begun to take place — computers are not used just at home or at the office; people who don't yet own a computer need access to one on occasion; internet users want faster access times than they can get at home or work; users want to use new or specialized hardware or software that they don't have private access to; business travelers and students carry their own laptop computers with them, but need a location from which to go online; etc. In all of these situations, there is a real and unfulfilled need for a public place where computers, and the online access that goes with them, are available and reasonably priced.

Enter the growth industry dedicated to providing what consumers need — Public Computer Access. There are a few forward-looking entrepreneurs which are beginning to fill this void. Kinko's Copy Centers are probably the best known. They have built a large and growing business around selling computer time to business people and others who need to be able to generate a document, print it, copy it, and distribute it. Kinko's theme, "Your branch office" is appropriate — they intend to fill a business production need by providing public computer access. The other most common public computer access provider is probably the local public library. Many now offer computer terminals for in-house data-base searches, and a growing number also offer full internet access at some of their stations. There is usually no charge at the library, although there are time limits and sometimes long waits to get to the limited number of available online computer stations. Still, there is a significant gap in the availability of public computer access, and into that void has grown the marvelous combination of public computer access joined with a specialty coffee cafe — the cybercafe.

A cybercafe is any public business which combines food and beverage sales with public computer access and, typically, internet access. While cybercafes can be bars, restaurants, or fast food places, Jumpin' Java Cybercafe has obviously chosen to focus on the most exciting of the cybercafe formats, the specialty coffee cybercafe.

The first cybercafe is said to have been the Electronic Cafe in Santa Monica, California, opened in 1984. This was well before the internet had been born, and the cybercafe craze didn't really begin until 1994, when Cyberia opened in London, England. It was the first to open with the intention of having internet access and computers be the primary focus of their business. The National Association for Internet Cafes, the leading industry association, emphasizes the rapid growth of American cybercafes by noting that there were a mere 50 nationwide at the end of 1995, exploding to several hundred by mid-1996.

The cybercafe craze that began on the coasts has begun to work its way to the center, with several now located in the Minneapolis market: Al's Place, Calypso Coffee Company, and Dunn Brothers Coffee are three examples in the area. Each cafe has its own look, its own feel, its own product mix, and its own clientele. The cybercafe market is new, uncrowded, and ready for a new major player in SW Hennepin County.

Industry Participants

There are several groups of industry participants which must come together in order for the cybercafe industry to function well.

1. The Customer. Everything in this business begins and ends with the customer. Every successful cybercafe must first identify the base of customers from which business will be drawn. Their tastes, desires, and needs will and must be the genesis of each decision in building the business.

-10-

2. The Coffee Suppliers. For a specialty coffee cybercafe to succeed, it must serve outstanding coffee products, and that necessitates the procurement of outstanding roasted coffee. There are now hundreds of specialty coffee roasters in the U.S. In fact, the number of "micro-roasteries" has grown from 40 in 1979, to 385 by 1989, and is expected to expand to 1400 by 1999. Suppliers are not in short supply.

3. Computer Hardware Manufacturers. For a cybercafe to provide the technical excitement sought by its customers, it must stay on the very top of the technology wave. And that means it's got to have the latest gadgets, bells, and whistles as soon as they're available. The industry depends on the continued advancement of the hardware industry, pressing to ever higher levels of sophistication and fun.

4. Software Manufacturers. Like the hardware component, the specialized gaming and other software change rapidly, and the continuing improvements will impact on the use of public computer access.

5. Internet Access Providers. Internet access is one of the key attractions of public computer access, since home-users must tolerate slow connect times and slow data retrieval. The access speed that Jumpin' Java will provide will make internet access fun, fast, and exciting.

6. The retail cybercafe. This is the triangulation point where it all comes together. By offering a top-of-the-line combination of coffee service, hardware and software, high-speed internet access, and a unique and inviting ambiance, a serious cybercafe owner creates an appealing and profitable business niche.

TARGET MARKET

Who are the individuals and groups that are likely customers of a new, bright, fun, cheery, and stimulating cybercafe? Fortunately, there is some history to provide answers, even in this young industry. First, cybercafes are NOT simply hangouts for nose-ringed cyberpunks or pocket-protected technophiles. There is a great variety of customer types students, mothers with young children, business people. The most common coffee house patrons look, demographically speaking, almost exactly like computer users: Baby boomers, young adults, teens; metropolitan/suburban, upscale, well-educated, light drinkers or non-drinkers, medium-to-high household income level (over $35,000 per year).

Each cybercafe develops its facilities, ambiance, products, and services around its target audience. Jumpin' Java will target several distinct groups of potential customers, all of which fit the basic demographic characteristics, in order to maximize revenues and distribute sales more evenly throughout each business day. The specific groups are:

1. Local Residents. Approximately 75,000 people live within a five-mile radius of Jumpin' Java, including part or all of the cities of Eden Prairie, Bloomington, Edina, and Minnetonka. With an average of 2.94 persons per household (1990 U.S. Census), this equates to over 25,000 households in the target area. Each of these households is a target.

2. Eden Prairie Shopping Center Patrons and Employees. Jumpin' Java is located on a prime corner of Flying Cloud Drive, adjacent to this major mall. The traffic in the center averages 9,000 vehicles per day on weekdays and 12,000 per day on weekends.

3. H.C.C.C. Students and Faculty. Hennepin County Community College is one mile from Jumpin' Java, and the HCCC faculty and students are clear targets for the cafe. 673 faculty and over 14,000 students constitute a market that, if properly exploited, would alone generate a successful sales volume.

4. High School Students and Faculty. Five major high schools are located within five miles of Jumpin' Java. St. John's High School (1248 students) and Eden Prairie High School (1450 students), both in Eden Prairie; Bloomington High School (2392 students) in Bloomington; Edina High School (1202 students) in Edina; and Minnetonka Township High School (2400 students) in Minnetonka house thousands of students and hundreds of faculty who are primary members of the target demographic groups. These will be targets for Jumpin' Java.

5. Daytime Commuters. Flying Cloud Drive (U.S. Rt. 212) is one of the busiest arterial four-lane routes in the Southwestern Twin Cities area. The Minnesota Department of Transportation reports the following 24-hour traffic counts on Flying Cloud as it passes Eden Prairie Shopping Center:

    — Northbound: 117,400 vehicles per 24 hours.

    — Southbound: 123,200 vehicles per 24 hours.

    — East leg Anderson Lakes Parkway: 28,200.

    — West leg Anderson Lakes Parkway: 24,700.

    The cafe's location at the Northeast corner of the intersection puts it in the path of roughly 300,000 motorists per day. Since a significant percentage of the American population can't, or won't, start the day without their morning shot of java, Jumpin' Java will help fill that morning need.

6. Businesses. There are over 20,000 businesses in the target area. Estimates are that at least half, or 10,000, use computer technology in the course of their business. While these may not seem to be natural targets for Jumpin' Java, they are primary targets for the Technology Training Center (TTC) located within Jumpin' Java.

These six primary target groups provide fertile ground for growing Jumpin' Java into a profitable operation within one year. In fact, Jumpin' Java will become the top stop for morning Joe, the daytime respite from the normal hum-drum existence, the best-known Southwest Twin Cities area corporate technology training location, and the long-needed Hot Spot for young adults at night and on the weekends.

Market Trends

Jumpin' Java Cybercafe is located at a key location in the southwestern Twin Cities area. The households and businesses within a five-mile radius match the demographic target profile exactly — baby boomers, young adults, and teens; metropolitan/suburban; upscale; well-educated; light drinkers or non-drinkers; medium to high household income. In fact, it is difficult to conceive of an urban or suburban locale that could surpass the demographic match and growth potential of Jumpin' Java's five-mile radius target market. The market trends for Jumpin' Java's target area reflect those of SW Hennepin County generally and central Eden Prairie specifically, and the trends couldn't be much better.

The Twin Cities Planning Commission (TCPC) reports that the 1990 population of Southwestern Hennepin County was 516,401, with expected growth by 2020 expanding that total to 772,411. This growth of 49.6% is double that forecast for the Twin Cities region as a whole, and ranks the target area as one of the fastest-growing in the state. A casual drive through the area will establish the fact that this growth is underway NOW, and will continue for years to come. It is interesting to note that, according to a survey conducted by Bell Federal Savings and published in the March 15, 1997 Minneapolis Tribune, three target-area cities ranked in the top 15 cities in the entire Twin Cities area for number of 1996 new home permits. Eden Prairie placed ninth with 394, Minnetonka ranked 11th with 346 permits, and Shakopee was 14th with 324 permits.

With new people come new jobs, and SW Hennepin County is no exception. The TCPC forecasts that the number of jobs in this segment will grow even faster than the population, expanding to over 471,000 in 2020 from less than 229,000 in 1990, an astounding 106% growth over the period. This compares to same-period growth in Hennepin County at 46%, Ramsey County at 53%, and Dakota County at 81%.

Income levels in the target area are high and growing. 1995 tax returns indicate an average adjusted gross income (AGI) in Southwest Hennepin County of over $62,000, placing it in the top 1% of counties nationwide (Transactional Records Access Clearinghouse, Minneapolis Tribune, 4/12/97). While city-specific household income data for 1995 are not available, 1989 data from The Towery Report indicate that the average household income in the four primary target-area cities was equal to that in the county at large. All expectations are for incomes to follow the growth in population and jobs — higher.

-13-

Educationally, the target area ranks significantly above the national average. The Towery Report states that in 1990, 21% of Americans 25 years and older held a four-year college degree, while in our target area, the figure is 32%, more than 50% above the national average.

Technologically, the target market is right where it should be — on or ahead of the curve. Plainsman Press conducted a recent survey of its readers in suburban Minneapolis, and found that 44% of its households owned personal computers, compared to only one-third of households nationwide. Conversely, 56% of Plainsman Press households do not own a PC, fertile ground for Jumpin' Java to build customers. While 44% of Plainsman Press households own a PC, only 6.3% subscribe to an online service. The remaining "unconnected" computer owners are prime targets for Jumpin' Java's online capability. In fact, of the 6.3% who do use an online service, virtually none of them have access to the supersonic T-1 speeds offered by Jumpin' Java.

The trends are clear. The Jumpin' Java target market is perfectly suited to accept and patronize a specialty coffee cybercafe, and Jumpin' Java will quickly become the leading cybercafe in the market.

COMPETITION

As noted in the Industry Analysis, the phenomenon called cybercafes has grown from roughly 50 stores nationwide in 1995 to several hundred today. Early growth was heavily concentrated in the major coastal cities in California, Washington State, and New York, and spillover into the center of the country has begun to occur just over the last year. Therefore, there is little established competition from other cybercafes in Jumpin' Java's target area. In fact, there is little competition from any established specialty coffee houses, with or without public computer access.

We view the competition as weak and easily overtaken. Jumpin' Java will be the dominant market participant at launch.

Primary Competitors

The competition within the target area will be examined at four different levels: 1) direct competition from cybercafes, 2) competition from other specialty coffeehouses which do not provide public computer access, 3) competitors which offer public computer access with no accompanying food or beverage service, and 4) other safe, wholesome young-adult entertainment centers.

1. Other cybercafes.

    — Connie's Internet Cafe. Opened in December 1996, Connie's is located in downtown Shakopee in a renovated small house. Roughly 800 square feet, it is warm and cozy, with oak floors and fixtures, and features four computers and a printer in a side nook, plus several tables. Connie's offers espresso-based drinks and other drinks, along with bakery items, chili, snacks, and sandwiches.

2. Non-cyber specialty coffeehouses.

— Something's Brewing. This 1200 sq. ft. downtown Eden Prairie coffeehouse offers a nice selection of hot and cold drinks, bakery items, chocolate candies, and ice cream. It has a comfortable ambiance and seven tables for customers.

— A Special Cup. This 1500 sq. ft. Olympic Hills coffeehouse opened in May 1997 in a building owned by Olympic Ford, next door. It has a classy appearance and serves a traditional mix of specialty coffee items.

— Oasis. This is a tiny (<100 sq. ft.) drive-through specialty coffee shop on eastbound Pioneer Trail in Eden Prairie.

3. Public Computer Access, no food/beverage.

— Eden Prairie Memorial Library, Eden Prairie. Two internet access terminals, no cost.

— Edina Public Library, Edina. Four internet access terminals, no cost.

— Hennepin County District Library, Bloomington. Six internet access terminals, no cost.

— Hennepin County Community College, Grayslake. 35 internet access terminals, no cost, $.25 per page printed.

4. Young-Adult Entertainment Centers. These are difficult to define, but include any place that 16- to 25-year-olds gather in the evenings and on weekends for safe and appropriate fun and entertainment. Extensive discussions with school officials, police, parents, and teens have underscored the lack of young-adult entertainment centers in SW Hennepin County. The only location which might currently qualify as a center is Eden Prairie Shopping Center. However, the establishment of Eden Prairie S.C. as a youth "hang-out" is more by default than by design. In fact, Mall Management welcomes the appearance of another high-quality option where teens can congregate.

Barriers to Entry

The cybercafe industry is new, and change is the only constant. There will be new entrants in Jumpin' Java's target market, and those newcomers must overcome several barriers:

1. Startup Costs. Technically, a cybercafe is any business which sells food or drinks and offers at least one public computer terminal. Therefore, a cybercafe could be opened on very little capital. However, to launch a substantial operation, particularly one which would be able to compete head-to-head with Jumpin' Java, would require an investment of hundreds of thousands of dollars. Compared to traditional coffeehouse startups, a cybercafe with a significant commitment to technology requires a substantial level of startup capital.

2. Technological Expertise. Due to the technical aspects of the cybercafe, management of any new venture must possess, or be able to buy, significant technological expertise.

3. Costly Continuous Upgrading of Hardware and Software. Ideally, a cybercafe needs access to very low-cost hardware and software. While this is not an absolute requirement, any cybercafe which is forced to pay retail prices for its hardware and software will find that the continuing costs of repeated upgrading will strain profitability to the utmost.

4. Specialty Coffee Expertise. The knowledge and techniques involved in the specialty coffee trade, especially espresso-based drinks, are significant. The "barrista", who brews the individual espresso drinks, is vital to the success of the cyber-coffeehouse. These individuals must come into the business with this specialized knowledge or undergo substantial training.

Future Competition

While there is little doubt that there will eventually be competitors to Jumpin' Java, there is little evidence of anything brewing at the present time.

The greatest direct future challenge to the dominance that Jumpin' Java will enjoy is probably the possibility of a large chain such as Starbucks, Brewster's, or perhaps others, making a substantial commitment to the cybercafe business. If one of these was to open one or more stores in SW Hennepin County, it could be detrimental to Jumpin' Java's sales and profit. However, given the differences between Jumpin' Java and "traditional" coffee cafes, even these major coffee providers could be effectively defended against. The experience in Seattle has been that multiple coffeehouses can thrive even in very close quarters, if demand is high. We expect the same trend in this arena.

SWOT ANALYSIS

An examination of the company's strengths and weaknesses, and the market opportunities and threats, will help to identify areas of concern and areas of additional potential.

Company Strengths

Jumpin' Java brings to the marketplace a number of strengths which give it advantage over competitors:

1. Visionary Ownership. Ethan Stanley has demonstrated his leadership and vision by building Datatech into the dominant computer assembler in its market. He has the ability to recognize and seize opportunities well ahead of the pack, realizing the early profits that accrue to innovators.

2. Low Cost Access to Technology. A firm long-term agreement with Datatech gives Jumpin' Java access to hardware and software at two percent over manufacturer's cost. This is a major strength which will be hard for others to match.

3. Knowledge of Computer Gaming. The Jumpin' Java Management Team has developed detailed knowledge of the computer gaming field, and is prepared to plug that knowledge into the leading computer gaming center in Minnesota — Jumpin' Java Cybercafe.

4. Strong and Dedicated Management Team. Jumpin' Java is led by three top-flight managers who know their roles, know their business, and know how to get things accomplished.

5. Location. Jumpin' Java is in a particularly advantageous location which provides exceptional visibility from the road and is known to virtually everyone in the target area.

Company Weaknesses

While recognizing the strengths that Jumpin' Java possesses, it is just as important to be honest about any weaknesses within the operation. We see the following weaknesses presently:

1. Jumpin' Java is new and untested. Every business development step has been carefully planned, and the management team has confidence in themselves, their concept, and the market's readiness. However, until the doors are open, and sales, cash flow, and profit begin, the fact that Jumpin' Java is an untested

-17-

enterprise must be viewed as a weakness. Clearly, the only way to correct this weakness is to launch the business successfully, and that is what we intend to do.

2. Lack of Large-Group Corporate Training Experience. Jumpin' Java will contain a 24-terminal Technology Training Center (TTC), a hub for public and corporate computer training in the target market. While staff have had extensive experience in one-on-one and small group training, groups of 24 in-house "trainees" represents a new challenge. In order to professionally address these training needs, Jumpin' Java has contracted with a computer skills training company to provide the large-group training.

The management team realizes that throughout the launch phase, additional weaknesses may be exposed. As weaknesses become known, proper steps will be taken immediately to alleviate them before damage occurs.

Market Opportunities

Market opportunities are abundant, since Jumpin' Java is entering a new industry in an undeveloped market. The main opportunities facing Jumpin' Java are:

1. Young adults, ages 16-21, in the target market are looking for a place to "hang out" in a safe and fun environment. There are currently very few, if any, good locations for teens to meet with each other in the evenings and on weekends. They need and want an interesting environment where they can meet their friends, eat and drink together, and do something fun that is reasonably priced. Market surveys indicate a high interest level in a center like Jumpin' Java.

2. Eden Prairie Police and Schools strongly support Jumpin' Java. Numerous meetings with various government officials show a great need and desire for a center like Jumpin' Java. Reflecting the opportunity detailed in #1 above, adults also recognize the need for a safe public hang-out for target-area youth.

3. There is a growing interest in specialty coffee, and all indications are that demand will continue to grow.

4. There are few specialty coffee outlets in the target area. There is only limited competition for the gourmet coffee customer. With specific regard to morning drive traffic moving north on Flying Cloud Drive, and East on Anderson Lakes Parkway, Jumpin' Java will be the biggest, best, and most accessible specialty coffee location for miles.

5. Excitement is building for the new socialization/information/food outlet called the "cybercafe." Its popularity is growing, and the target market is ready for a new, exciting entrant.

6. The entire target area is experiencing rapid and unabating growth in population, housing, and jobs. Jumpin' Java can be one of the primary beneficiaries of this growth.

7. There is a growing need for unique solutions to corporate computer skills training requirements. Companies are discovering that they have invested tens of thousands or even hundreds of thousands of dollars in computer hardware and software, yet if their staff can't run the systems correctly, it's wasted money. These businesses are looking for creative and effective ways to train employees properly. Jumpin' Java can be that creative and effective way.

8. Individuals need and want computer training. Datatech is queried continuously by its customers about inexpensive large-group training. Jumpin' Java will fill that need.

9. Cue 'N You is a billiards and games center next door to Jumpin' Java. The owners are very interested in creating an alliance with Jumpin' Java to increase the young adult traffic for both businesses. Cue 'N You is busy, especially nights and weekends, but has limited ability to appeal to minors because of alcohol issues.

10. Current plans are for a 16-theater complex to be constructed on the south side of Anderson Lakes Parkway, directly across from Jumpin' Java. Discussions have already begun into ways that Jumpin' Java and the theater could run combination offers.

Market Threats

We currently see no specific and identifiable threats in the marketplace.

NEEDS ANALYSIS

Jumpin' Java has been developed as a business intended to meet customer needs. We believe that the market presents current opportunities based on unfilled needs (and wants) within the target customer groups detailed in the Target Market section. Specifically, the following are current unmet needs within the target groups:

1. There is a strong unfilled need for a safe teen and young-adult "hangout". This is a need that is voiced repeatedly throughout the target area.

2. There is an unfilled need for a high-quality ready-to-drink specialty coffee provider in the target area and within the target customer base.

3. There is an unfilled need for high-speed public computer access in the target area.

4.   There is an unfilled need in the target area for high-quality public and corporate large-group computer training.

PRODUCTS AND SERVICES

Any description of the products and services offered by Jumpin' Java must begin with the store itself. An examination of the floor plan demonstrates that Jumpin' Java will be an interesting and stimulating environment. All the senses will be engaged from the moment a person comes through the door. Visually, a spacious and beautifully designed cybercafe with comfortable chairs — a high-tech look, yet warm and inviting. For the ears, the sound of steam foaming milk for a smooth cappuccino or cafe mocha; quiet conversations in some corners, interactive multi-player computer gaming in others. Savor the invigorating aroma of the best coffees, freshly and properly brewed. Indulge in the satisfying flavor of sweet baked-this-morning pastries paired with a cup of your favorite gourmet tea. Unwind in the warmth of a cozy fire in the winter, and relax in air-conditioned comfort on a sweltering summer day. Just to step inside Jumpin' Java Cybercafe is to have experienced at least part of the "product" that is offered. Without spending a dime, a customer can enjoy the ambiance. But once inside, there are a number of delightful ways to spend not only time, but money as well.

Product and Service Description

All Jumpin' Java products and services have been designed and selected to meet customer needs. Everything presented for customer use is intended to enhance the overall experience — to make their visit to Jumpin' Java so enjoyable that a return trip, with friends, is inevitable. We will review the products and services in three separate subgroups: Coffee and Food Service, Public Computer Access, and the Technology Training Center.

Coffee and Food Service

As a cybercafe specializing in gourmet coffee, Jumpin' Java will prepare and serve a variety of high-quality hot and cold drinks, focusing on espresso-based coffee drinks and fine teas. Exceptional coffee is one of the two "twin tracks" that will make Jumpin' Java a success (the other is public computer access). The coffee service center-piece will be the espresso bar, and each barista will be trained to be technically excellent and dedicated to outstanding customer service. In addition, Jumpin' Java will use automated espresso makers in order to maximize consistency and reduce user error to virtually zero. Jumpin' Java management is fully aware that the business's future is on the line with each cup of coffee sold. Therefore, extreme care will be taken in the equipment purchased, in personnel recruitment and training, and in the selection of coffee and tea suppliers.

Specifically, the store will open with five different decaffeinated varieties and twelve regular coffee choices. These will be selected with the aid and advice of our coffee suppliers. Four or five different varieties per day will be brewed and ready at the coffee bar. Other varieties will be available as espresso drinks. All coffee varieties will be available in bulk for home brewers. Jumpin' Java may eventually roast coffee on premise to enhance ambiance, aroma, and atmosphere, but the coffee served at Jumpin' Java will be primarily, if not exclusively, roasted off premise. In addition, Jumpin' Java will carry eight to ten varieties of fine teas, again with the help of our suppliers. Iced drinks will be featured as well, especially in summer months, including Granita, Iced Tea, Iced Cappuccino, and Iced Coffees. Other cold drinks will include milk, a variety of juices, and fountain soft drinks.

As a business serving excellent products to an upscale customer, Jumpin' Java will offer top-quality fresh baked goods delivered each morning by Twin Cities Bakery. Twin Cities will supply a mix of morning pastries: muffins, coffee cake, croissants, etc., in regular and low-fat varieties. Twin Cities will also supply their award-winning cheesecakes and tortes. "After breakfast" food service will consist of a controlled menu of pre-made quality sandwiches, pastries, and gourmet chocolates from Something's Brewing, along with packaged snack and candy items. To top off the lunch, dinner and late-night food service, Jumpin' Java will proudly serve fresh pizza ordered and paid for at Jumpin' Java, and delivered seamlessly from Rosati's Pizza next door.

Gift and accessory items will include electric coffee mills, filter coffee makers and supplies, insulated carafes, tea kettles, espresso makers and supplies, mugs/cups/creamers/sugar bowls, etc.

Public Computer Access

This is the second of the "twin tracks" that are vital to success. Jumpin' Java will be the largest cybercafe in the State of Minnesota, and one of the top ten in the entire country. Fifty-five eventual terminals, each of them with T-1 internet service, will beckon computer users to surf at speeds they've never experienced before. (For the uninitiated, T-1 lines are direct server lines — not phone lines — that deliver the internet directly to the computer at speeds up to hundreds of times faster than a modem!) Computers will be everywhere — some will be singles at desks or in quiet corners; some will be set as "doubles" for one-on-one computer gaming; others arranged as "quads" for the most exciting multi-player technogaming available anywhere in the world!

We expect computer utilization to be divided into three primary groups — Student/Business Applications; Casual Internet Surfing; and Computer Gaming. There will be superior hardware and software for each type of user, as follows:

- Since high-tech, high-speed gaming requires the fastest and most efficient computer technology, Jumpin' Java will initiate service with three specially designed gaming "pods" of four computers each, 12 computers total. Each of the twelve gaming positions will be equipped with hardware and software specifically created for the most elaborate and complicated computer gaming. These systems will inspire awe in each "gamer" who grabs the joystick. Full details of these systems is included in the Supporting Documents. Two additional pods of four systems each will be added as required.

- In addition to the gaming systems detailed above, Jumpin' Java will initiate operations with eight "base systems"; fully equipped and lightning fast state-of-the-art desk-top computers. These eight base systems will be scattered throughout Jumpin' Java in singles and doubles, and will be used primarily for internet access and business/student use. Current plans call for an additional five notebook computers to be mounted to the coffee bar as business grows. Complete details are available in the Supporting Documents. *(Editor's note: supporting documents are not reproduced.)*

- Laser and color printing will be available, along with fax service, a high-speed copier, and a limited variety of supplies such as special papers, pens, markers, etc.

- Individual e-mail accounts will be available.

Technology Training Center

Incorporated into this exciting and engaging cybercafe setting is the Technology Training Center (TTC), a state-of-the-art computer training classroom initially equipped with 19 networked computer terminals (18 for student use plus one for the instructor). Each terminal will be loaded with the latest interactive teaching software and all of the peripheral equipment needed to provide cutting-edge technology training. A glance at the floor plan reveals the care that has been taken in the design of this facility, including a color projection system for the instructor's terminal. Learning will be facilitated by having the right hardware, the right software, the right furnishings and layout, and the right setting — the friendly and intellectually stimulating environment of Jumpin' Java Cybercafe. The design of the TTC anticipates expansion to 24 student stations as utilization requires.

The TTC will offer two basic types of classroom training: 1) Private classes for groups of corporate employees. These may be companies which have purchased systems from Datatech and need large-group training, or other customers which need large-group training. 2) Public training classes provided at appropriate times covering a variety of topics. Individuals will register for various classes held in the TTC. A current list of classes is included in the Supporting Documents. *(Editor's note: supporting documents have not been reproduced).*

A variant on the normal "adult" technology training is the possibility of using the TTC as a site for children's' technology parties. Jumpin' Java is exploring this avenue for certain evening and weekend morning hours.

Competitive Comparison

Jumpin' Java Cybercafe will have competition in all three of its major product offering areas; specialty coffee cafe, public computer access, and corporate computer training. Each competitor has worked hard to build a business based on a unique selling advantage, a new and different angle, or a geographical superiority. Likewise, Jumpin' Java will have competitive advantages over others in the market. In fact, we believe that Jumpin' Java will have such overwhelming advantages in what it offers to customers, compared to the offerings of the competition, that current and future competitors will be hard pressed to compete for market share. Jumpin' Java intends to establish a new definition of "cybercafe" in Minnesota, and to maintain its position as the market leader. Compared to the competition, Jumpin' Java is:

- Newer. It's the newest.

- Bigger. There's nothing else even close.

- Faster. The fastest computer connections around.

- More Exciting. The newest games, the best networking.

- More Innovative. Contests and promotions to drive interest.

- Better Tasting. Only the best coffee, correctly brewed, plus great food.

- Easier to Find. Located at one of the best-known intersections in SW Hennepin County.

Sourcing

We will address sourcing of products and services in the three primary product groups, Coffee and Food Service, Public Computer Access; and Technology Training Center.

Coffee and Food Service Sourcing

All coffee and food vendors have been selected with great attention to quality and service. Each of the following suppliers has demonstrated that they have the ability to provide outstanding products, exemplary service, and responsible pricing.

1. Coffees and Teas.

    — Cappuccino Pronto. A maker of espresso machines and fine coffees.

    — Wisconsin Micro Roaster. Offers some of the finest bulk and retail packaged coffees in the Midwest.

-23-

— Coffee Masters. A Minnetonka-based supplier of a complete line of fine coffees, teas, equipment, supplies and accessories.

— Alterra Coffee Co.

— Shangri-La. A wholesaler of fine iced teas in a multitude of flavors.

2. Food.

— Something's Brewing. An Eden Prairie-based retail specialty coffeehouse and maker of fine pastries, sandwiches, and chocolate candies.

— Twin Cities Bakery. A Minneapolis company which creates some of the best cheesecakes and tortes known to mankind.

— Rosati's Pizza. Next door to Jumpin' Java, Rosati's will deliver pizza directly to Jumpin' Java customers through the building service corridor.

— Cold drinks. Fountain service is being bid by Coke and Pepsi.

— Snacks and chip service will be provided by Frito-Lay.

— Consumable supplies, e.g. cups, plates, utensils, napkins, etc., will be supplied by Sysco.

Catalogs, brochures, and/or agreements from each of these suppliers is included in the Supporting Documents. *(Editor's note: supporting documents have not been reproduced).*

Public Computer Access Sourcing

All computer hardware and software will be supplied by Datatech, Inc.

Jumpin' Java is interested in using free hardware and software sponsored by the various manufacturers. In return for free publicity and use in one of the largest cybercafes in the United States, manufacturers would provide their newest products for showcasing in Jumpin' Java. Contact has been made with the manufacturers of the hardware and software products which will be used in the gaming systems and the base systems. Initial response has been extremely favorable.

Internet T-1 line support is being provided through a joint-venture with Techramp, a St. Paul-based internet access provider. The agreement between Jumpin' Java and Techramp is included in the Supporting Documents. *(Editor's note: supporting documents have not been reproduced).*

Technology Training Center Sourcing

All classroom training will be conducted by independent subcontractors. Jumpin' Java is currently in negotiations with companies which wish to provide this service.

-24-

Future Services

Future services will be dictated by customer demand.

- Current expectations are that the gaming portion of the business will grow rapidly to include organized competition, league play, tournaments, 24-hour "game-a-thons", etc.

- The Technology Training Center should also experience substantial growth, and this growth will spur new product development.

- Coffee and Food service will adjust and expand as demand builds.

MARKETING PLAN

The presentation of the Marketing Plan for Jumpin' Java Cybercafe will use the four-factor classification system popularized by McCarthy, The Four P's of Marketing — Product, Price, Place (Distribution), and Promotion.

Product

As reviewed in detail in the Products and Services description, Jumpin' Java is to be a wonderful blend of high-tech computerization with the relaxed atmosphere of a traditional coffeehouse. Throughout the experience, customers will enjoy the very finest products and services available. In all three key areas — Coffee and Food Service, Public Computer Access, and the Technology Training Center — quality will be the order of the day. There is no more effective marketing tool than a superior product or service. In every phase of operation, in every product selection, in each personnel decision, Jumpin' Java will focus on Quality. All employees will be trained and retrained to fulfill their responsibilities flawlessly and with impeccable customer service. Jumpin' Java will constantly be searching for new ways to please our customers.

Price

Pricing for each of the three primary areas will be reviewed individually.

Coffee and Food Service Pricing

Coffee and Food Service will be priced slightly higher than surrounding coffeehouse competition. Price lists from three competitors — Connie's Internet Cafe, A Special Cup, and Something's Brewing — have been utilized to establish initial prices.

1. Hot Drinks, 12 oz. and 16 oz.

   — Drip-brewed coffees-of-the-day; $1.20 and $1.40.

   — Cafe Americano; $1.60 and $1.90.

   — Hot Chocolate; $1.70 and $2.25.

   — Cafe Latte; $2.30 and $2.75.

   — Cappuccino; $2.30 and $2.75.

   — Cafe Mocha; $2.60 and $2.90.

   — Teas; $1.20 and $1.40.

2. Cold Drinks, 16 oz.

   — Soda; $1.00.

   — Milk; $1.20.

   — Bottled Water; $1.20.

   — Bottled Juices; $1.20.

3. Baked Goods.

   — Brownies; $1.00.

   — Bagels; $1.00.

   — Giant Cookies; $1.20.

   — Muffins; $1.40.

   — Biscotti; $2.00.

   — Eclairs; $2.50.

   — Cheesecake; $2.75.

   — Tortes; $2.75.

4. Sandwiches. A pre-made fresh selection each day will include a variety of breads, meats, and cheeses. All condiments will be available at the food service bar.

   — Full Sandwich; $3.75.

   — Half Sandwich; $2.75.

5. Pizza.

— One topping; $3.50.

— Two toppings; $3.75.

— Three toppings; $4.00.

6. Other.

— Chips; $.80.

— Candy; $.80.

Public Computer Access Pricing

All public computer access will be priced at sixteen cents per minute, $9.60 per hour. There will be no differentiation between gaming terminals and base terminals, nor will there be any differentiation based on how the computer is used. The cost is the same whether the customer is gaming, typing a report, or doing an online search. While this may seem unusual based on the different costs of providing different types of service, flat pricing will be much more customer-friendly than a tiered pricing system.

- Laser printing, $.40 per page.

- Color inkjet printing, $1.25 per page.

- Photocopying, $.15 per page.

- Fax service, $1.00 per page outbound; $.50 per page inbound.

- Volume discounts will be available on printing and faxing services.

- E-mail accounts, $5.00 per month.

- Miscellaneous supplies such as paper, markers, highlighters, etc. will be available at full markup.

All computers, printers, and copiers will be activated by an online magnetic card swipe system mounted to each unit. Customers will purchase and add value to their cards at the service desk. Payment will be made by cash, check, Visa, Mastercard, or Discover. A full service cash machine will be located in the store.

Technology Training Center Pricing

Training prices will be divided into two segments — Public Groups and Private Groups.

-27-

- Public Groups. As detailed in the Products and Services description, public training classes will be held on an ongoing basis. Generally, classes will be either 1 hour, priced at $19.95; or 2 1/2 hours long, priced at $49.95. Advanced classes are being developed which will be priced at $79.95.

- Private Groups. Companies will pay for professional training at a 20% discount from the public rate. Custom training programs will be available. Children's' parties will pay a "Party Pack" price of $14.95 per child for a 30-minute training session, an additional 30 minutes of computer time, and then pizza and soda in the Jumpin' Java Conference Room. Groups will be limited to ten children. Another option for large groups is to rent the TTC alone (no trainer) for $135 per hour. The Ultimate Computer Bash is also available — rent all of Jumpin' Java for a private party for just $275 per hour!

Place (Distribution)

Obviously, all products and services will be delivered at Jumpin' Java's location in Eden Prairie. While Jumpin' Java cannot take its ambiance, products, and services "on the road", there is a way to significantly differentiate Jumpin' Java distribution patterns from those of all the competition — hours of operation. In order to accommodate the lifestyle and daily living patterns of young people in high school, college, and young adulthood, Jumpin' Java will maintain the following hours:

- 7 a.m. to 1 a.m. Monday through Thursday.

- 7 a.m. to 2 a.m. Friday.

- 7 a.m. to 2 a.m. Saturday.

- 7 a.m. to 1 a.m. Sunday.

These hours of operation will enable Jumpin' Java to become the night and weekend "hangout" that the youth of SW Hennepin County are so desperately waiting for. If research shows that morning drive traffic is sufficient to warrant an earlier opening time on weekdays, that will be done as well.

Promotion

We will divide the review of Jumpin' Java's promotional plan into its four distinct variables: Advertising, Sales Promotion, Public Relations, and Personal Selling. In addition, we outline the Launch Promotional Plan.

-28-

Advertising

Advertising consists of nonpersonal or one-way forms of communication conducted through paid media under clear sponsorship. Jumpin' Java's advertising campaign will be designed for and aimed at the target market as defined in the Target Market section, above: local residents, Eden Prairie Shopping Center patrons and employees, HCCC students and faculty, target-area high school students and faculty, daytime commuters, and SW Hennepin County businesses.

For the purposes of advertising, the target customer groups have been divided into "adult public," "non-adult public," and "business." The advertising objectives and key messages for each include:

1. Adult public.

    — Inform about what a "cybercafe" is.

    — Inform of Jumpin' Java, a new specialty-coffee cybercafe at Flying Cloud Drive and Anderson Lakes Parkway.

    — Inform that Jumpin' Java is the biggest and best cybercafe in the state.

    — Persuade that Jumpin' Java has the best coffee, best computers, and best atmosphere.

    — Persuade that Jumpin' Java is so different that it is worth a visit.

    — Give a reason to visit NOW.

2. Non-adult public.

    — Lament the lack of local hangouts.

    — Inform of Jumpin' Java, a new hangout designed specifically for them.

    — Inform of specialty coffee, sandwiches, pizza.

    — Inform of high-tech, "way cool" computer stuff.

    — Inform of late night hours just for them.

    — Persuade that Jumpin' Java is the new place to be.

    — Give a reason to visit NOW.

3. Businesses.

    — Inform of the new Technology Training Center.

-29-

— Inform of the size and capabilities.

— Inform of services available.

— Give way to get more information.

— Give reason to contact NOW.

With the advertising objectives and key messages established, the question turns to the selection of specific advertising vehicles. Jumpin' Java plans to use the following vehicles to accomplish its advertising objectives:

1. Print advertisements. Plainsman Press, Eden Prairie Review, Twin Cities Bulletin, Market Journal, Advertiser, HCCC in-house paper, high school in-house papers.

2. Broadcast advertisements. Radio spots on adult and youth stations, KFMC and KXLC.

3. Direct mail. Consideration is being given to a series of direct mail pieces for target households.

4. Posters and leaflets. These will be used to reach HCCC and high school students and faculty, as well as Eden Prairie Shopping Center shoppers and employees.

5. Billboards/display Signs. Investigation is underway regarding the placement of roadside billboards in the target area. In addition, investigation is planned with regard to the placement of display signs inside HCCC and target area high schools.

6. Jumpin' Java's Internet homepage. Currently under construction, the homepage will be the cyberspace version of the real thing.

7. On-screen advertising. Patrons using Jumpin' Java terminals will see randomly spaced advertisements for Jumpin' Java products and services.

Sales Promotion

Sales promotion consists of a diverse group of short-term incentive tools designed to stimulate quicker and/or greater purchases of a product or service by customers. In contrast to Advertising, which offers a REASON to buy, Sales Promotion offers an INCENTIVE to buy. Jumpin' Java has designed its sales promotion program around the lifestyle, needs, and wants of its target customers. Current plans call for the use of the following sales promotion vehicles:

1. Couponing. Jumpin' Java will make extensive use of discount coupons and "package" coupons with HCCC and high school students. Package coupons will provide discounts on the combined purchase of computer time and food/beverage items, and coupons will be available offering simple time volume discounts.

2. Gaming Tournaments. These will be tournaments sponsored by Jumpin' Java which will take various forms. Some will be ongoing over weeks or months; others will be short-term events over several hours, or 24-hour marathons.

3. Competition between opposing high school teams is a possibility, as is competition between the Jumpin' Java team and other cybercafe teams.

4. Sampling. Free samples of computer time and coffee products may be used during non-peak hours or with certain target groups.

5. Demonstrations. The TTC will be used for no-charge technology demonstrations during non-peak hours.

6. Live Entertainment. Consideration is being given to sponsoring live entertainment in the lounge area during evening and night hours.

7. Tie-ins. A multitude of options are available for tie-ins with other area businesses, and Jumpin' Java will make the best of them. Current targets for tie-in promotion partners include McDonald's, Walgreens, Cue 'N You, Shell gasoline, theaters, and Rosati's Pizza.

8. Gift Certificates. These will be available to be used for any product or service in the store, including training classes.

Public Relations

Marketing Public Relations is an often misunderstood part of the marketing mix. Marketing PR involves securing editorial space, as differentiated from paid space, in all media read, viewed, or heard by a company's customers or prospects, for the specific purpose of assisting in the achievement of sales goals.

Jumpin' Java will use a number of publicity tactics, including:

1. Marketing Plan Contests at HCCC and 5 target-area high schools. The staff and students of these schools are key target customers. Each of these schools has classes in business and or marketing. Each of these schools has at least one teacher/professor who is creative, realistic, and eager to give their students a REAL educational experience. What Jumpin' Java will do is partner with one teacher (or more) in each institution to create a class project which will consist of developing a marketing plan for Jumpin' Java, specifically with regard to the staff and students of that school. This may develop into a contest within a school or between schools.

-31-

Awards/Grants/Endowments/Prizes will be developed to reward each contributing school/class/individual, etc. (the details will be worked through as the project unfolds). Each participating class will conduct their class time in the Technology Training Center, and will use Jumpin' Java's hardware and software resources to build their plans. The publicity opportunities presented by this type of promotion are almost endless:

— Newspaper editorials about the marketing plan contest, including Jumpin' Java as the sponsor.

— Strong marketing impact within the staff and faculty of each participating school.

— Strong marketing impact within the student body of each participating school.

— Newspaper editorials w/pictures to introduce the winning team(s).

— Student assistance in implementing the plan elements.

— Radio interviews with winning student teams and Jumpin' Java management.

— Students can earn "extra credit" by creating publicity events.

— Managed properly, this could become an annual event in each school.

2. News. By the nature of its size and novelty, Jumpin' Java is perfectly suited to create newsworthy material. We will carefully and promptly notify the area press of special events and ongoing programming. In fact, a number of events will be designed specifically with their "publicity value" in mind. In fact, the news of Jumpin' Java is already newsworthy — the May 8, 1997 edition of the Plainsman Press ran a story on cybercafes which makes substantial mention of Jumpin' Java's planned opening in 1997.

3. Events. As noted in the previous section on sales promotion, Jumpin' Java will sponsor ongoing and special gaming tournaments. These are perfect vehicles for generating press attention, and we will be sure that the media is aware of each event.

4. Public Service Activities. Jumpin' Java will work to maximize its public image by contributing cash, products, and/or services to worthwhile causes.

Personal Selling

Personal Selling consists of an oral presentation in a conversation with one or more prospective purchasers for the purpose of making sales.

-32-

The high cost of including Personal Selling in the marketing mix makes it more appropriate for high-ticket items, and less appropriate for low-ticket items. While Personal Selling may not be the most frequently used tool in Jumpin' Java's marketing plan, there are two specific areas where it will be highly valued.

First, personal selling will be used in the marketing of the Technology Training Center (TTC) to corporate customers. Ethan and Dan will head up this effort.

Second, there may be opportunity for large-group sales presentations to students and/or faculty at HCCC and the five target-area high schools. This is under investigation.

Launch Promotional Plan

The opening of Jumpin' Java Cybercafe will be big — VERY BIG! A business concept as new and different as Jumpin' Java deserves a launch equally new and different. Exceptional effort has been put into the launch plan, and it will instantly put Jumpin' Java into the forefront of the minds of target area consumers.

1. Pre-opening "Intro Nights". These will be conducted during the week prior to opening and will be conducted on four consecutive evenings for four specific groups; HCCC faculty and staff; target area high school faculty and staff; Eden Prairie Shopping Center store owners and employees; and target area parents. Each Intro Night will feature all menu items and unlimited computer use, all at no charge.

2. Pre-opening newspaper ads. These will be teaser ads placed in local papers.

3. Grand Opening Extravaganza. The BIG opening weekend bash, including:

    — Open 60 hours non-stop — noon Friday until midnight Sunday night.

    — Newspaper ads in all local papers, Friday, Saturday, and Sunday.

    — Targeted radio ads, Friday, Saturday, and Sunday.

    — Two full-day live radio remote broadcasts; one on KFMC for adults, the other on KXLC for non-adults.

    — Daytime full-sized hot air balloon in the parking lot, labeled "Jumpin' Java Cybercafe".

    — Nighttime "Hollywood-style" searchlights scanning the sky.

    — Free samples of brewed coffees, sponsored by Alterra's.

    — Free pizza buffets during live broadcasts, sponsored by Rosati's Pizza.

-33-

— Mascot Model Contest. During the Extravaganza, customers will be able to audition to be the model for the official store mascot, "Jumpin' Java". The winning model will receive 100 hours of free computer time at Jumpin' Java.

— Registration for prizes. Winners to be drawn at the close of the 60-hour Extravaganza. Grand Prize, a complete computer gaming system just like those in the Jumpin' Java gaming pods; Second Prize, 100 hours of Jumpin' Java computer time; Third Prize, 10 hours of free Jumpin' Java computer time.

MANAGEMENT SUMMARY

At launch, Jumpin' Java Cybercafe will be directed by a senior management team consisting of the President, Executive Vice President, and Food Service Manager, as follows:

President, Ethan Stanley. As President of Jumpin' Java, Ethan will take the leadership role in conceptual issues, strategy, and finance. Ethan comes to Jumpin' Java with an exceptional background in establishing and growing businesses. At the University of Minnesota School of Technology, Ethan led the Entrepreneurial Technology Team to a National Championship in the 1994 New Product Development category. His vision and leadership have been a vital contributor to the success of his current project, Datatech, Inc., which he helped found in 1995. As a result of an unusual agreement with Datatech which enables him to reduce his Datatech workload to only 30 hours per week, Ethan will be able to devote roughly 30 hours per week to Jumpin' Java responsibilities. A business biography of Ethan is located in the Supporting Documents. *(Editor's note: supporting documents have not been reproduced.)*

Executive Vice President, Dan Victor. Dan spent 10 years operating his own business as a computer systems builder and integrator. Throughout his career, Dan has demonstrated the ability to effectively manage in a retail setting, and has dealt expertly with sales, personnel selection and development, cash management, scheduling, cost control, merchandising and store appearance, etc. Dan has extraordinary expertise in assembling, networking, and maintaining computer hardware and software. Dan will have day-to-day responsibility for ongoing operations at Jumpin' Java, and will devote 100% of his effort to those responsibilities. A resume and job description is included in the Supporting Documents.

Food Service Manager, Carolyn Schwartz. Carolyn joins Jumpin' Java directly from a Chicago-area Starbucks Coffee, where she had been Store Manager for two years. Carolyn brings obvious expertise in the food service arena — expertise that neither Ethan nor Dan has.

Carolyn will have responsibility for all aspects of food and beverage. This includes menu selection, procurement, pricing, preparation, equipment maintenance, etc. Carolyn's resume and job description may be found in the Supporting Documents.

OPERATIONS

Jumpin' Java Cybercafe is located in a single-store building at 3200 East Flying Cloud Drive, adjacent to Eden Prairie Shopping Center, an established and nearly fully occupied shopping center on the northeast corner of the busy intersection of Flying Cloud Drive and Anderson Lakes Parkway. As noted in the section regarding the target market, this location puts Jumpin' Java on the path of some 300,000 motorists daily.

The store is comprised of 4800 sq. ft., with a capacity of 200 people, divided as follows:

- Customer Seating, Computer and Gaming Stations, Food Service, and Office: 2400 sq. ft.

- Technology Training Center: 600 sq. ft.

- Rest Rooms, Storage and Computer Server Rooms: 1000 sq. ft.

- Executive Offices and Conference Room: 800 sq. ft.

The negotiated lease calls for the first four months free, with subsequent 12-month periods at the following monthly rates:

- Year 1 — $4,188 per month.

- Year 2 — $5,400 per month.

- Year 3 — $6,100 per month.

- Year 4 — $7,800 per month.

- Year 5 — $10,400 per month.

The buildout for Jumpin' Java by the leaseholder, Income Properties, is nearly complete, at a cost of $40,000. This expense will be paid by Jumpin' Java as follows: 25% will be paid at completion, with the remaining 75% to be paid over the life of the 5-year lease at 10% annual interest. A copy of the floor plan and the lease and buildout agreement is included in the Supporting Documents *(editor's note: the supporting documents have not been reproduced)*.

Staffing and Production

The nature of Jumpin' Java Cybercafe demands personnel with two vital and specific abilities — technological expertise to work with computer gamers, internet users, and computer novices; and the capacity to staff the food service counter expertly and prepare a perfect espresso-based drink. While these two abilities may seem difficult to merge into one person, we at Jumpin' Java intend to do just that.

Each Jumpin' Java staffer will be trained to be able to perform all of the basic functions needed by customers. In other words, every person on the floor will be prepared to answer hardware and software questions, be able to flawlessly brew a cafe mocha or latte, know how to serve sandwiches and soda, and be prepared to show customers how to use the printers and copier, all within any given 5-minute period of time. Recruitment of capable people is essential, and is already underway.

Table 3: Personnel Plan			
	FY1998	**FY1999**	**FY2000**
Ethan Stanley	$ 42,000	$ 43,680	$ 45,430
Dan Victor	$ 38,004	$ 39,520	$ 41,110
Carolyn Schwartz	$ 27,996	$ 29,120	$ 30,280
Asst. Mgr. 1	$ 13,308	$ 13,840	$ 14,390
Asst. Mgr. 2	$ 13,308	$ 13,840	$ 14,390
Asst. Mgr. 3	$ 12,480	$ 12,980	$ 13,500
Asst. Mgr. 4	$ 11,748	$ 12,220	$ 12,710
C.S.A. 1	$ 10,752	$ 11,180	$ 11,630
C.S.A. 2	$ 10,752	$ 11,180	$ 11,630
C.S.A. 3	$ 10,752	$ 11,180	$ 11,630
C.S.A. 4	$ 10,752	$ 11,180	$ 11,630
C.S.A. 5	$ 10,080	$ 10,480	$ 10,900
C.S.A. 6	$ 10,080	$ 10,480	$ 10,900
C.S.A. 7	$ 7,728	$ 8,040	$ 8,360
C.S.A. 8	$ 7,728	$ 8,040	$ 8,360
C.S.A. 9	$ 5,152	$ 8,040	$ 8,360
C.S.A. 10	$ 3,220	$ 8,040	$ 8,360
Other	$ 0	$ 0	$ 0
Subtotal	$245,840	$263,040	$273,570

Current plans call for two levels of personnel in addition to the Senior Managers (SMs) introduced in the Management section. Four Assistant Managers (AMs) will provide 1st level supervision for the store. Eight Customer Service Associates (CSAs) will provide the primary coverage of the food service counter and the technology areas.

Initial staffing schedules call for a minimum of one manager to be on the floor at all times (either an SM or an AM), and a minimum of one CSA to be on the floor at all times. A review of the staffing and annual salary schedule appears above in Table 3; a full review appears in the appendix.

Inventory Control

The Executive Vice President is responsible for all technology-related inventory, equipment, and supplies. The Food Service Manager is responsible for all food service inventory, equipment ,and supplies.

Each manager will establish minimum stock, maximum stock, and reorder points for each line item. These points will be developed in consultation with the respective supplier and experience. A just-in-time inventory system will be the result of careful planning and constant care.

Customer Service and Order Fulfillment

When a customer enters Jumpin' Java, a welcome sign will direct him to proceed to the service counter. There, a CSA will introduce themselves and explain the products, services and procedures. The customer's needs will be handled promptly and professionally. Food service will be handled at the service counter, and any technology needs will be dealt with either at the counter or at the computer stations. Customers will receive instructions regarding the use of all systems.

All computers, printers and copiers will be activated by an online magnetic debit card swipe system mounted to each unit. Customers will purchase and add value to their cards at the service desk. Payment will be made by cash, check, Visa, Mastercard, or Discover. The use of an electronic debit system of this type has inherent profit potential — all usage is prepaid, and statistics indicate that 12-15% of "purchased time" is never used. A full service ATM machine will be located in the store.

Research and Development

Jumpin' Java is a cutting-edge business. As such, it will be an absolute necessity to be constantly searching for new and better ways of serving customer needs, new technologies, new ways of serving customers. The most obvious area where R&D will dominate is with regard to computer technology. The fact that Jumpin' Java's President and Executive Vice President are also computer assembly experts creates an avenue for constant inflow of new technology.

Risk Management

We have conducted a thorough analysis of the various risks associated with the operation of Jumpin' Java Cybercafe, and have taken the following actions to minimize and/or cover our exposure to these specific risks:

1. Fire, theft, robbery, vandalism. A business insurance policy has been secured which provides replacement-cost coverage for all assets. This policy includes coverage of fixed costs during rebuilding from a catastrophic loss for up to six months.

2. Personal injury liability. Included in the policy above, with $5 million total liability coverage.

3. All software, accounting data, and customer account data will be backed up on zip-drives and stored off-site.

4. Computer virus scans. Due to our constant internet use, and the networking of all Jumpin' Java hardware, virus scans will be conducted daily to identify and eliminate any damaging viruses.

FINANCIAL PLAN

The company anticipates rapid acceptance of Jumpin' Java in the marketplace, with first year revenues of $744,000, growing to $900,000 in FY 2000.

Important Assumptions

The following assumptions are used throughout the financial statements:

- Short-term interest rate, 11%

- Long-term interest rate, 10%

- Payment days, 30

- Inventory turnover, 50/year

- Tax rate, 0%. Profit is passed through to the owners.

- No sales on credit.

- Personnel burden, 15%

Breakeven Analysis

To evaluate our breakeven point as detailed below, we have used the "average" customer — one hour of computer time @ $9.60; one and one-half beverages @ $2.00 = $3.00; and two-thirds food item @ $2.50 = $1.67; for a grand total of $14.27 spent per average customer. Costs are $.60 for beverage, and $1.00 for food.

Monthly fixed costs have been estimated at $39,307, the Total Operating Expenses for each of the initial four months, including depreciation at the rate necessary to fully depreciate all computer hardware in just 12 months.

Using these projections, the breakeven point for Jumpin' Java is 3,102 average customers per month, or about 100 per day. Projected customer load is 3,750 average customers per month, 20% above the breakeven point.

Table 4: Breakeven Analysis	
Monthly units breakeven	3,102
Monthly sales breakeven	$44,271
Assumptions	
Average unit sale	$14.27
Average per-unit cost	$1.60
Fixed cost	$39,307

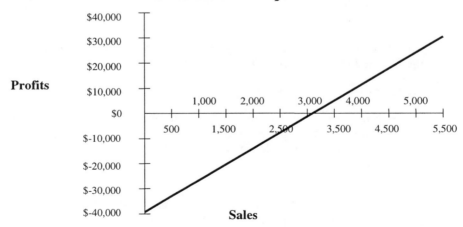

Breakeven Analysis

Projected Sales

Sales projections for Jumpin' Java have been based on aggressively pursuing and capturing the young adult market. The establishment of Jumpin' Java as THE Southwest Hennepin County young adult hangout will drive sales of computer time and food/beverage.

All sales projections are centered on the utilization of the computer terminals, and we have developed detailed utilization projections for all system terminals. The following review includes the basic concepts of the forecasting:

1. Computer Station Utilization Forecast.

   — Two stations will be used full-time during the weekday 2-hour morning drive.

   — Eight stations will be used full-time during the weekday 3-hour lunch window.

   — Sixteen stations will be used full-time during evening and night hours each day.

   — Two stations will be used full-time at all other times.

This rate of use generates 3,750 hours of use per month, at $9.60 per hour, for a monthly total revenue from computer utilization of $36,000. 3,750 use hours per month is 20% higher than breakeven. In addition, these forecasts DO NOT include use of the Technology Training Center (TTC) computer stations. TTC stations will be open for public use any time there is not a training class in session.

2. The forecast calls for an additional gaming pod to be opened in January '98, and the final pod to open in April '98.

3. We forecast a 20% "summer slump" in the months of June, July and August.

4. For each hour of computer time sold, we forecast 1.5 beverage sales @ $2.00 average purchase. The sales projections include ONLY beverages purchased in relation to computer use. That is, all "walk-in" beverage traffic will create sales beyond those included in the projections.

5. For each hour of computer time sold, we forecast two-thirds of a food purchase (one purchase every 1.5 hours) @ $2.50 average purchase. As in the case of beverage forecasts, the sales projections include ONLY food items purchased in relation to computer use.

6. The forecast calls for a conservative 60 TTC students per week @ $30 per student.

7. Sales of bulk coffee, gifts, and miscellaneous items are forecast to be 5% of combined food and beverage sales.

8. Sales in year two and three are projected to grow 10% per year.

9. The "average" customer will purchase one hour of computer time per visit, one and one-half beverages, and two-thirds of a food item.

The following chart and table indicate the first year sales projections. Full details are in the appendix.

Table 5: Sales Forecast			
Sales	**FY1998**	**FY1999**	**FY2000**
Computer Time	$439,400	$483,340	$531,670
Beverage	$131,820	$145,000	$159,500
Food	$74,720	$82,190	$90,410
Training Center	$87,880	$96,670	$106,330
Other	$10,410	$11,450	$12,600
Total Sales	$744,230	$818,650	$900,510
Cost of Sales:			
Computer Time	$0	$0	$0
Beverage	$22,590	$24,850	$27,330
Food	$44,910	$49,400	$54,340
Training Center	$43,940	$48,330	$53,170
Other	$6,230	$6,850	$7,540
Total Cost of Sales	$117,670	$129,430	$142,380

Total Sales by Month in Year 1

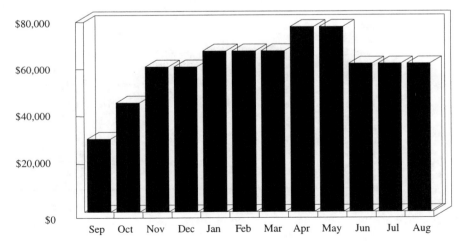

Projected Profit and Loss

The projections call for gross margin and net profit as shown in the accompanying chart, and Table 6 includes annual totals. Complete details are in the Appendix. Cost of Goods Sold as a percentage of Sales is as follows:

- Computer Time   0%.

- Beverage   20%.

- Food   60%.

- Training Center   50%.

- Other   60%.

Table 6: Pro-forma Income Statement			
	FY1998	**FY1999**	**FY2000**
Sales	$744,230	$818,650	$900,510
Direct Cost of Sales	$117,670	$129,430	$142,380
Other	$0	$0	$0
Total Cost of Sales	$117,670	$129,430	$142,380
Gross Margin	$626,560	$689,220	$758,130
Gross Margin Percent	84.19%	84.19%	84.19%
Operating Expenses:			
Advertising/Promotion	$12,000	$13,200	$14,520
Phone	$2,400	$2,640	$2,900
T-1 Line	$12,000	$13,200	$14,520
On-Line Subscriptions	$1,200	$1,320	$1,450
Other	$0	$0	$0
Payroll Expense	$245,840	$263,040	$273,570
Leased Equipment	$0	$0	$0
Utilities	$36,000	$39,600	$43,560
Insurance	$3,000	$3,300	$3,630
Rent	$33,504	$59,950	$70,400
Depreciation	$132,500	$132,500	$132,500
Payroll Burden	$36,876	$39,456	$41,036
Contract/Consultants	$0	$0	$0
Other	$0	$0	$0
Total Operating Expenses	$515,320	$568,206	$598,086
Profit Before Interest and Taxes	$111,240	$121,014	$160,045
Interest Expense ST	$3,388	$5,082	$5,082
Interest Expense LT	$29,407	$53,065	$61,024
Taxes Incurred	$0	$0	$0
Net Profit	$78,445	$62,867	$93,938
Net Profit/Sales	10.54%	7.68%	10.43%

In addition, please note that all computer hardware is being depreciated in just one year. This aggressive posture is being used for two primary reasons: 1) The hardware will be used intensely by generally young non-owners (who may not use adequate care) in a setting including food and beverage items. Accidents will happen, and equipment wears out. 2) A primary draw of Jumpin' Java is that it maintains the absolute top-of-the-line hardware and software. In order to keep up, we will have to rotate new equipment into the operation continuously after year 1. Despite this very rapid depreciation, we expect that Jumpin' Java will make an operating profit beginning in month 2.

Business Plan Highlights

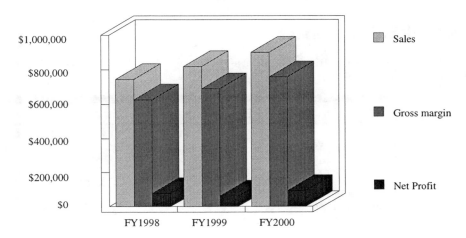

Projected Cash Flow

Cash flow projections are shown graphically in the chart and table below. Detailed projections appear in the appendix.

Table 7: Pro-Forma Cash Flow			
	FY1998	**FY1999**	**FY2000**
Net Profit:	$78,445	$62,867	$93,938
Plus:			
Depreciation	$132,500	$132,500	$132,500
Change in Accounts Payable	$30,083	$3,853	$2,638
Current Borrowing (Repayment)	$0	$0	$0
Increase (Decrease) Other Liabilities	$0	$0	$0
Long-Term Borrowing (Repayment)	$53,064	$53,064	$53,064
Capital Input	$0	$0	$0
Subtotal	$294,093	$252,285	$282,141

-43-

Less:			
Change in Accounts Receivable	$0	$0	$0
Change in Inventory	($2,559)	$244	$269
Change in Other ST Assets	$0	$0	$0
Capital Expenditure	$0	$0	$0
Dividends	$0	$0	$0
Subtotal	($2,559)	$244	$269
Net Cash Flow	$296,652	$252,041	$281,872
Cash Balance	$356,652	$608,693	$890,564

Projected Balance Sheet

Table 8 presents annual Balance Sheet projections. The complete projected balance sheet appears in the appendix.

Table 8: Pro-forma Balance Sheet			
	FY1998	**FY1999**	**FY2000**
Short-Term Assets			
Cash	$356,652	$608,693	$890,564
Accounts Receivable	$0	$0	$0
Inventory	$2,441	$2,685	$2,953
Other Short-Term Assets	$300	$300	$300
Total Short-Term Assets	$359,393	$611,677	$893,818
Long-Term Assets			
Capital Assets	$265,325	$265,325	$265,325
Accumulated Depreciation	$132,500	$265,000	$397,500
Total Long-Term Assets	$132,825	$325	($132,175)
Total Assets	$492,218	$612,002	$761,643
Debt and Equity			
Accounts Payable	$30,083	$33,937	$36,575
Short-Term Notes	$30,800	$30,800	$30,800
Other ST Liabilities	$0	$0	$0
Subtotal Short-Term Liabilities	$60,883	$64,737	$67,375
Long-Term Liabilities	$318,389	$371,453	$424,517
Total Liabilities	$379,272	$436,190	$491,892
Paid-In Capital	$100,000	$100,000	$100,000
Retained Earnings	($65,500)	$12,945	$75,812
Earnings	$78,445	$62,867	$93,938
Total Equity	$112,945	$175,812	$269,751
Total Debt and Equity	$492,218	$612,002	$761,643
Net Worth	$112,945	$175,812	$269,751

SOURCES AND USES OF FUNDS

Jumpin' Java needs $396,125 in total capital to initiate operations, as follows:

Startup expenses	$65,500
Startup assets	$65,300
Computer hardware/software	$132,500
Furniture/fixtures, other LT assets	<u>$132,825</u>
Total startup costs	**$396,125**

We seek funding as follows:

Direct owner investment	$100,000
Working capital line of credit for start-up expenses and assets	$30,800
Long term debt for LT assets	<u>$265,325</u>
Total funds sourced	**$396,125**

Appendix

Sales Forecast

	Sep 97	Oct 97	Nov 97	Dec 97	Jan 98	Feb 98	Mar 98	Apr 98	May 98	Jun 98	Jul-98	Aug 98	FY1998	FY1999	FY2000
Sales															
Computer Time	$18,000	$27,000	$36,000	$36,000	$40,000	$40,000	$40,000	$46,000	$46,000	$36,800	$36,800	$36,800	$439,400	$483,340	$531,670
Beverage	$5,400	$8,100	$10,800	$10,800	$12,000	$12,000	$12,000	$13,800	$13,800	$11,040	$11,040	$11,040	$131,820	$145,000	$159,500
Food	$3,060	$4,600	$6,120	$6,120	$6,800	$6,800	$6,800	$7,820	$7,820	$6,260	$6,260	$6,260	$74,720	$82,190	$90,410
Training Center	$3,600	$5,400	$7,200	$7,200	$8,000	$8,000	$8,000	$9,200	$9,200	$7,360	$7,360	$7,360	$87,880	$96,670	$106,330
Other	$430	$640	$850	$850	$950	$950	$950	$1,090	$1,090	$870	$870	$870	$10,410	$11,450	$12,600
Total Sales	$30,490	$45,740	$60,970	$60,970	$67,750	$67,750	$67,750	$77,910	$77,910	$62,330	$62,330	$62,330	$744,230	$818,650	$900,510
Cost of Sales															
Computer Time	$0	$0	$0	$0	$0	$0	$0	$0	$0	$0	$0	$0	$0	$0	$0
Beverage	$1,080	$1,620	$2,160	$2,160	$2,400	$2,400	$2,400	$2,760	$2,760	$2,210	$2,210	$2,210	$22,590	$24,850	$27,330
Food	$1,840	$2,760	$3,680	$3,680	$4,090	$4,090	$4,090	$4,700	$4,700	$3,760	$3,760	$3,760	$44,910	$49,400	$54,340
Training Center	$1,800	$2,700	$3,600	$3,600	$4,000	$4,000	$4,000	$4,600	$4,600	$3,680	$3,680	$3,680	$43,940	$48,330	$53,170
Other	$260	$380	$510	$510	$570	$570	$570	$650	$650	$520	$520	$520	$6,230	$6,850	$7,540
TotalCost of Sales	$4,980	$5,840	$7,790	$9,950	$11,060	$11,060	$11,060	$12,710	$12,710	$10,170	$10,170	$10,170	$117,670	$129,430	$142,380

Personnel Plan

	Sep-97	Oct 97	Nov 97	Dec 97	Jan 98	Feb 98	Mar 98	Apr 98	May 98	Jun 98	Jul 98	Aug 98	FY1998	FY1999	FY2000
Ethan Stanley	$3,500	$3,500	$3,500	$3,500	$3,500	$3,500	$3,500	$3,500	$3,500	$3,500	$3,500	$3,500	$42,000	$43,680	$45,430
Dan Victor	$3,167	$3,167	$3,167	$3,167	$3,167	$3,167	$3,167	$3,167	$3,167	$3,167	$3,167	$3,167	$38,004	$39,520	$41,110
Carolyn Schwartz	$2,333	$2,333	$2,333	$2,333	$2,333	$2,333	$2,333	$2,333	$2,333	$2,333	$2,333	$2,333	$27,996	$29,120	$30,280
Asst. Mgr. 1	$1,109	$1,109	$1,109	$1,109	$1,109	$1,109	$1,109	$1,109	$1,109	$1,109	$1,109	$1,109	$13,308	$13,840	$14,390
Asst. Mgr. 2	$1,109	$1,109	$1,109	$1,109	$1,109	$1,109	$1,109	$1,109	$1,109	$1,109	$1,109	$1,109	$13,308	$13,840	$14,390
Asst. Mgr. 3	$1,040	$1,040	$1,040	$1,040	$1,040	$1,040	$1,040	$1,040	$1,040	$1,040	$1,040	$1,040	$12,480	$12,980	$13,500
Asst. Mgr. 4	$979	$979	$979	$979	$979	$979	$979	$979	$979	$979	$979	$979	$11,748	$12,220	$12,710
C.S.A. 1	$896	$896	$896	$896	$896	$896	$896	$896	$896	$896	$896	$896	$10,752	$11,180	$11,630
C.S.A. 2	$896	$896	$896	$896	$896	$896	$896	$896	$896	$896	$896	$896	$10,752	$11,180	$11,630
C.S.A. 3	$896	$896	$896	$896	$896	$896	$896	$896	$896	$896	$896	$896	$10,752	$11,180	$11,630
C.S.A. 4	$896	$896	$896	$896	$896	$896	$896	$896	$896	$896	$896	$896	$10,752	$11,180	$11,630
C.S.A. 5	$840	$840	$840	$840	$840	$840	$840	$840	$840	$840	$840	$840	$10,080	$10,480	$10,900
C.S.A. 6	$840	$840	$840	$840	$840	$840	$840	$840	$840	$840	$840	$840	$10,080	$10,480	$10,900
C.S.A. 7	$644	$644	$644	$644	$644	$644	$644	$644	$644	$644	$644	$644	$7,728	$8,040	$8,360
C.S.A. 8	$644	$644	$644	$644	$644	$644	$644	$644	$644	$644	$644	$644	$7,728	$8,040	$8,360
C.S.A. 9					$644	$644	$644	$644	$644	$644	$644	$644	$5,152	$8,040	$8,360
C.S.A. 10								$644	$644	$644	$644	$644	$3,220	$8,040	$8,360
Other	$0	$0	$0	$0	$0	$0	$0	$0	$0	$0	$0	$0	$0	$0	$0
Subtotal	$19,789	$19,789	$19,789	$19,789	$20,433	$20,433	$20,433	$21,077	$21,077	$21,077	$21,077	$21,077	$245,840	$263,040	$273,570

Pro-forma Income Statement

	Sep 97	Oct 97	Nov 97	Dec 97	Jan 98	Feb 98	Mar 98	Apr 98	May 98	Jun 98	Jul 98	Aug 98	FY1998	FY1999	FY2000
Sales	$30,490	$45,740	$60,970	$60,970	$67,750	$67,750	$67,750	$77,910	$77,910	$62,330	$62,330	$62,330	$744,230	$818,650	$900,510
Direct Cost of Sales	$4,980	$5,840	$7,790	$9,950	$11,060	$11,060	$11,060	$12,710	$12,710	$10,170	$10,170	$10,170	$117,670	$129,430	$142,380
Other	$0	$0	$0	$0	$0	$0	$0	$0	$0	$0	$0	$0	$0	$0	$0
Total Cost of Sales	$4,980	$5,840	$7,790	$9,950	$11,060	$11,060	$11,060	$12,710	$12,710	$10,170	$10,170	$10,170	$117,670	$129,430	$142,380
Gross Margin	$25,510	$39,900	$53,180	$51,020	$56,690	$56,690	$56,690	$65,200	$65,200	$52,160	$52,160	$52,160	$626,560	$689,220	$758,130
Gross Margin Percent	83.67%	87.23%	87.22%	83.68%	83.68%	83.68%	83.68%	83.69%	83.69%	83.68%	83.68%	83.68%	84.19%	84.19%	84.19%
Operating Expenses:															
Advertising/Promotion	$1,000	$1,000	$1,000	$1,000	$1,000	$1,000	$1,000	$1,000	$1,000	$1,000	$1,000	$1,000	$12,000	$13,200	$14,520
Phone	$200	$200	$200	$200	$200	$200	$200	$200	$200	$200	$200	$200	$2,400	$2,640	$2,900
T-1 Line	$1,000	$1,000	$1,000	$1,000	$1,000	$1,000	$1,000	$1,000	$1,000	$1,000	$1,000	$1,000	$12,000	$13,200	$14,520
On-Line Subscriptions	$100	$100	$100	$100	$100	$100	$100	$100	$100	$100	$100	$100	$1,200	$1,320	$1,450
Other	$0	$0	$0	$0	$0	$0	$0	$0	$0	$0	$0	$0	$0	$0	$0
Payroll Expense	$19,789	$19,789	$19,789	$19,789	$20,433	$20,433	$20,433	$21,077	$21,077	$21,077	$21,077	$21,077	$245,840	$263,040	$273,570
Leased Equipment	$0	$0	$0	$0	$0	$0	$0	$0	$0	$0	$0	$0	$0	$0	$0
Utilities	$3,000	$3,000	$3,000	$3,000	$3,000	$3,000	$3,000	$3,000	$3,000	$3,000	$3,000	$3,000	$36,000	$39,600	$43,560
Insurance	$250	$250	$250	$250	$250	$250	$250	$250	$250	$250	$250	$250	$3,000	$3,300	$3,630
Rent	$0	$0	$0	$0	$4,188	$4,188	$4,188	$4,188	$4,188	$4,188	$4,188	$4,188	$33,504	$59,950	$70,400
Depreciation	$11,500	$11,000	$11,000	$11,000	$11,000	$11,000	$11,000	$11,000	$11,000	$11,000	$11,000	$11,000	$132,500	$132,500	$132,500
Payroll Burden	$2,968	$2,968	$2,968	$2,968	$3,065	$3,065	$3,065	$3,162	$3,162	$3,162	$3,162	$3,162	$36,876	$39,456	$41,036
Contract/Consultants	$0	$0	$0	$0	$0	$0	$0	$0	$0	$0	$0	$0	$0	$0	$0
Other	$0	$0	$0	$0	$0	$0	$0	$0	$0	$0	$0	$0	$0	$0	$0
Total Operating Expenses	$39,807	$39,307	$39,307	$39,307	$44,236	$44,236	$44,236	$44,977	$44,977	$44,977	$44,977	$44,977	$515,320	$568,206	$598,086
Profit Before Interest and Taxes	($14,297)	$593	$13,873	$11,713	$12,454	$12,454	$12,454	$20,223	$20,223	$7,183	$7,183	$7,183	$111,240	$121,014	$160,045
Interest Expense ST	$282	$282	$282	$282	$282	$282	$282	$282	$282	$282	$282	$282	$3,388	$5,082	$5,082
Interest Expense LT	$2,248	$2,285	$2,322	$2,358	$2,395	$2,432	$2,469	$2,506	$2,543	$2,580	$2,616	$2,653	$29,407	$53,065	$61,024
Taxes Incurred	$0	$0	$0	$0	$0	$0	$0	$0	$0	$0	$0	$0	$0	$0	$0
Net Profit	($16,828)	($1,974)	$11,269	$9,072	$9,776	$9,740	$9,703	$17,435	$17,398	$4,322	$4,285	$4,248	$78,445	$62,867	$93,938
Net Profit/Sales	-55.19%	-4.32%	18.48%	14.88%	14.43%	14.38%	14.32%	22.38%	22.33%	6.93%	6.87%	6.82%	10.54%	7.68%	10.43%

Pro-Forma Cash Flow

	Sep 97	Oct 97	Nov 97	Dec 97	Jan 98	Feb 98	Mar 98	Apr 98	May 98	Jun 98	Jul 98	Aug 98	FY1998	FY1999	FY2000
Net Profit:	($16,828)	($1,974)	$11,269	$9,072	$9,776	$9,740	$9,703	$17,435	$17,398	$4,322	$4,285	$4,248	$78,445	$62,867	$93,938
Plus:															
Depreciation	$11,500	$11,000	$11,000	$11,000	$11,000	$11,000	$11,000	$11,000	$11,000	$11,000	$11,000	$11,000	$132,500	$132,500	$132,500
Change in Accounts Payable	$21,442	$350	$1,898	$2,102	$5,157	$0	$0	$1,606	$0	($2,472)	$0	$0	$30,083	$3,853	$2,638
Current Borrowing (Repayment)	$0	$0	$0	$0	$0	$0	$0	$0	$0	$0	$0	$0	$0	$0	$0
Increase (Other Liabilities)	$0	$0	$0	$0	$0	$0	$0	$0	$0	$0	$0	$0	$0	$0	$0
Long-Term Borrowing (Repayment)	$4,422	$4,422	$4,422	$4,422	$4,422	$4,422	$4,422	$4,422	$4,422	$4,422	$4,422	$4,422	$53,064	$53,064	$53,064
Capital Input	$0	$0	$0	$0	$0	$0	$0	$0	$0	$0	$0	$0	$0	$0	$0
Subtotal	$20,537	$13,798	$28,589	$26,596	$30,355	$25,162	$25,125	$34,463	$32,820	$17,271	$19,707	$19,670	$294,093	$252,285	$282,141
Less:															
Change in Accounts Receivable	$0	$0	$0	$0	$0	$0	$0	$0	$0	$0	$0	$0	$0	$0	$0
Change in Inventory	($3,805)	$206	$468	$518	$266	$0	$0	$396	$0	($610)	$0	$0	($2,559)	$244	$269
Change in Other ST Assets	$0	$0	$0	$0	$0	$0	$0	$0	$0	$0	$0	$0	$0	$0	$0
Capital Expenditure	$0	$0	$0	$0	$0	$0	$0	$0	$0	$0	$0	$0	$0	$0	$0
Dividends	$0	$0	$0	$0	$0	$0	$0	$0	$0	$0	$0	$0	$0	$0	$0
Subtotal	($3,805)	$206	$468	$518	$266	$0	$0	$396	$0	($610)	$0	$0	($2,559)	$244	$269
Net Cash Flow	$24,342	$13,592	$28,121	$26,078	$30,089	$25,162	$25,125	$34,067	$32,820	$17,881	$19,707	$19,670	$296,652	$252,041	$281,872
Cash Balance	$84,342	$97,933	$126,054	$152,132	$182,220	$207,382	$232,507	$266,574	$299,394	$317,275	$336,982	$356,652	$356,652	$608,693	$890,564

Pro-forma Balance Sheet

	Sep 97	Oct 97	Nov 97	Dec 97	Jan 98	Feb 98	Mar 98	Apr 98	May 98	Jun 98	Jul 98	Aug 98	FY1998	FY1999	FY2000
Short-Term Assets															
Cash	$84,342	$97,933	$126,054	$152,132	$182,220	$207,382	$232,507	$266,574	$299,394	$317,275	$336,982	$356,652	$356,652	$608,693	$890,564
Accounts Receivable	$0	$0	$0	$0	$0	$0	$0	$0	$0	$0	$0	$0	$0	$0	$0
Inventory	$1,195	$1,402	$1,870	$2,388	$2,654	$2,654	$2,654	$3,050	$3,050	$2,441	$2,441	$2,441	$2,441	$2,685	$2,953
Other ST Assets	$300	$300	$300	$300	$300	$300	$300	$300	$300	$300	$300	$300	$300	$300	$300
Total ST Assets	$85,837	$99,635	$128,223	$154,820	$185,175	$210,336	$235,461	$269,924	$302,745	$320,016	$339,723	$359,393	$359,393	$611,677	$893,818
Long-Term Assets															
Capital Assets	$265,325	$265,325	$265,325	$265,325	$265,325	$265,325	$265,325	$265,325	$265,325	$265,325	$265,325	$265,325	$265,325	$265,325	$265,325
Accumulated Depr.	$11,500	$22,500	$33,500	$44,500	$55,500	$66,500	$77,500	$88,500	$99,500	$110,500	$121,500	$132,500	$132,500	$265,000	$397,500
Total LT Assets	$253,825	$242,825	$231,825	$220,825	$209,825	$198,825	$187,825	$176,825	$165,825	$154,825	$143,825	$132,825	$132,825	$325	($132,175)
Total Assets	$339,662	$342,460	$360,048	$375,645	$395,000	$409,161	$423,286	$446,749	$468,570	$474,841	$483,548	$492,218	$492,218	$612,002	$761,643
Debt and Equity															
Accounts Payable	$21,442	$21,793	$23,691	$25,793	$30,950	$30,950	$30,950	$32,556	$32,556	$30,083	$30,083	$30,083	$30,083	$33,937	$36,575
Short-Term Notes	$30,800	$30,800	$30,800	$30,800	$30,800	$30,800	$30,800	$30,800	$30,800	$30,800	$30,800	$30,800	$30,800	$30,800	$30,800
Other ST Liabilities	$0	$0	$0	$0	$0	$0	$0	$0	$0	$0	$0	$0	$0	$0	$0
Subtotal ST Liabilities	$52,242	$52,593	$54,491	$56,593	$61,750	$61,750	$61,750	$63,356	$63,356	$60,883	$60,883	$60,883	$60,883	$64,737	$67,375
Long-Term Liabilities	$269,747	$274,169	$278,591	$283,013	$287,435	$291,857	$296,279	$300,701	$305,123	$309,545	$313,967	$318,389	$318,389	$371,453	$424,517
Total Liabilities	$321,989	$326,762	$333,082	$339,606	$349,185	$353,607	$358,029	$364,057	$368,479	$370,428	$374,850	$379,272	$379,272	$436,190	$491,892
Paid-In Capital	$100,000	$100,000	$100,000	$100,000	$100,000	$100,000	$100,000	$100,000	$100,000	$100,000	$100,000	$100,000	$100,000	$100,000	$100,000
Retained Earnings	($65,500)	($65,500)	($65,500)	($65,500)	($65,500)	($65,500)	($65,500)	($65,500)	($65,500)	($65,500)	($65,500)	($65,500)	($65,500)	$12,945	$75,812
Earnings	($16,828)	($18,802)	($7,533)	$1,539	$11,315	$21,055	$30,757	$48,193	$65,591	$69,913	$74,197	$78,445	$78,445	$62,867	$93,938
Total Equity	$17,672	$15,698	$26,967	$36,039	$45,815	$55,555	$65,257	$82,693	$100,091	$104,413	$108,697	$112,945	$112,945	$175,812	$269,751
Total Debt and Equity	$339,662	$342,460	$360,048	$375,645	$395,000	$409,161	$423,286	$446,749	$468,570	$474,841	$483,548	$492,218	$492,218	$612,002	$761,643
Net Worth	$17,672	$15,698	$26,967	$36,039	$45,815	$55,555	$65,257	$82,693	$100,091	$104,413	$108,697	$112,945	$112,945	$175,812	$269,751

A Final Word

If you need any more convincing of the value of writing a business plan for the success of your business, Steve Crow, our planning expert, offers the following words of advice.

The Bottom Line

As I look back at the five plans used as examples in this book, I think of the hours invested in each one of them. Hard hours of research, thinking, talking, evaluating, testing ideas, writing and rewriting. I try to put myself in your shoes: a new or hopeful entrepreneur, a reader of this book. What must you be thinking? What are the questions you're asking yourself right now? What will it take to convince you and enable you and encourage you to create a solid business plan for your new venture? My answers always come back to one central issue: You've got to be truly convinced that the process and product of business planning will add to your bottom line.

Everyone in "the business world" seems to be interested in the bottom line. Dollars and cents. The real value of a business, or an expansion, or a new product. The bottom line is sometimes easy to predict and simple to measure. But what about the "bottom line" when it comes to the value of a carefully developed, well-written business plan? How is that value to be measured? Do business owners who plan well really have a better bottom line than those who don't? Not easy questions. But there *must* be an answer, and there *is* an answer.

In January of 1995, the *Journal of Small Business Management* published a paper entitled "A Nonfinancial Business Success Versus Failure Model for Young Firms." The purpose of the study was to develop and test a nonfinancial model that will predict a young business's success or failure.

Fifteen variables that may have predictive value were isolated and measured to determine how each variable does or does not affect a young business's success. The 15 variables studied were drawn from 20 previous articles on the same subject, and included those variables one might expect: having or not having adequate capital, having or not having previous management experience, etc.

Two matched sets of companies were examined. Set one included 108 companies which had failed (Chapter 11 bankruptcy), while set two included 108 viable companies. Importantly, for each failed company included, the researchers included a matching successful company that was similar with regard to size, age, location, and industry.

Of the 15 variables tested, only four had a statistically significant impact on these firms' success:

1. Businesses that used <u>professional advisors</u> were more successful than those that did not.

2. Businesses that developed <u>specific business plans</u> were more successful than those that did not.

3. Businesses that had <u>more difficulty filling staff positions</u> were more successful than those that had less difficulty.

4. Businesses with <u>owners with less formal education</u> were more successful than those with more education.

What's the bottom line on business planning? If you're serious about succeeding in your new venture, I think you already know the answer. Accept what you already instinctively know is true: Businesses that start without a written plan are statistically more likely to fail. Period. End of debate. So, grit your teeth, square your shoulders, and just do it.

As you work, remember:

- This is not rocket science; it's words and numbers.

- By the mile it's a trial, but by the inch it's a cinch. Little steps are OK, but start walking!

- Start with the industry, then the target market, then your competition. Then decide what the market needs that you can provide better than your competition does.

- Determine the four or five key issues that you must successfully address in order to win.

- Think and plan as if your success depends on it — because it does.

Here are four concrete suggestions that might help you get started. Try the one that matches your talent, time, and money. You may want to combine two or more of these to get the job done.

1. Use this book as a guide to organize and guide your thoughts. If you aren't a good typist, write your ideas, then hire someone else to do the typing for you.

2. If your computer skills are decent, some basic business planning, accounting, or spreadsheet software can help you to format the plan and generate the financial statements.

3. Visit your local Small Business Development Center/SBA office. You'll find free help and advice.

4. If you still need more assistance, there are probably consultants in your area that can work

with you, for a fee, to help you design and complete your plan. Don't let them tell you how you should run your business. Instead, they should help guide you through the important questions and issues, allowing you to build your answers carefully at your own pace. Check in your yellow pages under "Business Consultants."

Finally, let me simply say that I wish you the best as you embark on the journey to plan your business. Seeing a new business planned, launched, and succeeding is one of the greatest pleasures of my profession. If you need to talk with me, call me anytime. I'll do my best to help.

Steve Crow
A Better Business Plan
847-247-1213

Index